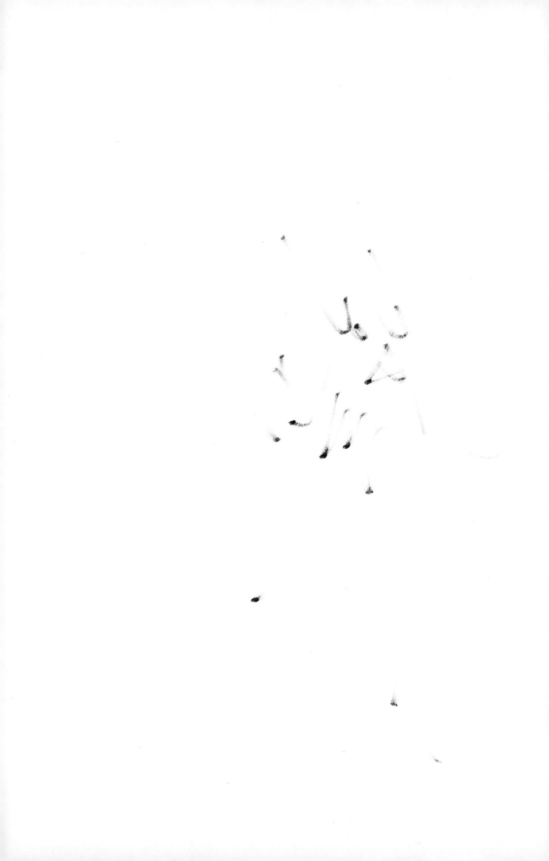

Making the Mentalist

Gerry McCambridge

MAKING THE MENTALIST
BY GERRY MCCAMBRIDGE

All Rights Reserved © 2014

ISBN: 978-1-936759-37-8
Library of Congress Control Number: 2014952556

Published in the United States of America

www.houdinipublishing.com

Dedication

To my Mom, for always supporting me and always being my number one fan.

To my beautiful children: Please forgive me for not always being there. I was so focused on trying to give you a better life, sometimes I forgot to enjoy the life we had.

To Tommy Perry, I am so sorry.

Contents

And Away We Go

The NBC Television Special

Heading to the Desert

Persistence Achieves Goals

Making the Mentalist

Introduction

When the lights dim in the V Theater at the Planet Hollywood Resort and Casino, the audience expects to be amazed and entertained by the mystical skills of The Mentalist. Few, if any, know the real story behind the longest-running mentalist act in the history of Las Vegas. Everyone in Las Vegas has a tale, and this is mine.

But the book you're holding is more than a recounting of my life story and how I came to be The Mentalist. I think there are two major parts of my life that others can possibly learn from: how I set and accomplished goals, and how I constantly overcame adversity and grew from it instead of using it as an excuse for any of my failures.

In 1988, my master goal was to be a professional entertainer. More specifically, I wanted to be one of the world's most successful mentalists. I broke my master goal down into three mini-goals:

1. I wanted to have my own one-hour NBC television special.
2. I wanted to have my own Off Broadway show in New York City.
3. I wanted to be a Las Vegas Strip headliner.

These were three things my mentor Doug Henning accomplished in his career, and they were also three things I wished to accomplish in my career. I knew they were attainable goals for me, and I refused to stop trying until I finally achieved them. I am a very driven person who always succeeds with what I set my mind to.

My ability to achieve my master goal rested on those mini-goals, which I conquered in part by setting up plateau rewards for myself to celebrate my progress along the way. I hope that by sharing how I set my goals, how I developed the ability to keep a laser-like focus on them, and how I finally figured out a way to achieve them, I can motivate others to achieve theirs.

However, goal-setting wasn't the only factor in my success. My achievements are rooted in my ability to constantly overcome adversity and grow from it instead of using it as an excuse for any of my failures. Whenever I would candidly tell my story of childhood sexual abuse to friends, it had a magical way of causing some of them to open up and share their stories as well. I knew I had to tell my own story and write this book to possibly help others struggling with the burden of sexual abuse.

After years of living silently with my own guilt and shame, I have come to terms with what has happened to me. I've decided, through self-exploration and therapy, that what happened to me at the hands of my abusers was not my fault. I was an innocent child who was taken advantage of in unthinkable ways. When I finally realized how wrong it all was, I was too ashamed to talk about it to anyone. It took almost twenty-five years before I would come to terms with the events. I eventually put it all behind me and finally felt like a new man.

Being a father of six, and a grandfather to many, I wanted to teach my children, as well as the rest of the world, that it is okay to talk about such things. In fact, you have to talk about it to be able to work through the pain. Ignoring heartache does not make it go away. It's like having a disease: left untreated, it will take over your entire body and eventually kill you. You have to eradicate the disease completely before moving on towards healing.

It is my hope that by sharing my story of sexual abuse, others will be able to open up and talk about theirs as well. I also hope that people can learn from what happened to me and possibly spare their children from the same fate. I want to encourage victims like me to investigate the local laws in their area to see if they have any recourse against the injustices they may have encountered.

As you read this book, you'll notice that I include very specific details about dates and events. Motivational speaker Tony Robbins taught me that "a life worth living is a life worth documenting." On March 9, 1981, I began doing just that—documenting my life by keeping a daily journal. My journal also includes events prior to that date thanks to conversations with family members, dated family photos, and old home movies. My mother kept detailed records of my younger years, so I was able to add specific information about my life with tremendous accuracy. I also added events that came from my childhood friend Steve's memory. (I call Steve my personal "Rain Man" because of his extraordinary ability to recall numbers and dates.) We have been best friends since childhood, and he has stored many of my life's events in his unique brain.

I knew that when I finally accomplished my goals, I might be able to use the details in my journal to motivate others to accomplish their goals. That information became the basis of this book. I hope you find it helpful.

Gerry McCambridge
October 31, 2014
Las Vegas, Nevada

What Is Mentalism?

Every week, millions of people tune into CBS to watch the hit television series *The Mentalist* starring Simon Baker. The show starts by giving the viewer a very brief description of what a mentalist is:

> Mentalist – Someone who uses mental acuity, hypnosis and/or suggestion. A master manipulator of thoughts and behavior.

I have booked myself on thousands of performances over the course of my career, and many of the people I sold my act to would ask the very same question: "What is a mentalist?" The producers of the television series were very smart for putting a brief description at the beginning of the show.

The description was accurate yet short because of the time constraints of television. Since I do not have time or space limitations, I can embellish on the description so my reader fully understands what a mentalist is, and what a mentalist does.

For starters, mentalism is a form of magic that doesn't require big boxes or assistants. The average mentalist can perform an entire show with a few envelopes, sketchpads, and markers. Mentalism is not a supernatural ability, nor does it involve any type of supernatural powers. Most mentalists start out as magicians, and they eventually gravitate to mentalism because it is a "thinking man's" form of entertainment. It packs small, yet plays big.

Some principles authentically used by a mentalist are: memory, magic, verbal guidance, understanding of human behavior, psychology, hypnosis, power of observation, mathematical calculations, verbal manipulation, illusion, statistics, cold reading, intuition, and common sense. Mentalism allows the performer to create the illusion that they can actually read minds and see your innermost thoughts, predict future events, gain telepathic information using clairvoyance, talk to the dead, move objects using psychokinesis, and see into the future using precognition. In fact, they can't.

Performing Was In My Blood

Chapter 1

My Magical Appearance

I made my debut into the world on October 31, 1962 with the name of Scott Thomas Burns. Ironically, it is the same calendar date that legendary magician and escape artist Harry Houdini passed away in Detroit, Michigan. He died on October 31, 1926. The reverse of 26 is 62. The reverse of death is life. I guess from the start, I was destined to begin where he left off.

My seventeen-year-old unwed mother was an American Caucasian, Roman Catholic of Irish and German descent from Brooklyn. She was a high school graduate who worked part-time for an insurance company and was living with her parents when she gave birth to me. She was described as being very attractive, with dark brown hair, brown eyes, and a fair complexion. She was 5'5" tall, weighed 116 pounds, and was very shy and sensitive.

I was a full term pregnancy, born by low forceps delivery. I was eight pounds and two ounces at birth and twenty inches long. My birth mother's father was fifty-seven years old and worked as a bridge operator; her mother was forty-five and unemployed. They were both born in the United States, and that is all that I know about my biological mother and her parents.

My (alleged) biological father was also seventeen. He was an American Caucasian, Roman Catholic of Irish descent, 5'8", 147 pounds, with black hair, blue eyes, and a fair complexion. At the time of my birth, he was an unemployed high school graduate. He was fully aware of my birth and contributed towards my biological mother's care. I do not have any information about his parents.

Adoption seemed to be the best plan for me since my biological parents were young, unmarried, and unable to plan for my future. After my birth, I spent almost one month in the hospital, but I don't know why I was there for such a long time. On November 26, 1962, I was admitted to the nursery at the Angel Guardian Home through the Department of Welfare, directly across from the hospital. Two days later, on November 28, I was baptized at the Angel Guardian Chapel by Reverend John H. Walker. For my first three and a half months of life, I was living alone in an orphanage.

Studies show that taking a baby away from its mother at birth has a profound effect on the child. The child loses not only its mother, but also part of the self. If an infant is deprived of its mother soon after birth, its brain does not develop normally.

The babies in these studies were found to have serious adjustment problems in adolescence, and all seemed to have a sense of abandonment by the birth parents. It's been suggested that the wound can be healed in a loving adoptive family, but the scar will always remain. Adopted adults tend to experience more alcoholism, sexual acting out, and suicide attempts. But at the time, no one knew how adoption would affect my life.

Gerard Alexander McCambridge, Sr., who was twenty-one years old, and twenty-year-old Frances Ann Pantaleo were married on May 4, 1957. They purchased a modest house on his police officer's salary in Bayside Queens, New York, which is a small suburb about thirteen miles outside of New York City.

For the first few years of their marriage, Frances was a housewife trying unsuccessfully to have a child. After giving up hope of a natural conception, Frances and Gerard started the grueling one-year application process (and the numerous home inspections required) to adopt a newborn child from the Angel Guardian Home. The couple had a special love for this home since Gerard was also adopted from there as a young child. On March 19, 1963, when I was four and a half months old, Gerard and Frances brought me home.

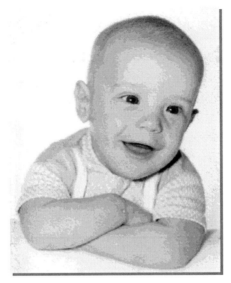

Gerard Alexander McCambridge Jr.

They immediately renamed me Gerard Alexander McCambridge, Jr. after my father. Gerard, who was Irish, and Frances, who was Italian, cared for me as if I were their own child, while the adoption agency made periodic surprise visits to check on my welfare. My soon-to-be adoptive parents would walk on eggshells for fifteen months before the adoption became final. The lawyer who handled the entire adoption process for them was a close friend.

While my adoptive parents were going through the adoption process with me, they heard about a seven-year-old boy named Malcolm and his eleven-year-old sister, Maureen. The siblings, who recently lost both their parents, were distantly related to my parents by marriage. They were staying with an uncle when my mother and father invited them to stay with us for a few weeks in the summer. This was a great decision, because as it turned out they became a part of our family permanently. Malcolm and Maureen fit in with our family so nicely that my parents soon became their legal guardians.

My adoption was finalized on June 23, 1964 in Queens County. My biological mother didn't have any contact with the adoption agency after she signed the surrender document in February of 1963. Research shows that after the physical separation and legal formalities are complete, there has to be a period of mourning and adjustment for a baby's mother. Separation is unnatural and painful, and the pain must be recognized, accepted, and expressed. Young unmarried mothers who have surrendered their babies for adoption often have difficulties in their later personal adjustment and relationships.

Other problems for an adopted baby's biological mother include depression, anxiety, insomnia or excessive sleep, loss of appetite or excessive appetite, personality disturbances, vague fears and doubts, loss of self-confidence, strong feelings of rejection, regret at having surrendered their baby for adoption, and feeling that they have "destroyed" their child by surrendering him or her. Research like this makes me curious if my biological mother experienced any of this pain when she had to give me up, or if I was just an accidental burden to her that she was glad to be rid of.

In less than one year, my adoptive mother went from having no children at all to having three children, one of them being a preteen. In 1968, the adoption agency called again and said they had a baby girl for my parents to adopt if they were still interested. They jumped at the chance and adopted the baby whom my parents named Toni Francine, after my grandfather Tony Pantaleo and my mother Frances. Toni completed our middle class family.

We lived in a small, 1,400 square foot, three-bedroom, semi-attached corner house on 200th Street and 33rd Avenue in Bayside Queens, New York. My brother Malcolm and I shared a bedroom that measured seven feet by ten feet, and my two sisters shared the other bedroom, which was about the same size.

Frances, Gerard Jr., and Gerard Sr.

Malcolm and Maureen knew who their biological parents were. The two of them were related by blood and seemed to have a special bond between them. They also had close contact with their three older biological siblings. This was a blood bond I could not feel, and I desperately wanted to know what it was like. When I was older, I knew the only way I could feel that blood bond with another human being was to have kids of my own.

Toni and I, on the other hand, did not know who our biological parents were. I didn't really care, but I did not know it was eating away at Toni. When she was a little older, she decided to search for her biological parents. She found and contacted her biological mother who was living in Massachusetts at the time; her biological father had passed away many years prior. Toni also made contact with her biological grandparents and uncle.

My adoptive parents were very up front with Toni and me, telling us when we were old enough to understand what adoption meant. Our adoptive father was also adopted, but he knew who his biological parents were. He and our mother made sure that our being adopted was never a stigma or an issue. In fact, they made it into a source of pride. "We wanted you guys," they often told me. They were the most loving parents a child could ever want.

I felt that searching for my biological parents would somehow be a slap in the face to my adoptive parents. But I couldn't help but be haunted by the actions of my birth mother, especially after having children of my own. I always wondered how she could just walk away and leave me. I attribute her actions as a sign of the times. In the early 1960s, if you were an unmarried teenager and you got pregnant, you instantly had a scarlet letter painted on your chest. Most girls that age would disappear for the summer under the guise of staying with an out-of-town family member, while secretly giving birth to a child and keeping the pregnancy hidden from society.

While I have never had any desire to find my biological mother, I tried to process why she did what she did. Her abandoning me was sometimes confusing and painful. Since my sister Toni was successful with her search, she offered to help me find my biological parents. As far as I was concerned, my biological mother was now most likely married with a family. And chances are, she did not tell her husband that she put a child up for adoption when she was seventeen.

Who was I to contact her and possibly upset her life, just to satisfy my own curiosity? I told Toni I did not want her to search for my biological parents; however, when I was twenty-four, I did give her permission to fill out an adoptee registration form with the New York State Department of Health on my behalf. If my biological parents were searching for me, that form gave the agency permission to use my information and match us up, and to notify me if and when they found a successful match.

As a child, my adoption wasn't kept a secret from anyone; everyone in the neighborhood seemed to know it. My two best friends were my neighbors Lois and Susie. Lois lived in the house connected to ours and Susie lived across the driveway from Lois. Susie was a tomboy who kept up with everything I did, so we played the most together. Lois was very feminine and only participated in half of what Susie and I did. Neither of them treated me any different because I was adopted. Another childhood friend, Brian, lived across the street from me. When he introduced me to other kids, he would say, "This is Gerard." And when he did not think I was listening, he would follow it up by whispering, "He's adopted."

That made me feel different from the other kids, but not in a good way. I always wondered what else he was whispering about me to the other kids. I would fantasize about being able to read his mind so I would know what he really was saying about me. It felt as if my biological mother secretly removed the scarlet letter from her chest and plastered it on mine. My parents made adoption seem right, and my best friend made it seem wrong.

Gerard Sr., Gerard Jr. and Frances

Chapter 2

I Was Born to Entertain

My mother loves to tell the story that I was a little ham at the age of two. When we had late night visitors over to the house, my father would come into my bedroom, wake me out of a sound sleep, and bring me downstairs. He'd stand me on the kitchen table and I would perform rehearsed routines for our company. I had a soldier routine that included standing at attention and pulling my stomach in, marching in place, and saluting on command. My repertoire also included a hobo routine in which I acted drunk and had a cigarette in my mouth. I would bet my bottom dollar my father never asked me to do my hobo routine in front of the adoption agency inspector!

During the day, my mother often dressed me up in different military outfits, and I would play the part of either a soldier or a sailor. Since the Vietnam War was on everyone's mind, the patriotic clothes seemed to fit with the times.

On September 9, 1967, at the age of five, I attended school for the very first time. (Luckily for me, my mother dressed me in regular clothes and not one of my military uniforms.) I attended kindergarten at P.S. 159 in Queens about five blocks from my house. I was a very shy child and small, standing only forty-three and a half inches tall and weighing just forty-one pounds.

My mother walked me to my class. I was frightened and did not want her to leave. I started to cry as the teacher insisted she leave the classroom. I could see her peeking through the window on the classroom door; she was crying as well. I hated it every day when she left me in the class. The only thing that helped get me through the pain was that my friend, Brian, was in the same class as I was.

After my first year of school was over, my parents decided to take a cruise to the Caribbean with my mother's only brother, my Uncle Joe and his wife, Aunt Lucretia. My father's brother and his wife, Uncle Eddie and Aunt Peggy, stayed at our house to watch me while my parents were away. I remember going to see my parents off at the docks, and crying my eyes out as the boat slowly pulled away. I thought they were leaving me forever. Up to that point in my life, it was the saddest I'd felt since watching my mother leave me at school. I still remember the heartache as I watched the ship move away, and I saw my mother's face fade away into the distance.

While staying at the house, my Uncle Eddie decided to make a few minor repairs since my father did not know the difference between a hammer and a screwdriver. I watched Uncle Eddie as he worked his repair magic. His craftsmanship and attention to detail fascinated me. I asked him a lot of questions, and he taught me how to use his tools and allowed me to help him with the repairs. Uncle Joe and my grandfather were also very handy. As I was growing up, all three of them taught me how to design, build, and repair things—a skillset that would come in very handy in years to come.

When my parents returned from the cruise, they had a bunch of souvenirs for us kids. I received a big sombrero hat, and a marionette of a drunk Mexican man wearing a sombrero, holding a bottle in one hand and a maraca in the other. I hung the big hat up in my bedroom because it was too big for me to wear, but the puppet had me totally intrigued. With a little practice I was able to make the marionette walk, drink from his bottle, play the maraca, bow, and sit. Then I started putting on little shows. My mother noticed my interest, and for Christmas that year she gave me a few more marionettes, some hand puppets, and a puppet theater.

I would kneel behind the puppet theater and put on puppet shows for my family and friends. I really enjoyed making everyone laugh, but did not like the fact that I wasn't able to watch them laugh and smile during my performance. During the show, I tried to peek through a crack in the wood of the puppet theater to see my audience's reaction.

Eventually I discovered ventriloquist puppets, which I could sit on my knee to put on my show rather than kneeling behind the puppet theater. I remember seeing ventriloquist Willie Tyler and his puppet, Lester, on *The Ed Sullivan Show*. From that point on, I wanted a Lester puppet! When I finally got one, it was only a miniature version of the one I saw on TV. I wanted a full-size ventriloquist doll, so I begged my mother to get me one. Willie Tyler and Lester were African-American, and my father used to make fun of the ethnicity of my little doll. So my mother got me a full-sized Charlie McCarthy and a Mortimer Snerd ventriloquist doll as well.

After receiving the two ventriloquist dolls, I practiced as much as I could trying to talk without moving my lips. I actually became pretty good at manipulating the puppets and telling jokes. In spite of my shyness, standing up in front of my family and friends while performing with the puppets did not seem to intimidate me in the least.

Every summer, my family took a trip to Connecticut to visit my mother's friend, Annette. My mother and Annette had worked together at the AT&T phone company. Annette and her husband, Charlie, had three children: Susan, Bruce, and Scott. I loved to visit them but hated taking the long drive because I had terrible motion sickness.

Our little red Dodge Dart did not have any air-conditioning, and my father was a heavy smoker. Between the smoke filling up in the back seat and the movement of the car, every drive would cause me to puke my brains out. Eventually my mother started giving me half of a Dramamine motion sickness pill about a half hour before each long trip. The pill usually knocked me out for the entire drive and kept me groggy for half of the day.

We usually slept over at the house for the weekend. My favorite part of the trip was walking to a local milk farm and playing hide-and-seek in the hayloft. I always wanted to be a farmer when I grew up because I figured as a farmer, I could play in the hay all day long. "Aunt" Annette and "Uncle" Charlie also hosted a big backyard barbecue with local friends dropping by during our weekend stay. One tradition was to boil live lobsters in a huge fifty-five gallon steel drum. I distinctly remember hearing the poor lobsters scream as they were dumped into the boiling hot water. Then I heard them banging their claws on the inside of the drum until they eventually were scalded to death. Knowing how the poor lobsters died so horribly scarred me enough to never eat seafood again for the rest of my life.

During one of those Connecticut weekends in 1972, when I was nine years old, I met a man who was a guest at the annual barbecue. I was entertaining him with my puppets, and in return he decided to show me a disappearing coin trick.

Chapter 3

Bitten by the Magical Bug

I didn't know the man at the barbecue, but he moved a coin from his left hand to his right hand, and the coin suddenly disappeared right before my eyes. Both of his hands were completely empty! Then, at will, he made the coin reappear behind my ear. I was totally mesmerized by that coin trick. I didn't even feel the coin there, and suddenly there it was!

I asked him to repeat the trick, and again the coin reappeared behind my ear. I told him I would teach him how to talk without moving his lips if he would teach me the coin trick in exchange. I did not let up until he eventually told me how the trick was done. He made me promise not to tell anyone the secret. "Being a good magician means you never reveal the secrets to a magic trick," he whispered.

Once he told me how the trick was done, I could not believe it was so simple. The coin was never really in his right hand; he only *pretended* to shift it from his left hand to his right hand. He deceived me. He lied to me. He manipulated my thoughts into believing the coin was actually in his right hand. After watching him perform it again for my little sister Toni, I couldn't believe that she did not realize the coin never left his other hand! She couldn't see how he was doing it, yet it was now perfectly obvious to me.

The trick was very deceiving except for the fact that when he performed it, he had to be sitting down in a chair to accomplish the miracle. When I looked at his right hand thinking the coin was there, he was secretly dropping it into the small cuff he made on his pants leg; he could then show both his hands empty. It was my first lesson in mental misdirection.

When I returned home from Connecticut, I put the puppets aside and practiced that trick over and over again until I perfected it. Now I was eager to show my brother, Malcolm, the disappearing coin trick. I performed it perfectly and fooled him!

"How did you do that?" he asked.

I refused to tell him. "Being a good magician means you never reveal the secrets to a magic trick," I explained with a sly grin.

A week later, Malcolm came home from a date with one of our neighbors, Cindy, who happened to live three houses away from us. Mal showed my father and me a magic trick that Cindy accidentally received in the bathroom vending machine at the Bay Terrace movie theater. It was called the *Wonder Wallet*, and it was a little three-inch red cardboard wallet with a picture of a dragon painted on the outside. My brother opened the wallet, placed a coin on the inside, and closed it. He turned the wallet over a few times, said the magic word, and opened it up. The coin had vanished. I was completely amazed! I thought I was the master of the disappearing coin trick, but now I was totally astonished all over again. When did my brother all of a sudden become a magician? I was fooling him only days earlier.

Malcolm then closed the wallet again, spun it around, said another magic word, and *presto!* The coin reappeared.

"How does it work?" I asked.

"Being a good magician means you never reveal the secrets to a magic trick," he repeated back to me with a snicker.

The next day I decided to go through my brother's dresser drawers, and there I found the *Wonder Wallet*. Since he wasn't around, I had a chance to sit on my bed and play with it. I opened it up and noticed that the coin was still inside. I closed the wallet and spun it around a few times as I recalled Mal doing. I didn't remember the magic words, so I made some up. And when I opened the wallet, *the coin vanished!* I almost fell off the bed. How did I do this?

I tried to make the coin reappear but was unsuccessful. Since I learned that magic usually has a very simple explanation, and I was an inquisitive little kid, I needed to figure out what was going on, so I inspected the wallet. Eventually I determined the wallet had two sides: one with a coin, and the other without a coin. As long as you kept track of which side you were opening, you could either show the coin was there or show the empty side, making it seem as if the coin had vanished.

Since the first coin trick I learned in Connecticut required me to be sitting down and to make an unnatural cuff in my pants, I wasn't able to show the trick to my friends at school. So I practiced the wallet trick until I perfected it, then I took it to school to show my friends. Adding a little showmanship and flair, I performed the disappearing coin trick and instantly became the center of attention. They were amazed! My friends and the other school children were shocked that I was able to do magic. I went from being quiet little Gerard to "Gerard the Magician"! That was the very moment that I was bitten by the magic bug.

My parents liked to sleep in on Saturdays. My mother left me a Tupperware soup bowl filled with cereal, and a Tupperware cup in the refrigerator filled with just the right amount of milk. I would dump the cup of milk into the bowl and enjoy my breakfast before watching hours and hours of cartoons.

I remember seeing a television commercial with magician Marshall Brodien, a TV pitchman who sold decks of *TV Magic Cards*. His thirty-second commercial completely captivated me.

"With these cards you, too, can become a magician, as long as you know the secret," he said.

I was so amazing to my friends with the *Wonder Wallet*, I couldn't imagine how surprised they would be if I had these magic cards! My *Wonder Wallet* only performed one trick, but this deck of cards performed lots of miracles. I begged and pleaded with my mother until she finally gave in and purchased the trick deck for me. Then I practiced and practiced and practiced. I watched TV all day long, just waiting for the commercial to come back on so I could study the moves exactly the way Marshall demonstrated them. Eventually I was able to duplicate the TV commercial flawlessly. Noting my growing interest in magic, my mother bought me the entire Marshall Brodien Magic Set for Christmas that year.

I remember sitting on my bed, laying out all the new tricks from the kit. I scanned the instruction booklet to see which magic trick explanations contained the most photos. From the photos, I was able to figure out how to perform the tricks. My favorite trick was the *Color Vision* mindreading cube trick. Later that night, my brother Malcolm came home from his date with Cindy and I proceeded to show him the tricks I had just learned. He was genuinely astounded when I read his mind correctly!

Over time, the magic kit made me forget all about my puppets. I was now totally consumed with magic. I went to the library on a regular basis and took out every book that I could find on the subject of magic. When I tried to read the books, though, I did not have enough focus to make it past one or two paragraphs without getting totally distracted. I'd have to keep reading the same sentence over and over again until I absorbed the content, so the books I usually checked out were the ones with the most photos. If the trick I was reading about didn't contain a lot of descriptive pictures, I couldn't learn it.

Sometimes I made up my own trick based on the limited number of photos the explanation contained.

Back when I was a child, the teachers always told my parents that I was a smart kid, but I just did not apply myself. They did not understand learning disorders like they do today. I am sure if I were a child in school today, they would have a diagnosis for my reading problem. I am sure there is a logical reason why I was never able to stay focused enough to understand and read a complete book. But even though I could not focus on one specific thing while reading a book, I was very good at hearing all conversations going on around me. It would prove to be a great skill to have later on in my life, but I didn't know it yet.

After I learned the secrets in the books, I didn't want any other kids to uncover the mystery, so I snuck the books out of the library without the librarian noticing. As a result, many of the magic books in the public library disappeared and permanently reappeared in my personal library. It's ironic that the books taught me how to be a magician and make things disappear, so the first thing I would make disappear were the library books that taught me the secrets! Many of those books are still in my library today.

One of my two favorite TV shows was *The Magician* with Bill Bixby. Bill played the part of millionaire Tony Blake, who drove a sharp-looking Corvette and lived on a jet airplane. While Tony unjustly spent some time in jail, he met a man who later died and left Tony with a considerable sum of money. Tony performed his magic shows in Las Vegas. When he was not on stage, he used his brains and his magical skills to help people out of unusual situations. I always dreamed about living in Las Vegas and driving a Corvette, just like Tony Blake did.

My second favorite show was *Kung Fu* with David Carradine. I loved the way he remained calm while kicking butt.

This show prompted me to start taking Kempo karate lessons at the age of eleven. I only made it to the orange belt before losing interest. I would rather stay home practicing my magic instead of being beat up by other kids in the dojo. I guess I was destined to be a performer, not a fighter.

Bill Bixby

Chapter 4

My Best Friend Vanishes

We always had big holiday parties at our house. My parents were very social people and they had a lot of friends who attended the parties. Every year for my birthday on Halloween, our place was the house everyone would eventually wind up partying. People came from all around to celebrate the holiday and my birthday. Even for the smallest occasion, our house always seemed to be packed with friends and family. Whenever my parents threw a party, my father would tell me to go get my little bag of magic tricks and perform for everyone.

One couple my parents were very close to was Tommy and Gail. Our families were so close that I came to call them my uncle and aunt, even though we were not related. They had two children, Kelly and Little Tommy. Kelly was a few years older than Little Tommy, and they lived close enough that Little Tommy was able to ride his bike to my house and come play with me often. Little Tommy was a special person. He had a speech impediment, and he was a little slower than other kids his age. I felt the need to watch over him and defend him when other kids made fun of him and picked on him because of the way he talked. He loved to collect Matchbox cars and baseball cards, and he had a great memory for recalling baseball players' statistics. We were like brothers.

Little Tommy's father was the President of Labor Union 32J. Unfortunately, Uncle Tommy died of a heart attack at a very young age. After he passed, Little Tommy began to spend more and more time with my family.

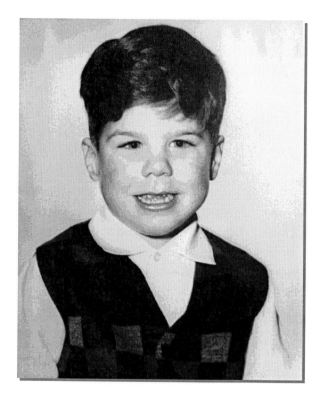

Little Tommy

In the summer of 1974, my family rented a house by a lake in Connecticut and Little Tommy came to live with us for the entire summer. My father's dad, Grandpa Alex, also spent the summer with us. My father was at the summerhouse only on the weekends because he had to work during the week. That summer it was just Little Tommy and I playing together, because most of my magic tricks stayed home. Every day, Little Tommy and I fished off of the dock a block away from our rental house. We played on the beach with the other kids and swam in the water.

One day while swimming in the lake, I felt a stinging pain in my stomach, a burning pain like I had never experienced before. While I was getting out of the water, I realized there was a jellyfish floating near me. It was close enough to sting me multiple times. I was in such excruciating pain, I wanted to tear the flesh off my stomach. I ran back up to our summer house hoping my mother could offer some form of relief. I don't recall exactly what she did to ease the pain, but I never forgot how much that jellyfish sting hurt. From that day on, I have hated jellyfish with a passion, and I do not like swimming in the ocean. To this day, if I see a jellyfish in an aquarium or in a photo, I cringe with disgust and am reminded of that painful episode from my childhood.

Another day while Little Tommy and I were swimming in the lake, I noticed that most of the other kids were wearing identical white bracelets that looked like they were made out of rope. I asked one of the kids where they all got them, and he said another kid's father was making them. Little Tommy and I begged him to make us each a matching sailor's nautical turk's head knotted bracelet. We always looked for matching items like that to show our brotherly bond.

Near the end of the summer, everyone was preparing to return to their homes. It was the winding down of a perfect summer until one starry night when the unthinkable happened.

A guy with a pickup truck was giving all the kids in the area a tour around the lake. The kids piled into the back of his truck, and he'd take everyone for a joy ride. Little Tommy and I took the tour along with many other kids. After returning from the first tour, Little Tommy and I boarded the pickup truck for a second tour. I was sitting at the very back of the truck with my legs straddled over the tailgate. Little Tommy was facing the front of the truck, talking to some of the other kids.

At the last minute, I decided I did not want to take the lengthy ride again and jumped off the back of the truck before it pulled away. I casually walked towards the lake and decided I was going to walk along the shoreline until everyone returned from the tour. Little Tommy must have turned around and noticed I was gone and also jumped out. But the truck was already moving. He fell to the ground and hit his head on the street, fracturing his skull.

Suddenly I saw the truck, still full of kids, backing up and returning to the spot where it started. It stopped abruptly, and everyone jumped off and crowded around something in the middle of the street. I also heard a loud, horrible moan. I ran over to find out what everyone was looking at, and there was my best friend, Little Tommy, lying in the middle of the street. The awful noise was coming from him. He was looking up at me like a wounded baby, not saying a word, merely moaning in pain with sad confusion in his eyes. The sound of his deep-throated groans still haunt me to this very day.

Someone called for an ambulance and Little Tommy was rushed to the local hospital. A few days later, all of the lake rental houses were deserted as vacationing families returned to their homes. I went back to New York with my grandfather. My parents stayed behind to go to the hospital and sit with my Aunt Gail and Little Tommy, who was in a coma. I don't remember many details about his condition because I was kept in the dark with his diagnosis. That fall I started school a few days later than everyone else, and I had to explain the delay to my teacher, Sister Albon. She was very sympathetic to the situation and helped me catch up to the rest of the class.

A week later I was practicing my magic in my bedroom while my brother Mal was watching me perform. I heard people downstairs coming into our house. My parents were returning home from Connecticut, but it did not sound like they were receiving a happy welcome. The energy in our little house quickly turned dark. When I heard my father's voice as he said hello to my grandfather, I immediately had a vision in my mind: My father was going to walk into my bedroom, sit on the bed next to me, and tell me that Little Tommy had died. The vision was very strong and crystal clear in my mind's eye. I was shocked at how strong the feeling was, and I had to snap myself out of the painful daydream.

A few moments later, my father came upstairs and asked me to sit on the bed next to him. In a soft voice, he asked my brother to leave us alone in the small bedroom. He then proceeded to tell me in the kindest way possible that Little Tommy was no longer with us. Little Tommy was now with his father in heaven. On September 10, 1974, my best friend Little Tommy passed away.

I sat in stunned silence. The vision I had moments earlier had just become my reality, exactly how I imagined it in my mind. Before he started talking, I knew exactly what my father was going to say and exactly how he was going to say it. He misinterpreted my long silence and told me it was okay to cry. It took me a minute or two to process what he just said and then I broke down crying in his arms. My best friend was gone, and I was the reason for his death. If I had not jumped off the back of the truck, he would not have followed me, and he would still be living today.

The untimely loss of Tommy left a huge void in my heart that practically destroyed me. It was a pain no eleven-year-old boy should ever have to experience. The guilt slowly ate away at me like a cancer devouring my insides. It caused me to sink into depression. Focusing on my magic was the only way to distract my thoughts and try to forget the pain of the death I seem to have caused. It wasn't bad enough my aunt lost her husband a year earlier; now I caused her to lose her only son.

Years later, Aunt Gail invited me over to her house because she was going through all of Little Tommy's belongings that were stored in her basement. She told me I could have whatever I wanted from all of his toys. I remembered how much his collection of Matchbox toy cars meant to him, so I took his favorite yellow car and told her I didn't want anything else. Since the day I took that car, it has always been on display somewhere in my house. I want to be able to see it every day as a constant reminder of the love I have for my best friend, Little Tommy.

Gerard and Tommy blowing out birthday candles

Chapter 5

Paying for My Magic

The only way I could distract myself from thinking about Little Tommy's death was with my magic, but I needed to find a way to earn money so I could buy new magic tricks and books to keep my mind occupied. The only way for a kid my age to make money was to have a paper route. I went down to the *Long Island Press* newspaper office, and the route foreman told me I couldn't have a paper route because I needed to be twelve years old, and I was only eleven at the time. There had to be a way to get the job. Since I already admitted my age to the route foreman, I needed to find some other way to get the job before my twelfth birthday.

My older sister, Maureen, was dating a guy named Charlie who happened to work for the *Long Island Press*. I told Charlie I would wash his car once a week for a month if he would help me get the job. He agreed. After making a few calls, pulling a few strings, and going over the route foreman's head, he was able to get me a paper route a year earlier than I was allowed.

Every day after school at three thirty, a huge stack of newspapers was delivered to my house. I'd fold them, put rubber bands around them, and stuff the folded papers into a huge canvas bag attached to my bicycle handlebars. Seven days a week, I delivered newspapers to people's houses. I dreaded the Sunday paper, because it was so big and heavy and contained so many additional sections. A year later, I was also able to get a paper route delivering *The Daily News*. The routine for delivering that paper was the same as the *Long Island Press*, except *The Daily News* had to be delivered first thing in the morning before I went to school.

Snow had fallen the night before the very first morning I was to deliver *The Daily News*. It was freezing cold, and the streets were covered in snowflakes and ice that had not yet been plowed. I wasn't able to ride my bicycle that morning, so I had to use my mother's folding shopping cart to deliver the papers. Wheeling the shopping cart full of newspapers a half-mile to my first delivery was grueling. The streets were empty and no one was out that early in the morning. I was never so cold in my life, and I cried as I walked—not a baby type cry, but more of a painful cry because of the blistering cold.

I started to visualize sitting in my warm house, sipping a hot chocolate with whipped cream on top while talking to my mom. The entire time I was delivering the newspapers, I kept that image in my mind to help distract me from the pain of the cold. Taking my mind out of my body and projecting it into the future, to ease the pain of the present, was a skill I would come to use quite often as I grew up.

Once a week on Friday, I went from house to house collecting the money owed to me for the week's newspaper delivery. Most of my profit was generated from people tipping me. If I put the paper on their front steps so they didn't have to step outside of their house to fetch it, I was tipped more. If the paper was far from the stoop or lost in the bushes, I wasn't tipped at all. I became a master at speedily riding my bicycle past houses and tossing papers with extreme accuracy, so they landed directly on the top step of each customer's stoop.

When I collected money, I started to notice that customers' attitudes would sometimes correlate to how much they were going to tip me. If they answered the door with a bad attitude and started complaining to me, I knew I was about to be stiffed and they were justifying their cheapness with excuses. I started playing a game in my head to predict how much I would be tipped before they tipped me. As time went by, reading people from their body language and tonality of their words became a game I got better and better at playing.

When I was done collecting from my paper route, I went to Bux Candy Store on Francis Lewis Boulevard for a fresh egg cream and a glazed donut. After a while, the candy store owner noticed my weekly routine and asked why I was there every Friday at the same time. I told him I had a paper route and needed to earn money so I could buy new magic tricks for my hobby. He realized I was very responsible for a young boy and asked me if I wanted a job working in the candy store after I completed my paper route. I gladly took the job knowing I would be earning more money, which meant more new magic tricks to add to my collection.

Every day, I woke up at five-thirty in the morning and delivered *The Daily News*. I came home and had breakfast, then went to school until three o'clock. After school I walked home, changed out of my Catholic school uniform, and delivered the *Long Island Press* newspaper. Then I'd go work at the candy store until dinnertime. After dinner, I would struggle through my homework and eventually go to bed. Every week, I took my pay and went to a store called Top Value Discounts on 35th Avenue and Francis Lewis Boulevard, where I'd buy my trick of the week.

The candy store had two owners, Jack and George, who lived together in an apartment above the shop. Jack was older then George, and it showed in his appearance. Jack always looked like he was mad at the world; he had a resting mad face. The customers knew Jack as the grumpy one and George as the nice one. I spent most of my time working in the candy store with Jack, because George drove an oil delivery truck from house to house, pumping oil into basement storage tanks. I always knew when we were getting an oil delivery from George because the filling process made a high-pitched whistling sound that indicated how full the storage tank was getting. Jack and George told me they were "brothers from different mothers." Much later I found out that they were a gay couple.

Jack enjoyed sitting at the counter reading the newspaper while I took care of all the customers. If the store got busy, he would stop reading his newspaper and reluctantly come behind the counter to help me with the customers. When there were no customers in the store, I restocked the soda display and refilled the candy racks. I also refilled the greeting card display and dusted them all off, organized soda deliveries in the basement, and wiped down all the counters. Eventually Jack taught me how to make egg creams, malteds, and ice cream sundaes. After I was done refilling the soda and candy racks, I worked behind the counter as a soda jerk. When I got older, I quit the *Long Island Press* paper route and worked exclusively at the candy store from three thirty in the afternoon to nine o'clock at night, six days a week. My salary was five dollars a week. Jack and I seemed to get along really well because I understood him, so he was not really that grumpy to me. One of the things he and I did for fun was to give all the regular customers nicknames: The Alley Girls, Old Lady Osmond, Steve Square, Dirty Joe, Tin Can, Slow-Motion Mike, Giraffe Neck, El-Cheap-o, John Peanuts, Brillo Hair, Bill Coke, The Midget Lady, The Peppy Lady, and Blinky are the ones I recall.

Jack liked the fact that I was always looking for a way to earn a buck. He thought my best idea was during the gas shortage in the 1970s. People would get up really early in the morning, hours before the gas station opened, and form a line with their cars to get their daily ration of gas. Barney's Gulf

Station was two blocks from my house, and the line of cars started at the gas pumps and went past my house. I told Jack that a lot of the people waiting for gas were sleeping in their cars. Using a shopping cart borrowed from our local Waldbaum's Supermarket, I'd go to the candy store at six a.m. when it opened and fill the cart with newspapers, magazines, donuts, and coffee. Then I walked up and down the line of cars selling them to the waiting motorists. My sales were so good, my weekly salary from the candy store doubled. I think I was the only one in New York who was disappointed when the gas shortage eventually ended. My best friend Brian would always proclaim, "If there's a way to make a buck, Gerard will figure out how to do it."

Brian was one of my best friends from the day I met him at the age of four. He lived right across the street from me with his grandparents and his older brother, Ty. Brian and I were born one day apart in the same year, he on October 30, and I on October 31. Having our birthdays so close always gave us a special bond, and he never let me forget that I had to respect my elders. If I wasn't with Little Tommy, I was usually with Brian. Since Ty was a little older, I didn't hang out with him as much. Growing up we all had nicknames. Brain dubbed me "The Chiseler" because he said I was able to chisel anybody out of anything.

Brian would sometimes hang out at the candy store with me when I was working. Jack was an amateur painter, so he tried to make extra money by displaying and selling his paintings in the candy store. He was very proud of his artwork, but Brian and I thought they looked like a first-grader painted them. I guess everyone else shared our opinion because Jack never sold any of his artwork.

But I discovered that whenever Jack was in a bad mood, all I needed to do was talk to him about his paintings and he would cheer up. I learned you can change someone's attitude by directing their thoughts and the focus of the conversation onto something they were interested in. That skill combined with my "chiseling" abilities led my mother to declare that I should be a lawyer. "You are so good with words and manipulating people," she said. "You definitely should be a lawyer."

Another way to make money at my age was to become an altar boy at the church. My family members were practicing Catholics who attended weekly Mass at the Our Lady of the Most Blessed Sacrament church, which had a church, rectory, convent, and a school where I attended grades one through eight. Half of my teachers were nuns who were allowed to hit pupils if they felt that physical discipline was necessary. Sister Victor was the one nun who comes to mind as being the most physically abusive of all the nuns teaching in the school.

The sixth-grade boys were allowed to become altar boys, which meant assisting the priests during the Mass. It also meant making money from tips when we worked weddings and funerals. Another perk of being an altar boy was getting out of school for one day a year to go on a field trip to Rye Playland, an amusement park just outside New York City. I heard from other altar boys that Rye Playland had a great magic store. My desire to make extra money and my need to shop at that magic store prompted me to become an altar boy.

Little did I realize that I would be getting up in front of large groups of people each week during the Mass. If I served Sunday Mass, there was a chance I'd be up on the altar in front of at least five hundred people. The priest would do all the talking, making my duties as an altar boy silent and easy, but I'd still be doing things in front of a large audience. It was like a silent, well-choreographed performance. We became so comfortable with our duties on the altar that we found ways to goof around without the priest seeing what we were doing.

By the time I was thirteen, I had purchased all the parlor magic tricks from the local Top Value store. Then I learned that there was a magic shop on Long Island, about thirty minutes from my house. Whenever I saved up enough money, I begged my brother or my sister to give me a ride to Esposito's Magic Shop in Rockville Center. With my busy work schedule, I didn't have much time to focus on my school studies, but my collection of parlor magic tricks and books was growing at an impressive rate. My first purchases from the magic store were *Hyrum the Haunted Handkerchief*, *Chinese Sticks*, a *Milk Pitcher*, the *Siberian Chain Escape*, the *Vanishing Candlestick* and the *Glass Penetration Board*. My next purchase included *Nickels to Dimes*, *Linking Rings*, a *Wonder Signal*, and the *Magic Sponge Balls*.

The *Siberian Chain Escape* was one of my favorite tricks. I would ask a spectator to secure my wrists together with a chain and a padlock. A cloth was placed over my hands, and I'd instantly escape from the chains. I wanted to make it seem more difficult, so I'd ask someone to tie a blindfold over my eyes in addition to placing the cloth over my hands before I escaped. I became fascinated with having to perform the trick without actually seeing it.

I started doing things in my life without my sight. While walking home from school, I chose a house halfway up the block and made it my target. Then I'd close my eyes and slowly walk up the block, trying to imagine how far I traveled. Before I shut my eyes, I took notice of anything that would help me figure out my position, like a dog in someone's front yard that I could hear when I came closer to it, or people sitting on their front steps talking. When I was in my house, I walked up the stairs to the second floor with my eyes closed to see if I could remember how many steps remained without counting them. Then I tried to make it all the way into my bedroom without banging into anything before I finally opened my eyes. I also played the same game walking from room to room. I became quite good at approximating what was around me and how far I traveled while keeping my eyes shut.

My mother and I usually watched the Mike Douglas show while she was getting dinner ready. I remember Mike and an actress plotting against the next guest on the show. When the guest came out and told a show business story to Mike, the actress started to cry. I was confused and asked my mother why the woman was so sad and crying. My mother explained what actors and actress were, and how they were able to control their emotions and play the parts of others.

Every day, my schoolteacher would read one chapter from a book to my class if we were well behaved. At that time she was reading from *The Wind in the Willows*. My teacher not only read the book to us, she added emotions to her voice when she read the part of Mr. Toad. Her voice stimulated my imagination, and I visualized the entire scene from the book in my head as she read it to us. I asked my mother if that was also considered acting and she said, yes, it was. The ability to become someone else fascinated me. I started to read books on acting, thinking it could help my own performance.

Mike Douglas often had magicians on his show, which I enjoyed, but another regular guest that interested me was *The Amazing Kreskin*. Instead of performing magic tricks, he read minds. I asked my mother if Kreskin was acting or if he really had the ability to read minds, and she said she wasn't sure. I was amazed by Kreskin's tricks, but I did not like his nerdy schoolteacher appearance and his aggressive personality.

Chapter 6

Destined to Be an Entertainer

On Saturday mornings, I loved to watch a television show called *Wonderama* with host Bob McAllister. One of the magicians I saw on the show was a long-haired illusionist named Doug Henning. He had a new, fresh approach to performing magic. He did not dress in a suit or a tuxedo, nor did he have a top hat and tails. He dressed like a hippie from the sixties. After *Wonderama*, I often saw him on television promoting his Broadway show, *The Magic Show*. My brother Mal gave me a ticket to see Doug's Broadway show for my twelfth birthday in 1974. This would be my first of many times seeing this show.

The tickets were for a performance a week or so after my birthday. I remember we parked about two blocks from the theater and walked in the cold air down 48th Street. I saw the huge Cort Theater marquee that read *The Magic Show - A New Musical* with a big eyeball that had hypnotic rays shooting from it. I was so excited!

When we entered the theater, the usher sat us center stage in the fifth row. The curtain rose and the show began and suddenly an unexplainable charge of electricity exploded in my spinal cord like nothing I had ever felt before.

There were six people sitting on stage, three on either side of a little box that had a curtain draped across the front. The six-member cast started to sing, and a few moments later the little curtains parted and we could see Doug Henning kneeling inside the box, making his entrance. Again, I felt like a lightning bolt of electricity shot down my spine when I saw him for the first time. I was about twenty feet away from Doug Henning, the magician I watched on TV. This was the first time in my life I was star-struck.

Midway through the performance, Doug performed the legendary trunk trick called the *Metamorphosis*. In this trick, his assistant climbed inside the trunk and stood in a mailbag. Her wrists were handcuffed and the mailbag was tied shut with a piece of rope. Doug then stood on top of the trunk, and in less than three seconds, they would magically switch places. I knew the trick well because I saw him perform it on television many times. I also knew that Doug loved to have audience members inspect the trunk for trap doors, so as soon as he walked to center stage and started to ask for an audience volunteer, my hand shot up. It was almost as if the hand of God reached down and lifted my arm before Doug was able to finish his sentence. I was the first in a theater full of kids to raise his hand.

Doug looked over at me, pointed at me, and invited me on the stage. Once more I felt as though a jolt of electricity raced down my spine. I quickly made my way up to the stage, where he greeted me and shook my hand. I was shaking the hand of Doug Henning! I couldn't believe I was standing there in his presence. It was the first time I touched a real live celebrity, and I remember thinking he was actually smaller than I thought he would be.

He took me over to the trunk and asked me to bang on all four sides to prove they were solid. While his assistant tilted the trunk so I could inspect the bottom, Doug said, "Kick the bottom as hard as you can." I did exactly as he said, and gave the bottom of the trunk a good solid kick. He made a face at the audience as if he was totally surprised by my forceful actions. The entire audience laughed at his expression and what seemed to be an enthusiastic kick by a rambunctious little kid. The audience's laughter broke the hypnotic spell that Doug had seemingly cast upon me. I looked up and realized I was on stage with hundreds of people staring at me.

I guess the average twelve-year-old would have been scared standing there on that large Broadway stage, but every week during Sunday Mass, I stood in front of hundreds of people as an altar boy. Being on stage in front of a group that size didn't seem to bother me in the least.

Doug handed me the key to the lock that just secured the trunk closed. He then asked me to step over to the side while he and his assistant performed the magical switch. As soon as they switched places, the assistant took the key from me and I was quickly escorted off the stage. The assistant unlocked the trunk, to reveal Doug inside.

As I returned to my seat, I noticed all the other kids in the theater were looking at me with envy. I knew they secretly wished they were on stage with Doug. I could feel my heart pounding with excitement. It was like a drug that gave me some sort of magical high, an awesome, euphoric feeling I never felt before. If people other than priests and nuns could have life callings, this was clearly mine. I realized at that very moment I wanted to be on stage performing and entertaining people with my magic for the rest of my life. It was not only the act of doing a trick, it was also acting and performing that allowed the audience to enjoy the show. I made myself a promise and set my very first goal: Someday I was going to be on stage performing for a live audience just like Doug Henning.

Immediately following the show, I needed to find the stage door so I could talk to Doug. When we exited the theater, I noticed a big metal gate outside the theater that led down a long alleyway. At the very end of that alleyway was the stage door. I waited on the sidewalk by the gate with everyone else who also wanted to meet Doug and the rest of the cast members. The crowd was excited, and every time a cast member exited the self-locking gate, he or she was immediately swarmed by fans seeking autographs and photos. I realized getting any "alone time" with Doug was going to be impossible this way. I was the one who was on stage with him, so I felt I should at least have a few minutes with him. Time to think outside the box and figure out how to get one-on-one time with Doug Henning.

The very next time the big metal gate opened and a cast member emerged—this time the piano player from the band—I looked him in the eye and confidently said, "Doug is expecting me." I swung the gate open and started walking down the alley. It was the first time I used my acting skills, and I bluffed my way right past him. He never even tried to stop me! (Unbeknownst to me, Paul Schaffer was the piano player who let me slip past the gate—the same Paul Schaffer who would eventually become the bandleader for David Letterman.)

I walked down to the stage door and knocked on it. I figured since the confidence routine worked once, I would try it again. The stage doorman answered and said, "Can I help you?"

I replied, "Yeah, I'm here to see Doug."

"Is he expecting you?"

"Yes, I was the one on stage with him tonight inspecting the trunk," I said in the most confident voice I could muster.

"Hold on a minute," he said, and disappeared into the theater. While I waited, I was able to look inside and see a few of the illusions on the wings of the stage. Standing there, looking at the illusions lined up backstage, knowing I was seeing something that most audience members don't get a chance to see, was an exciting moment for me.

The stage doorman returned and said, "Doug will be with you in a minute."

A few moments later, Doug Henning appeared. He was wearing a long brown leather coat, a blue plaid scarf wrapped around his neck, and he had a brown leather messenger type bag over his left shoulder.

He walked over to me and said, "Hey Gerard, you did a great job in the show tonight." He remembered my name from the show!

I said, "Thank you, and so did you." He laughed.

I proceeded to tell him I was a magician just like he was and that I never knew what I wanted to do with my magic, but now I knew. I wanted to be on stage every night making people laugh and smile just like he did. Doug told me never to let anything get in the way of my dreams, and to learn as much as I could about the art of magic, as well as acting. He said it was not necessarily the tricks themselves that were so important to entertain your audience, but how you performed them for an audience is what mattered.

"My brother and I built the *Zig-Zag Illusion* that you performed in the show," I said, "but it didn't turn out very well."

Doug took a piece of paper out of his pocket and scribbled the words *Victory Carton Illusions*. "This is a book that will show you how to make inexpensive illusions out of cardboard boxes. It'll be a great place for you to start building your act."

I took the paper. "Thanks! Is it okay if I get a picture with you?"

"Sure. I'd love to."

I sprinted back up the alleyway, opened the fire escape door, and told my brother to come on in. I introduced Malcolm to Doug as if we were long-lost friends and had him snap a picture of Doug and me together.

A few weeks after meeting Doug Henning, he mailed me a letter saying that I could visit him at the theater any time I wanted. If I let him know in advance I was going to be there, he would let the doorman know when I was coming. That picture and letter have always hung proudly in my house as a reminder of the day that my life found its meaning. Standing on stage with Doug, looking out at the audience and feeling their energy, made me realize that was what I wanted to do with my life. I wanted to be a magician.

But I didn't want to be just any magician—I wanted to be one who was different from the rest. Now that I knew what I wanted to do with my life, it was time to get cracking. Seeing Doug Henning's Broadway show filled me with the desire to practice my magic tricks as much as I could so I could start to perform for audiences and once again experience that euphoric feeling from their applause.

Doug Henning and Gerard backstage

One Saturday night, February 14, 1975, my sister Toni was invited to attend a sleepover birthday party for our neighbor, Linda Leone. My father and I walked my seven-year-old sister across the street to the party. Linda's father, Ben, had planned for all the men to play poker in the kitchen during the slumber party.

"Hey, Gerard," Ben said. "How would you like to perform a magic show for the girls?"

"I'd love to!" I quickly replied.

"Great! So how much do you charge?" he asked jokingly.

I confidently replied, "Two dollars and fifty cents for a half hour performance."

He handed me a five-dollar bill and told me to keep the girls busy for an hour while the men played cards.

I ran home and got my suitcase full of magic tricks. I had been practicing consistently for three months, but I knew I didn't have an hour's worth of tricks to keep the girls busy. The last thing I wanted to do was give Linda's father any change, so I decided to do my tricks slowly, and I added a lot of patter to my presentation like I saw Doug do.

I loved performing for the girls, and the applause at the end of each trick was exhilarating. I had not felt that good since I was on stage with Doug Henning. I thought this was a much better way of making money than working in the candy store. I was making five dollars for a one-hour show, and it took me an entire week to make that much as a soda jerk and refilling shelves.

After the show was over, I had a decision to make: Do I use the money to purchase another trick from the store, or do I invest the money in advertisement to get more shows? I decided to invest the money and took my five dollars down the block to a sign store on 34th Avenue. I spoke to the artist who was hand-painting the signs.

"I need a big sign for the window of the candy store I work in," I said. "A sign that says *Gerard the Great, Magic for all Occasions*, along with my phone number on it."

"That'll cost you fifteen dollars," he said.

"I don't have fifteen bucks. All I have is five." I thought about it for a moment. "Could you just make me the best sign possible for five dollars?"

A few days later, the sign painter presented me with a small, hand-painted cardboard sign. I rushed to the candy store and asked Jack if I could place the sign in the store window. Now I was officially in business! I was a professional magician advertising my services for the world to see—or at least advertising to the people who passed by the little candy store.

From that day on, I started performing everywhere I could: children's hospitals, birthday parties, Bar Mitzvahs, and Boy Scout Blue and Gold Dinners. I built a small theater in my mother's basement so I could rehearse there and put on occasional shows for the neighborhood children.

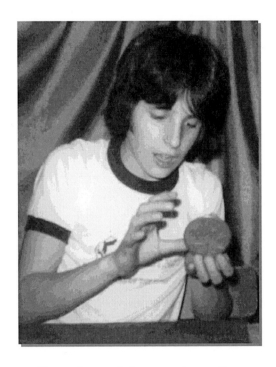

Gerard practicing a coin routine

Chapter 7

Things Are Not What They Seem

February 25, 1975 was my mother's birthday. On that day, my father secretly told her he had met someone at work named Geraldine. She was a divorced mother of two and he wanted to "help her out." He told my mother he wanted to keep his current family, and have Geraldine as his girlfriend on the side. In his mind, he did not see anything wrong with his proposal; he basically wanted his cake and he wanted to eat it, too. I would later come to realize that was the type of man that my father really was—he broke the news to my mother on her *birthday*. My mother wanted no part of his twisted fantasy arrangement and told him he needed to make a decision: He could have his wife or his girlfriend, but he could not have both. My mother never shared his disturbing news with anyone else in the family.

My brother Mal continued to date Cindy, and eventually they decided to tie the knot. Before Mal was married, he had a bachelor party at our house. Everyone attending the party was someone I knew. This was going to be a fun night! Soon after the party began, my father sent me up to my bedroom and ordered me to stay in my room with the door closed. He said that a twelve-year-old was too young to be at the party. I was completely humiliated in front of my friends. While I argued my point to stay at the party, they were setting up a movie screen and projector.

"I love home movies. Can I please stay?" I begged my father.

My father insisted I go to bed and close the door. The men started to watch the movies, and from my room I heard all the guys laughing and making jokes. I did not remember our home movies ever getting that kind of reaction, so I snuck out of my bedroom. When I peeked down the stairs, I saw images of naked girls doing strange things to naked guys. The party guests were having a good time. I remember a few of the guys using words I never heard before.

On August 31, 1975, soon after his bachelor party, Malcolm and Cindy were married at Leonard's of Great Neck on Northern Boulevard. Everyone was happy at the occasion except for me. I was about to lose my brother, my roommate, and one of my best friends. Following the wedding reception, the newlyweds took a two-week honeymoon and visited California and Hawaii. I remember hearing some friends talking about what a honeymoon was, and how my brother was now having sex with his new wife. Is this why my brother left me? Did he want to do the things I saw in the bachelor party movies with Cindy?

Two weeks later I was sitting outside my house on my front stoop, eagerly waiting for my brother and his new wife to return from the airport after the honeymoon. Unfortunately, they were late and each minute that passed by seemed like an hour to me. I remember hearing the older kids sitting on the front stoop of the house next door, laughing and saying something about my brother being late because he was still enjoying sex with his wife.

They were also making fun of the fact that my cousin Mark would rather have sex with a man than a woman. I didn't understand why they were making these mean comments about my cousin, so I went over and asked why they were saying such hurtful things. My mean-spirited neighbors proceeded to explain to me that my cousin was gay. He didn't like to do things like that to a girl, he liked to do those things to another guy. Now I was totally confused about the description of sex, and annoyed because they were clearly making fun of my cousin. I returned to my own stoop in anger.

Again I fantasized about being able to read their minds so I knew what they were joking about. When my brother finally pulled up and stepped out of the car, I ran over and hugged him, and I burst out crying uncontrollably. I was happy to see him, but frustrated at what everyone was talking about. I felt embarrassed because all my friends were watching, and I was crying in front of them and I didn't know why. My father always told me not to cry, and now I was not able to control it.

Almost a month after my brother's wedding, on September 28, my father and mother called my little sister, Toni, and me into their bedroom. While he packed everything into his suitcase, my father proceeded to tell us he was leaving the house. I remember my mother sat on the bed, crying. My father made his decision, and decided he wanted to be with his girlfriend instead of my mother. He had also decided he was going to stay married to my mother until after my brother's wedding because he didn't want to disrupt a joyous occasion for the family. It was one of the first times in my life that I realized things are not always what they seem. "Your father is moving out for a while," is what my mother said.

My parents tried to reassure us that his moving out was not because they did not love us and, in fact, his decision to leave had nothing to do with us at all. I was completely heartbroken when my brother moved out for good because he got married, and now a few weeks later, my father was moving out for good as well. I was devastated. My dad was my rock, my hero, a big man with a big heart. He was a police officer who made me feel protected and loved. Not only did he adopt me, he gave me his name. So when he left, a part of me also went away. I did not want to make him feel bad about leaving, so I hid my feelings from everyone.

After he left, I was still able to spend time with him, but it was different. He was no longer my dad, living in my home. I had to share him with another family. Talk about a textbook midlife crisis: He left on September 28, which was his fortieth birthday, so he could start a new life with his girlfriend and her two sons.

My father's leaving was particularly hard for me because it left a tremendous void in my world. He had been a strong and reliable figure in my life. In fact, he may be one of the reasons why I am an entertainer today. I grew up idolizing him and wanting to be just like him.

My father was a loud, opinionated person who was always the life of the party. He was always the one who had to get the last word in during an argument. He would find a way to twist your words and make it seem like he was right. It was his way or the highway; he was never wrong and would scream and shout until you saw things his way. He did not perform or sing; he was a New York City detective who worked from nine to five every day. He never showed that he was proud of my skills when it came to performing magic. He only used my love of magic as a tool to punish me. If I wasn't a good boy, he would threaten to take away my magic props.

After he moved out, I vividly recall hearing my older family members talking about the situation. Everyone was completely in shock over his actions. Just one month ago he was dancing with my mother at my brother's wedding, and now they were getting divorced. They seemed like a happy couple celebrating their son's wedding day. How could he have kept a secret for so long without anybody figuring it out? How could he have pulled the wool over all of our eyes, and nobody had any idea what was going on in his secret life?

He seemed to have manipulated the thoughts of the entire family, but my mother refused to take any more of his manipulations and filed for divorce. For some strange reason I did not care why he was leaving, but I was intrigued with how he was able to screw with everybody's minds for so long. It seemed to be a form of mental misdirection. I remember frequently hearing my mother in her room crying. I did not know how to help her. I didn't know how to take away her pain.

My mother had to get a job to support us. My Aunt Gail worked as a cosmetician in a Madison Avenue cosmetic drugstore called Boyd's of Madison Avenue. She was able to get my mother a job there as a cosmetician. My father played his mind games to convince my mother to use his good friend, the same lawyer who took care of my adoption, to represent them both in the divorce. That was the biggest mistake my mother ever made.

While my family was falling apart around me, I continued to work at the candy store. In October 1975, a kid around my age used to come into the store a lot with his father. He would bring his acoustic guitar and play old Italian songs while Jack, the store owner, sang along. The kid seemed a little odd. He had an old-fashioned haircut, he wore old-fashioned clothes, he spoke with a stutter, and he seemed a little slow. In fact, he reminded me of Little Tommy. His name was Steve, and little did I know at the time, he would become one of my closest friends.

Steve lived around the block from the candy store. He was from an old-school Italian family, which is why he knew how to play all the old Italian songs on his guitar. After he and his father left, I asked the candy store owner who he was. Jack explained that every week at the same time, they came into the candy store to buy cigars and play Italian music.

The next time Steve came into the candy store, I introduced myself to him and we became instant friends. He started to hang around the candy store more often. Eventually Jack gave him a job compacting and tying up all the garbage boxes. After he was done, he was allowed to order a drink from the fountain. He always asked me to make him a C.E.C. (which stood for a chocolate egg cream). Steve loved the way I made them.

Steve and I started hanging out more and more together after work. He came to my house and we listened to records or watched TV together. I performed my newest magic tricks for him and he was always amazed. He was my best audience. Steve seemed to fill a void in my heart left by the untimely death of Little Tommy.

Steve and Gerard

Chapter 8

Discovering Different Types of Magic

Later that year, on December 26, 1975, Doug appeared in his first NBC television special called *The World of Magic with Doug Henning*. I watched the special and felt like I was watching my best friend on TV performing for the world. After seeing that show, I promised myself that someday I would have a live stage show as well as my own NBC television special just like Doug. My life had a purpose; I now had two dreams I needed to turn into reality.

In June of 1976 I was in eighth grade, and it was my final year in Catholic school before advancing to high school. I approached the principal, Sister Ellen Mary, and asked her if I could put on a magic show for the entire school. She said all of the students could not fit in the auditorium at the same time, so I would have to do my show twice. I confidently looked her in the eyes and said, "That's not a problem. I have done multiple performances in one day before." After she agreed to let me perform for the school, I started to write a script.

The play that I wrote was a direct copy of Doug Henning's Broadway show. It featured me as a magician and my friend, Peter, as a dark villain who wore a black top hat and cape with red satin lining. All of the kids loved our performance. I was graduating from the school on the top of my game. Everyone in school knew me as Gerard the Magician. I was now very popular, and I was no longer just a short, shy geek.

One day in July 1976, when I reported to work at the candy store, Jack told me about a young man who came in asking about my "Gerard the Great" sign in the window. He told Jack he was also a magician. To prove it, he took a little red scarf, waved it in the air, and instantly turned the scarf into a long cane. Jack said it was a really cool trick that I should be doing. I had never seen this trick before, and Jack's excitement over it intrigued me. Jack didn't know the kid's name nor had he ever seen him before, but he said he would be easy to recognize because he looked like a giant Q-Tip with his big Afro and long neck.

Eventually the young man returned to the candy store. He handed me his business card and introduced himself as Lance. He was a little older than me and seemed to be more advanced in the art of close-up magic than I was. We immediately became friends, and Lance invited me over to his house to check out all his tricks.

He had much bigger magic props than I did. He had *The Temple Screens*, a *French Arm Chopper*, and the *Lota Bowl Production*. They were professional props and nothing was made out of cardboard.

"Where did you get all these amazing props?" I asked.

"There's this magic store right in the center of Times Square called Tannen's Magic," Lance said. "I go there once in a while to buy new props."

I'd never heard of the place, but if they sold magic tricks and props, I had to see it. "Could you take me with you some time?"

"Yeah, of course."

I remember bragging to Lance that I wanted to be an illusionist like Doug Henning, and I had a *Zig-Zag Illusion* in my basement. Owning a *Zig-Zag Illusion* was much more impressive than all of Lance's tricks combined and he was very excited to see it. But when he came over to my house, as soon as he saw it he said it was a piece of junk. For some strange reason, he wanted to try it out and have me separate his middle from the rest of his body. So Lance climbed into the box, stuck his head out of the face hole, stuck his foot out of the foot hole, and stuck his two hands out of the hand holes. I slid two metal blades into the box and proceeded to slide Lance's midsection away from the rest of his body.

The box was not attached to any type of base, and the weight of Lance's body shifting around to avoid the blades inside the box caused the center of gravity to change. The entire box slowly tipped and started to fall. Lance could do nothing to prevent it from falling because the blades limited his movement. The box was too heavy for me to catch, so there was nothing I could do to help him, either. As I watched in horror, the box seemed to fall in slow motion. All I remember is feeling helpless to stop it while Lance screamed like a girl as he and the box crashed to the floor. That was the end of my *Zig-Zag Illusion.* It was completely destroyed. Once I realized Lance wasn't hurt, I started laughing my ass off even as Lance was screaming at me to get him out of the mangled illusion.

A week later, Lance and I took the Q28 bus from our neighborhood to Main Street Flushing. From there we took the number seven train to 42nd Street and Times Square. In total, it was about an hour's worth of traveling to get into New York City. We walked a few blocks from the train station to an office building on Broadway. After checking in with the building's doorman, we took the elevator up to the sixth floor where the secret magic shop was located. The shop occupied the entire floor, so when the elevator doors opened, it was like I was entering a magical dream world that was hidden away from the public—right in the middle of Times Square.

Everywhere I looked, I saw trick boxes, posters, silks, and props. And all the people in the store were either performing magic for each other or talking about magic. Their common bond was their love of and interest in magic, just like me. I remember the store being packed wall-to-wall with people young and old, short and tall, male and female, all gathering to discuss, perform, or purchase magic.

It took me a minute to take it all in. I saw props I never even knew existed. The showcases were full of tricks, all on display. And best of all, there was a handful of professional magicians behind the counter ready to demonstrate anything I wanted to see. Since Lance loved close-up magic, he was immediately drawn towards a group of "finger flickers" comparing card tricks. Since I wanted to be an illusionist, card tricks really didn't interest me, so I walked around the store and looked at the big props on display.

I approached one of the showcases and noticed somebody had just purchased a prop from the salesman. A customer could only learn the secret of the prop after purchasing it. The salesman started to demonstrate exactly how the trick worked and did not seem to mind that I was watching. By observing very closely, I was able to figure out how the trick worked as well how it was made. I knew I could make one of those at home and add that illusion to my magic show.

Another thing I found interesting about Tannen's Magic was its thick catalog, which contained descriptions of all the tricks they offered. They were scattered all around the counter, chained down so people could look at them but not walk away with them. Anyone who wanted a catalog could buy one for five dollars. While looking through the pages, I realized there were different categories of magic: dove magic, close-up magic, parlor magic, escapes, illusions, and mental magic. When I saw mental magic, I realized that's what *The Amazing Kreskin* was performing on the *Mike Douglas Show*. My mother did not know if he was really reading minds or not, but I just found the answer.

While we were in the shop, a magician walked off the elevator carrying a *Metamorphosis Trick*—the same type of trunk trick that I assisted Doug Henning with on stage. He was looking to sell it to anyone in the store. I had a chance to look at the trunk closely and figured out how the illusion actually worked before it was whisked to the back of the store to the "Illusion Room." I found out the Illusion Room was a hidden, ultra-private room to which only a few people were granted access. Lance said he had never seen the inside of this room.

A few minutes later, another illusion came into the shop called the *Sword Suspension*, which was also in Doug's show. This one was made by Chu's Magic Studio in Hong Kong. It was a lot smaller than the trunk trick and looked a lot more professional. It, too, quickly disappeared into the Illusion Room. Once I saw the *Sword Suspension*, I knew I had to own it. But where would I get the three hundred dollars to purchase it? With jobs as a paperboy, soda jerk, and altar boy, I would never be able to afford it.

Later that day, I called my brother Malcolm to tell him about the *Metamorphosis* trick and how I wanted that to be the next illusion that we built together. Malcolm only lived a block from us after he was married. He suggested that instead of building a *Metamorphosis* from scratch, we should buy a used trunk and alter it. I discovered that an elderly lady just a few blocks away was selling an old steamer trunk. Malcolm and I looked at it and decided we could use it, so I bought the trunk and we took it home. We worked on it for a while and made the proper alterations to enable me to perform the *Metamorphosis* trick.

While we were at Tannen's Magic, Lance heard about an upcoming magic convention called the "Larry Weeks Magic Convention" in New York City. All the local magicians would show up and shop for new tricks for their acts at a bunch of vendor tables and a magic auction. We attended the convention and I met Harry Blackstone, Jr. while we were there. When he entered the convention hall, all the magicians were in awe of him. He was kind enough to pose for a photo with me. When I asked if he had any advice for me, he said, "You need to be the best at what you do if you want to succeed." It was the same exact advice Doug Henning gave me.

During the convention, Larry Weeks needed someone to carry items out to him, one by one, as he auctioned them off. I volunteered for the job, figuring it would give me time to touch and inspect the props before they were sold at auction. I did not have the money to purchase any of them, but I could study them and fabricate them on my own. The final prop to be auctioned off was a *Dollhouse Illusion*. I remembered seeing the illusion performed on Bill Bixby's TV show, *The Magician*, and after inspecting it, I now knew the secret!

Following the convention, Lance and I started to hang out together more and more. Lance and his younger brother, Frank, whom Jack had nicknamed Blinky because he had a nervous twitch and constantly blinked his eyes, started hanging out with Steve and me on a regular basis. My old friend Brian and I started to drift apart.

I felt I needed to study all of the different types of magic until I discovered the one I wanted to focus on. Because Lance was more advanced than me in the art of close-up magic, I wanted to learn everything he knew, so I proposed a partnership: We would be a magical team instead of two solo acts. He would be the close-up performer and I would be the illusionist. We could give our audience two different types of magic in one show. By partnering up with him, I thought I could also learn all of his close-up routines and moves.

The first illusion Lance and I started to rehearse together was my *Metamorphosis* trick. The very first time we performed it in public was at his brother Frank's Bar Mitzvah. At the last minute, we decided to make the trick more incredible by adding an escape to it. Instead of Lance getting into a sack before being locked in the trunk, we decided I would tie up Lance with a long rope instead, but we didn't have time to rehearse the change. In our minds it would be more astounding, but in hindsight, it was not very well thought out by either of us.

After I had Lance all tied up, he had no way of getting into the trunk. He was at least a foot and a half taller than me, or at least it seemed that way with his Afro. He clearly should have been standing inside the trunk while I was tying him up. Eventually, a few men from the audience helped lift Lance up and place him into the trunk so we could finish the trick. That was a huge lesson to me. I learned the hard way never to perform any routine in front of an audience without blocking it out and rehearsing it first.

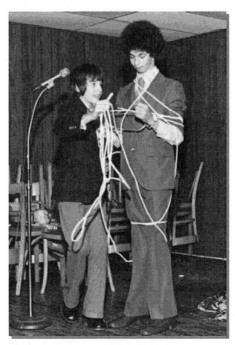

Gerard and Lance

Since illusions were expensive to purchase, and I only had one, I decided I would add a dove routine to my act. I took out the Yellow Pages and started calling every pet store in New York until I finally located one that claimed they had white doves. On September 1, 1976, I took two buses to a pet store in Brooklyn.

When I finally arrived, I didn't see any white magician-quality doves. Instead, I saw a cage full of grey ring-neck doves. Since I had counted on buying a bird that day, I decided to pay the ten dollars for one of the grey doves. I was so excited taking him home on the bus, imagining how I was going to train him to appear and disappear during my act. I wanted to take him out of the box and play with him on the bus!

Performing as a magical team was something Lance and I enjoyed doing together. Our summer day trips to Tannen's Magic in New York City continued on a weekly basis. I also stopped by the Cort Theater every week and talked to Doug Henning. He would tell me about his upcoming television appearances to watch for, and I would ask him for more advice with my budding magic career.

Chapter 9

Reflections on My Early Years

Sitting down and looking back on your entire life is an interesting process. If I had to sum up this chapter in my life, I would say my brain was programmed to think people who entered my life would eventually leave my life. People who loved me would eventually hurt or abandon me. My biological parents left me, my adoptive father left me, my best friend left me, and my brother left me. The only constant in my life has been my mother.

I was hard wired to believe that if I did not get close to people, it would not hurt as much when they eventually left me. My mind started to build a metaphoric wall around my heart and emotions.

I learned not to trust anyone, because the person I looked up to the most, my father, wound up being a huge liar. He manipulated me into thinking he was happy with his family when, in fact, he did not want me at all. He chose another family. When the average person meets someone, they give the other person the benefit of the doubt and allow them a little default trust. More trust can be earned over time as the relationship continues, or the default trust can be broken. But with me, I learned not to trust anyone. Trust is something you have to earn from me, and I always look at people and their motives with skepticism.

But before he left me, my father did teach me how to be comfortable performing for small groups. He had me doing it since I was one year old. When I was a little older, I would learn from him how to command attention at parties and in small gatherings. Being an altar boy also trained me to be comfortable in front of larger groups.

Learning how to take my mind out of my body and project it into the future to ease the pain of the present came in handy on that brutally cold day while I was delivering newspapers. Little did I know at the time how useful that skill would become.

At a very young age it was clear to my parents I was born to be a performer. We had no clue if my biological parents or anyone else in my biological family were entertainers or in any form of show business. I happened to be lucky enough to discover that show business was what I was destined to do with my life.

The day I stood on stage with Doug Henning before a packed audience in New York City's Cort Theater was the day my life changed forever. Some people go through their entire lives without knowing if they have a calling or a purpose in life. I was one of the lucky ones who knew mine by the age of twelve.

I learned there were different types of magic I could specialize in, and I also learned where I could purchase the magic props I needed to be able to build my show. I thought I wanted to be an illusionist like my mentor Doug Henning, but felt I needed to learn about the other types of magic just to make sure performing illusions was right for me. I learned there was a difference between fooling people and entertaining them.

Hearing all the professional magicians in the magic shop talking about booking their next gigs made me realize I needed to learn the "business" part of show business. I had to learn how to promote myself and my dream show when I eventually built it.

When I was twelve, I set my first goal: I wanted to be a successful performer like my mentor, Doug Henning; I wanted to perform on stage every night for a live audience; and I also wanted to have my own one-hour NBC television special.

Gerard putting on a music show

Discovering Mentalism

Chapter 10

The Sorcerer's Apprentice

For the first eight years of school I was a nobody. At the end of eighth grade, I performed for my entire elementary school and became a star. It was now time to attend my first year of high school, which would make me a nobody again.

In September of 1976, I felt like a fish out of water when I walked into Bayside High School for the very first time. It was the same Bayside High School that would later become the setting for the TV show *Saved by the Bell*.

The high school was full of new students I did not know. Many of the students were African-American. It was a new social mixture program that bussed in kids from different areas around the city. There were hardly any African-American students in my elementary school, or living in my neighborhood, so interacting with them was totally new to me. All the stories I'd heard from my father painted a negative picture about them. I was a little worried because I didn't know what to expect.

Lance and Steve both attended different schools, so I was alone while trying to navigate my way around the new, much larger school. Like so many young men my age, I was struggling simply to find my place. I was still quiet and shy, but unlike many other teens my age, I was undersized—barely 5'3" and 115 pounds. While many of my classmates' bodies had the whole puberty thing figured out, I was still waiting for the first signs of pubic and facial hair to sprout.

I did not think this was an issue until one weekend while visiting my father's apartment. I was in the kitchen when my stepbrother, Steven, and his friend, Kevin, decided that we should all pull down our pants and show each other our new genital hairs. I remember Steven saying, "Let's see the top of your flock." I didn't know that I was supposed to have hair down there; I was only fourteen. When they saw that I was bald, they both howled with laughter and teased me for the rest of the weekend. It was humiliating. If my lack of pubic hair was a source of humiliation in my own home, I was sure it was going to be a million times worse in the school gym locker room.

The very first day of school, I secured a gym locker in the corner. I learned how to get dressed and undressed in a hurry and keep all of my tiny private parts private. My underwear was the only thing someone would get to see. I was not going to change in front of a lot of guys who had "packages" while mine was still empty. I figured out how to avoid putting myself in a position to be teased.

The second day of school, I was in the lunchroom and saw a few girls walking around with balloon animals. Balloon animals meant there was a clown or another magician close by, so I searched until I found the student making them. His name was Floyd and he was a year older than me—and a lot taller, too. He had successfully made his way through puberty because he was clearly a ladies man. I introduced myself to Floyd and told him I was a magician and illusionist. I told him I was Doug Henning's friend, and he invited me to sit at his table and introduced me to all of his friends.

I was surprised that Floyd had befriended so many other students after only two days of school, but I quickly discovered that most of the kids sitting at his lunchroom table lived with him at Fort Totton, a military base at the foot of the Throgs Neck Bridge on the Hudson River. They all knew each other before school began. Everybody on the military base seemed to know his father. He was a big shot in the Navy, which explained why he had such a huge house.

I thought some of the girls Floyd introduced me to were cute, but I didn't exactly know why I felt this way. They adopted me into their group and we all instantly became friends. I felt very comfortable with Floyd and the girls and started to spend my daily lunch periods with them. Every day we all sat at the same lunchroom table. Floyd and I loved to perform our latest magic tricks for all the girls. Sometimes a small crowd of strangers would gather around our table to watch us perform.

Each day immediately after school ended, I'd hurry home to train my new dove to appear and vanish during my act, and to rehearse my latest magic tricks. I also looked forward to going into New York City on the weekends to hang out at Tannen's Magic with Lance and see Doug Henning at the Cort Theater.

In October 1976, not long after school began, Doug Henning left the *Magic Show* and actor Joe Abaldo took over his role as the magician. I had no interest in getting to know Joe, so my visits to the Cort Theater stopped, but my weekly visits to Tannen's Magic with Lance continued. In the mid-1980s, Doug retired from the stage and became increasingly interested in transcendental meditation. I never heard from him after his retirement. Unfortunately, on February 7, 2000, Doug passed away from liver cancer at the age of fifty-two. He lived in Los Angeles at the time of his death.

One day in the gym locker room, while changing in the corner, I met a short, heavyset fellow named Scott who was also embarrassed to change in front of the rest of the class due to his weight. Coincidently, Scott was also a magician. In the locker room we chatted and talked about the latest tricks we learned.

Scott approached me one day with a job offer. He told me he occasionally worked for a professional magician who specialized in illusions and dove work. The magician often had a show or audition in New York City and would have parking issues. The magician paid Scott twenty-five dollars to sit in the car while he was double-parked out in front of the venue loading or unloading all of his props.

Scott said he wasn't able to go with the magician to an audition that weekend and asked if I wanted the job. Since the magician specialized in the two types of magic that interested me, and since there was a three hundred dollar *Sword Suspension* I wanted to buy, I took the guy's number and called him when I got home. We made arrangements for him to pick me up in Main Street Flushing.

The magician's name was Charles Merrill, and he was very old school, still wearing a tuxedo and tails. After he picked me up, we needed to stop and pick up his agent, an older woman named Rose Adaire. She was a small-time theatrical agent who operated her business out of her New York City apartment. The gig was easy and the money was good. I was able to watch him put his illusions together and get a close-up look at his fine craftsmanship.

As time went on, I worked more and more for Charles, and eventually Scott stopped working for him completely. At first, I only sat in the car while Charles double-parked, loaded, and unloaded. Then he started asking me to run his music during the show.

Soon I wound up being his on-stage assistant. I pushed the empty illusion boxes on stage and, after the girl appeared in the empty box, I pushed the box off the stage. When he made a girl float, I was the one who would carry out the hoop. If he sliced a girl in half, I carried out the blades.

I started to get to know his agent and watched the way professional shows were performed. I was there for sound checks, lighting rehearsals, and blocking. While Charles was getting dressed and stuffing the poor doves into the secret pockets of his tuxedo, I talked to his agent and learned as much as I could from her. In my eyes, I was learning my trade while working for a professional. I was now a professional magician's apprentice.

Charles Merrill, his assistant, and Gerard

Charles had a big fantailed pigeon in his act that he would produce from under a handful of silk scarves during his dove routine. I really liked that effect, so I purchased a fantailed white pigeon to add to my own dove routine. My buddy Steve named the bird Fred Glataziano. For some reason Steve loved to make up crazy names. Both of my birds now shared a cage in my tiny bedroom, and I rehearsed with them all the time.

One of the illusions that Charles performed in his act was called the *Mis-Made Lady Illusion*. A girl climbed into a box, then the magician inserted a number of blades and divided the girl into four equal parts. I loved that illusion because I saw Doug Henning perform it on Broadway. I asked Charles where he purchased it, and he said he built it himself. He was a real craftsman who had the ability to build almost anything out of wood.

"Could you build me one?" I asked one day.

He shook his head. "I'm afraid not. It's a very tedious illusion to build, and I just don't have the time."

That wasn't the answer I wanted to hear. I really wanted that illusion; how could I get him to build it for me?

After some thought, I said, "How about this? You can take as long as you need to build it, and I'll cut my pay rate from twenty-five dollars a gig to twenty for six months."

He mulled it over. "All right. I'll build you a *Mis-Made Lady Illusion* for four hundred dollars, but you'll have to paint it yourself."

We made a deal agreeing that every time I worked for him, the twenty dollars I earned would be deducted from the four hundred for the illusion fabrication. When the illusion was complete, I'd use my savings from working in the candy store to pay off the remainder. It took Charles about a month to build the illusion for me. As soon as he delivered it to me, I set it up in my garage and painted it to look just like Doug Henning's *Mis-Made Lady Illusion*.

Chapter 11

Seeking a Male Role Model

In my first year of high school, I took a woodshop class. I was very excited to take this class because I wanted to learn woodworking so I could build illusions myself, and not have to pay Charles to fabricate more for me. But instead of making magic tricks like I thought I would be doing, our teacher, Mr. Levine (or as the kids called him, "Mr. Stoneface") had us making kitchen spice racks. "Stoneface" was a typical shop teacher in that one of his fingers had been partially cut off by a table saw.

Towards the end of the semester, I started to notice an African-American teacher named Mr. Hector Cuales who would enter the classroom and walk into the back office to prepare to teach the next woodshop class. At first he smiled whenever he passed me at my workbench. Soon the smiles turned to nods and then into hellos. When he walked by, he'd stop and compliment my work.

Mr. Cuales was a teacher in the Industrial Arts Department who taught woodshop, printing, ham radio operation, and metal shop. He was also in charge of the school's spotlights and theater projector. If there was a play that needed lighting, he was in charge of it. If the school was going to watch a movie in the main auditorium, he was in charge of that as well. He had a private office, well secluded in the upper level of the projection room in the back of the main auditorium.

Hector Cuales

I had a study period immediately following my woodshop class. One day Mr. Cuales asked me to stick around after class and watch his woodshop class. He was a good teacher, and all of his students really liked him. He went around and made sure they were making straight lines with their saws and using their tools correctly. He was equally attentive to all his students and gave them encouragement. Unlike my teacher, "Mr. Stoneface," he made his woodshop class fun. After class, several students stayed behind to hang out with him in the woodshop office. *What student ever wants to stay after class?* I wondered. *Why do the students like Mr. Cuales so much?*

Mr. Cuales said that he noticed the spice rack project seemed to be boring me. "What would you rather be building?" he asked.

"I want to build a *Dollhouse Illusion* like the one I saw at the Larry Weeks Magic Convention this summer," I replied.

"When the next semester starts, you should take my woodshop class," he said. "I'll let you build that illusion in class instead of a paper towel rack, and your final grade will be based on your craftsmanship."

Having Mr. Cuales say he was going to allow me to build an illusion during school time, and get passing grades from making it, seemed too good an offer to refuse. So when the next semester started in January 1977, I made sure I was in his class. He also talked me into taking his metal shop and printing classes.

The illusion is a dollhouse sitting on top of a small base. The house is opened to show it's clearly empty and then closed. A female assistant instantly appears inside the empty house. The secret of the trick is that the girl is hidden inside the small base. The base is constructed to look thin, but it is much larger than it appears. Mr. Cuales had never seen one of these illusions, so we built it without blueprints or a reference photo.

Since we were able to construct the illusion rather quickly, I thought possibly we could sell the *Dollhouse Illusion* and use the profit to buy me the *Sword Suspension Illusion* from Tannen's Magic. Then I could just build another Dollhouse. When I asked Mr. Cuales if we could take the illusion to New York City and try to trade it or sell it at Tannen's, he said we would have to do it the next weekend. Since we'd have to leave early on Saturday morning, it would be best if I slept over at his house so we could get an early start.

Before I could stay over at his house, however, I had to get permission from my mom. Mr. Cuales came to my house and told her that we were going to the city in the morning to sell my woodshop project. He also said he was giving me the opportunity to work with him and other students over the weekend. He did his best to put her at ease until she said, "No problem."

He did such a good job deceiving my mother that staying with Mr. Cuales did not raise any eyebrows for her. I was rarely home on the weekends anyway. Either I was in the city with Lance, or I'd visit my father in his tiny, smoke-infested, two-bedroom condo in Forest Hills, Queens. My mother just assumed that I was doing something constructive for school with a schoolteacher and wasn't concerned about anything bad happening. She had placed her trust in a person of authority who was in a trustworthy position in society. She thought I was in good hands, as did I.

Mr. Cuales lived in the Upper Brookville area, which was one of the wealthiest neighborhoods on Long Island. He claimed he built houses on the side and that was where his money really came from—not from his small schoolteacher's salary. His neighborhood was lined with palatial homes, manicured lawns, and very "normal" families. It was the kind of community that I dreamed of living in. Even when my dad lived with us, we lived pretty modestly in a small home with not a lot of money in the bank.

Going to Mr. Cuales's house opened up a whole new world for me. His basement was huge and secluded from the rest of the house. His workshop featured the latest tools and woodworking equipment. It also had a nice-sized guest bedroom and bathroom. I remember the guest room had electric heat and when it was bedtime, the room would be cold and clammy. I had to wait for the heat to come up to get comfortable.

The next morning, we packed up the *Dollhouse Illusion* in Mr. Cuales's van and took the drive into the city. This was the first Saturday in quite some time that I was not going to Tannen's with Lance. I proudly wheeled the illusion into Tannen's Magic and we were almost laughed out of the store by the employees and the customers. Tony Spina, one of the store's owners, said the base of the illusion was too big and looked obviously large enough to be able to hide a girl—not deceptive at all. They said it was horrible and they were not interested in buying it from us. However, the good news was they *did* like our quality of workmanship.

Tony offered to show us what the Dollhouse should look like, and invited us to go back into the Illusion Room to see how a deceptive base was supposed to look. The Illusion Room! Being allowed to go back there was like the Holy Grail to a young illusionist like me. The sting of being told my *Dollhouse Illusion* was nothing more than a piece of scrap wood quickly wore off knowing I was being taken into the secret room I heard about for so long, yet never had access to!

The secret space was pretty deep into the store. We passed through a huge stock room, then through the shipping room and staff offices until finally we entered the Illusion Room. I was in heaven! There was a *Zig-Zag Illusion*, a *Crystal Casket Illusion*, a huge *Guillotine*, a *Levitation Couch*, a *Dollhouse Illusion*, a *Houdini Milk Can Escape*, and the *Sword Suspension* and *Metamorphosis Illusion* I saw a few weeks ago. I fell in love with the *Mis-Made Lady Illusion* that was also there. But I didn't love the $1,750 price.

I asked Mr. Cuales if we could make the *Sword Suspension* in metal shop. He told me the swords were made of very thick steel and were chrome dunked to give the shiny metallic finish. He could work with metal, but this was something beyond his capabilities.

Tony heard us talking about having a metal shop and showed us the *Houdini Milk Can Escape*. He said it was for sale at a price of five thousand dollars, but the bullet catches on the secret duplicate trick lid were too flimsy and loose. He needed them repaired, but Mr. Cuales said he could not fix it. Tony also showed us a *Suspension Illusion* that was not very stable. He asked if we could fabricate a metal plate to reinforce the wood plate it currently used to properly support a person's weight. Mr. Cuales said that was something we could fix for him and offered to repair the wooden base at his home workshop. Before we left the magic store, Mr. Cuales purchased a book for me titled *The World's Greatest Magic* by Hyla M. Clark. Doug Henning was on the cover and it contained many photos of Doug performing, as well as a lot of other famous magicians. The book seemed to contain more photos than text, which is why I loved it so much. I looked at the photos often and imagined I was the one performing the illusions.

Since the people at Tannen's thought my *Dollhouse Illusion* wasn't very deceptive, it was no longer something I wanted to own. We left Tannen's Magic and took the oversized dollhouse to another place at the Mid-Island Plaza Mall where I shopped for new tricks. The store was owned by two men named Howie and Phil. They purchased the illusion from us for two hundred and fifty dollars and immediately put it on display in their window.

When we left the store, Mr. Cuales said I would have to help him repair the *Suspension Illusion* from Tannen's Magic. I insisted that I'd have to sleep over the following weekend also because we'd have to return the illusion to Tannen's Magic that Saturday morning. We worked on it during the week in school and drove into the city on Saturday to deliver the prop.

Tony was very pleased with our work and asked how much he owed us. I told him it was fifty dollars for the repair and then asked Mr. Cuales to give Tony the two hundred and fifty dollars we received from selling the *Dollhouse Illusion*. Tony could add the fifty dollars to that, and I could purchase the *Sword Suspension Illusion*. I remember Mr. Cuales made me carry it all the way back to his van. The swords were so heavy—they felt like they weighed a ton!

As soon as we returned to Mr. Cuales's house, I wanted a photo of me lying on the swords. He lifted me up and placed me on the swords and snapped a Polaroid photo so I could see what the illusion looked like. That night I was so excited because I finally made part of my dream come true. I was practically bouncing off the walls in the guest bedroom while swinging my new swords around. I could now perform the *Sword Suspension Illusion* and the *Mis-Made Lady Illusion*, just like Doug Henning performed. I could see myself on stage, amazing an audience!

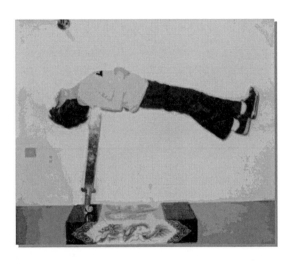

Mr. Cuales said his wife was complaining that he was not spending enough time with his own children. As a favor, he asked me to perform for his daughter Melissa and her friends at her birthday party the following week. I agreed, and again I slept over at his house.

Chapter 12

My Big Break

A short time after Mr. Cuales helped me build and sell the *Dollhouse Illusion*, he told me that his boss, Saul Caul, the head of the Industrial Arts Department, was really upset with me. Mr. Caul was wondering who was going to pay for all the wood that I had used to build the *Dollhouse Illusion*.

Mr. Cuales said that Mr. Caul wanted to send my mother a bill for all the wood I used, or I could sell my *Sword Suspension* to pay the outstanding bill. My mother was trying desperately to make financial ends meet since my father left. She had been forced to take a job in New York City as a cosmetician, and I could imagine how upset she would be if she received a bill in the mail from the school. I told Mr. Cuales I did not want to sell my *Sword Suspension*, so I would take money out of my bank account to pay back the school.

Mr. Cuales then told me he'd reached a compromise with his boss. First, I would have to perform a magic show at the Leonard's of Great Neck reception hall for Saul Caul's daughter's Sweet Sixteen birthday party. Then if I performed a magic show before the end of this semester, and gave all the proceeds from ticket sales to the Industrial Arts Department, the school would consider my debt paid in full. Again I offered to take money out of my bank account to pay back the school without worrying my mother, and to have Mr. Caul pay me for performing at his daughter's Sweet Sixteen party.

Mr. Cuales told me he had a friend who was a big talent scout in Hollywood looking to discover the new face of magic, and he was seeking a young illusionist. If I did the school show, he might be able to convince his friend to fly into New York and come watch the show. The scout would see my illusion act, which could be my big break in show business. After I expressed my excitement about that opportunity, Mr. Cuales said I needed a lot of work on my performance before the talent scout should see me. He volunteered to spend more time with me on the weekends to prepare for my big show and said he would work with me as much as needed. He even thought I was talented enough to be able to host the entire show.

I decided to take Mr. Cuales up on his proposal to do both shows. I performed for the Sweet Sixteen and started planning for the school magic show, which I wanted to name after Doug Henning's very first television show. His was called *The World of Magic with Doug Henning*; I would call mine *The World of Magic with Jerry McCambridge*. I invited Lance and Floyd to perform in the show with me. Floyd had a magician friend, Steve, who lived in Fort Totten. His stage name was Martini and he also agreed to be in the show.

Show Ticket

After I performed at the Sweet Sixteen, word started getting around school that I had an entertaining show. Two other teachers, Dr. Isaacson and Mr. Lucks, hired me to perform at their daughters' Sweet Sixteen parties. I used the money from those two shows to build a *Shadow Box Illusion.*

I went to the Mid-Island Plaza Magic Shop to ask Phil and Howie if they would put flyers for the show on display in their store. While I was there, I met an escape artist who billed himself as "Jimmy - The Spirit of '76," even though it was now 1977. He asked to be in the show. Since I felt connected to Houdini, who was an escape artist, I felt it was time I started learning about escapes, so I allowed him to be in the show as well. Mr. Cuales called the local newspaper and told them about the show, and they agreed to write a little blurb to help us sell tickets.

Students to Stage World of Magic

The Industrial Arts Department at Bayside High School will present "The World of Magic" tomorrow night at 8.

Jerry McCambridge will be master of ceremonies for the program, which will be held at the school. Tickets are $2 and may be purchased at the door.

Bayside High School had a television studio where students could learn the latest technology used to create a television show, and the function of each person behind the scenes. Mr. Cuales asked the TV studio teacher, Mr. Arnie Friedman, if he could have his students tape the show so I could watch it back and learn from it. Mr. Friedman agreed.

On April 29, 1977 at 8:00 p.m., my friends and I performed at Bayside High School.

The show was a complete train wreck.

We opened with my appearance, coming out of my *Shadow Box Illusion*. I welcomed the audience to the show and proceeded to produce my assistant from the *Dollhouse Illusion*. I then introduced Lance and assisted him with my *Metamorphosis Illusion*. I don't remember much about doing the trick because I was locked inside the trunk, but Steve told me that when Lance raised the curtain, which was attached to fly ropes, he got his neck tangled in the curtain and the audience laughed at his awkwardness.

After Lance was done performing, I returned to the stage and performed my new *Sword Suspension Illusion*. I wasn't strong enough to lift the girl up onto the swords myself, so I needed to have two of the other performers help me lift her. I felt like I was on top of the world. I was performing in front of an audience just like Doug Henning did. I was making my dream come true.

Later in the show I introduced Floyd, who would perform his magic act followed by Martini. Neither of those two acts stood out enough for me to remember them. My mind was preoccupied backstage trying to figure out if the talent scout had shown up or not.

Midway through the show, I introduced "Jimmy - The Spirit of '76," who was going to escape from a straitjacket while the entire audience watched. He asked for a volunteer from the audience. A stampede of young audience members ran down the aisle, all eager to be the first on the stage. One of them happened to trip and smashed his face into one of the seat backs. There was blood all over the place and the show had to be stopped.

While someone tended to the kid's wounds, I remember Mr. Cuales telling me to go out on stage and keep the audience busy until order was restored in the auditorium. That was the one

84

point in the show where I was scared, because I didn't know what to say. We hadn't rehearsed anything like this, so that three or four minute delay felt like hours. The boy was eventually removed from the auditorium and the show continued as planned. I was concerned the talent scout had seen this, but Mr. Cuales told me not to worry because it turned out his friend missed his flight.

The show was a financial success, however. Mr. Cuales said the director of the Industrial Arts Department was happy with ticket sales and would not send a bill to my mom. I didn't owe the school anything for excessive wood-shop supply usage. Later, I spent many hours after school in the TV studio watching the videotapes over and over and over again. I took notes on what I needed to do to change my performance. There are many things that I disliked, but there were some things that I liked as well.

One thing that I knew for sure was that Lance was never going to be a good performer. Technically he was awesome when it came to sleight-of-hand, but he didn't have the right look to be on stage. He was just too tall and too awkward. I felt he would hold me back if he stayed as my partner, and I knew I would have to sever our partnership if I was going to advance in my career. But I enjoyed hanging out with him, so I had to figure out how to tell him without hurting him or affecting our friendship.

I did notice, however, that Floyd was an awesome performer. He had a great look, the girls loved him, and he had good stage presence.

A few weeks later, my freshman year of high school ended. Mr. Cuales gave me excellent grades on my report card in all three of my classes: a 97 percent in woodshop, a 90 percent in printing class, and a 95 percent in Ham Radio class. During the summer, my weekend visits to Mr. Cuales's house stopped.

Gerard's homemade performing outfit

Chapter 13

The Sun Will Come Out Tomorrow

That summer I hung out with both Lance and Floyd, but never with them together. For some reason, Floyd did not like Lance. Floyd and I started traveling into New York City every week, and my time hanging around with Lance started to dwindle. The train ride from Main Street to Times Square was about forty minutes. We always tried to get the front train car so we could look out the window as the train rolled down the tracks. I stared at the scenery and daydreamed about success.

Floyd and I had a lot in common as we were both into magic and theater. We went to Tannen's every week to see the newest trick on the market and hang out with other magicians.

Tannen's closed at 3:00 p.m. on Saturdays, so afterward Floyd and I would go from theater to theater collecting Broadway show playbills. I took them home and hung them up in my bedroom. Weekdays, I'd work during the day and visit Floyd's afterward. On the weekends, I slept over at his house so we could travel to the city on Saturday morning together.

I remember on the night of July 13, 1977, I was skateboarding to Floyd's house to hang out with him after work. I didn't realize all the lights in the city had gone out. I went to Floyd's house and kept ringing the doorbell but no one answered. I eventually found him at the teen center, sitting with everyone in a candlelit room. There was a massive blackout in New York and I did not even realize it until they told me.

One of the girls was sitting close to me, casually rubbing up against me in the dimly lit room, and I liked it. That unexplainable charge of electricity that would explode in my spine when I was on stage happened again. I wasn't exactly sure why I liked her touching me, but I knew that I did.

Lance and I spent a lot of time at the local pool in Whitestone, Queens and I became quite an attraction there. The grand finale of Doug Henning's 1974 television special was Doug's attempt to escape from the *Houdini Water Torture Cell*. Seeing how much Doug admired Houdini, and since I had the Houdini birthday connection, I decided to study more about his escapes and his showmanship.

From watching old film footage, I learned that Houdini had a flair for the dramatic and was a perfectionist with timing. He knew how to pause at the exact moment and steal a glance at the audience, which was usually holding its collective breath, before making his move. I realized Houdini was the best of the best—a consummate showman, a pop culture icon, a trendsetter. Houdini was one of the greatest showmen to ever live.

Houdini escaped from a padlocked trunk after it was thrown into an icy cold river. He even escaped from a straitjacket while hanging upside down from his ankles, while suspended from an office building fifty floors above the city as thousands looked on. I decided to follow in his footsteps and challenged the adults at the pool. I allowed them to tie up this little fourteen-year-old and throw me into the deep end of the pool, which was about twelve feet deep. Luckily for me, one of the lifeguards was also a magician. He knew what I was doing, and knew I had the ability to escape. I started with ropes and eventually graduated to handcuffs.

Learning those escapes were easy because my father was a police officer and I had unlimited access to his handcuffs. I spent many hours in my bedroom studying the locking mechanism, figuring out how it worked, and then practicing, practicing, and practicing. I became quite good at picking locks using many simple household items like bobby pins, safety pins, and paper clips. I even created my own set of lock picks.

Once I was challenged to escape from a pair of police officer's handcuffs while underwater at the Whitestone pool. I practically had the locks picked before I hit the water after jumping off the high diving board. I stayed underwater for almost two minutes to build up the suspense—the same way Houdini did—and then I came up gasping for air to great applause. I was learning it was not about how fast I could pick open the handcuffs, but how much suspense I could create to make the audience feel anxious and excited. That summer, Whitestone pool became my stage.

One Saturday Floyd and I were making our usual rounds going from theater to theater, knocking on stage doors and asking for copies of playbills. That day we walked all the way up to 52nd Street to get the playbill for the new show *Annie*. As we approached the stage door, a taxi pulled up and out jumped a little redhead girl named Andrea McArdle—the star of the show. She said hello as she walked past us heading to the stage door. I suddenly felt that unexplainable electrical charge in my spinal cord again!

While we were standing there, two gentlemen named Stephen and Arnie approached us. They were groupies of the *Annie* show and asked us what we were doing and who we were. We told them we were collecting playbills and that we were magicians. They asked us to do some tricks and we obliged, as we always did for anyone who wanted to watch us perform.

While we were performing for Stephen and Arnie, other young girls in the cast arrived at the theater and entered through the stage door before their scheduled call time. Eventually,

Stephen and Arnie would introduce us to the entire cast. Between their matinee and their evening performance on Saturdays, the kids in the cast would usually go out for dinner together.

One week Stephen and Arnie invited Floyd and me to have dinner with some of the young cast members. We performed for them while waiting for our food to be served, and we were a big hit! From that point on, we were always invited to dinner with the cast members in between their Saturday shows, and we always performed for them. Neither Floyd nor I had much money, so we would usually wind up ordering one appetizer and split it between us.

Floyd and I walked up to Central Park and perform magic on the streets while the *Annie* kids were in the theater performing their matinee. After our performances, we'd pass the hat and make money so we could order a full meal at dinner with the cast. We made enough money performing on the streets that I quit my job at the candy store. Each week the cast ate at a different upscale restaurant in New York. Floyd and I were on cloud nine with our new friends—two magicians from Queens hanging out with real Broadway stars!

One of the kids we spent time with was Annie's understudy, Sarah Jessica Parker, who would grow up to portray Carrie Bradshaw in *Sex and the City*. Others included Danielle Brisebois, who landed a part in *All in the Family*, and also Diana Barrows, who later appeared in *Friday the 13th Part VII*.

We learned that some of the girls in the cast took weekly dance lessons at the Phil Black Dance Studios on Broadway. Floyd and I never wanted to be dancers, but we wanted to look good on stage while moving around—not awkward like Lance. So we started taking tap and jazz dance class every Saturday morning with various members of the cast of *Annie*. We took those dance classes the entire summer.

We especially liked cast member Bob Fitch, who played Rooster Hannigan. He was also a magician in real life and made a switchblade knife disappear during the play. He would say "Hi" to us when he passed by, but we never spent any quality time with him.

Since we were around the theaters so much, Floyd and I started to get bold. We figured out a way to sneak into the theaters and see the plays for free. When a show let out for intermission, we would walk into the theater and hide out in the bathrooms. When the second half of the show started, we came out of hiding and found empty seats in the balcony. If we liked the second half of a play, we'd carefully use duct tape to keep the latch of a fire exit door from locking. Then we would return later that evening and reenter the theater through the fire exit to catch the first act of the play.

91

Chapter 14

The Cost of His Friendship

When the school year began in September of 1977, I took another woodshop class with Mr. Cuales. Almost instantly, our weekend visits started up again. He said if I slept at his house on the weekends, he might have an opportunity for me to also earn some extra money. He said he had side jobs doing construction and always needed help. He hired students all the time to work on the construction sites and paid them handsomely. He made it seem like it was a privilege to be "chosen" to work with him, since so many other students wanted that chance.

Since I knew I wanted to be a television star like Doug Henning, I decided that I should learn how to produce television shows. I took Mr. Friedman's class and found him to be very nice and patient with his students. Occasionally he brought his young sons to class and I performed magic for them. I also wanted to try my hand at acting, so I took Play Production class. Floyd and I were in TV Studio class and Play Production class together. Ironically, we portrayed brothers in the play *Our Town*. I was Joe Crowell the paperboy, and Floyd was my younger brother. Rehearsing every day after school brought Floyd and me even closer.

Around this time, I officially ended my partnership with Lance. I asked Floyd if he wanted to be my new magic partner and he agreed. His mother made us matching sequined jumpsuits. Mine was red and Floyd's was blue.

Gerry and Sortani

I asked my friend, Arnie, to take head shots for me since I didn't have money to pay a professional photographer. I did not want to confuse my acting career with my magic career, so I officially changed my name. My acting name was "Gerard Alexander" from my first and middle names, and my magician name became "Jerry McCambridge."

After doing a photo shoot, Arnie came back with an eight by ten with one full-length pose and three smaller shots to show my versatility. Unfortunately, the only thing it showed was how bad he was in the darkroom. Either way, it was free, and I had them duplicated and tried to use them.

I signed with a manager named Peggy Bramson who had an agency in New York City. After I auditioned for her, she wanted to represent me as an actor, not a magician. She had me going on auditions in New York City, but she insisted I get better head shots. Floyd took some photos and they were much better than Arnie's. I had a dark room in my bedroom closet where I did my own developing, so I developed my own headshots to use. During the same photo shoot, I took a picture of Floyd in his jumpsuit, top hat, and cane for his promo photo.

Every time I went to an acting audition, I noticed I was the only kid at the audition who was alone. All of the other kids were accompanied by their stage mothers, who pushed the kids hard to succeed in show business. There were usually at least twenty other kids that looked just like me, so I decided that I needed a way for the people auditioning me to *need* me instead of *me* needing *them*. I had to come up with something all the other kids couldn't do to set me apart from them. That's when I decided to give up acting and focus on finding exactly what I was destined to do—what I could do better than anyone else. I would focus on my magic.

Gerard Alexander

95

Floyd and I continued our weekend visits to the city and became close friends with most of the *Annie* cast and their parents. We were invited to attend Andrea's fourteenth birthday party at an expensive restaurant in November of 1977. Floyd's mother made a cute ceramic statue of Little Orphan Annie for us to give Andrea for her birthday. It was very cold and the festivities were going to end late, so Floyd's father picked us up so we wouldn't have to take the bus and train home after the party. As Floyd and I were saying our good-byes to all of our friends, Andrea's mother told her to thank me for the statue. Andrea kissed me on the cheek, and suddenly it felt like lightning was blasting through my spine again. I was in heaven! I ran out to the car and told Floyd that she kissed me, and he became very jealous. Soon after her birthday, the producers decided she was getting too big for the part and Andrea left *Annie.*

A few weeks later while sleeping over Mr. Cuales's house, I went into the guest bedroom and cranked up the electric heat. I grabbed my pajamas and headed into the bathroom to change as I always did. Mr. Cuales asked me why I didn't undress in front of him, and I told him I was more comfortable changing in private. He'd nicknamed me "Little Squirt," and that night he asked if I knew why he called me that. I replied that it was because he thought I was short. He said no, it was because he assumed I had a "little squirt" in my pants, and I was embarrassed to change in front of him because he'd laugh at me. I told him he was wrong. He asked me to prove him wrong by letting him see it. I refused. He laughed and said he knew he was right after all.

Once I changed into my pajamas, Mr. Cuales pointed out an eight-millimeter movie projector in the corner of the bedroom hidden behind the bed. He explained a few of the kids from school who were there earlier in the week forgot to put it away.

Mr. Cuales then told me that the movie spooled on the projector showed people doing interesting things and that I could watch the movie while I was waiting for the room to warm up, but only if I remained very quiet. He said my classmates who came to his house always enjoyed watching the movies. Then he said good night and left the guest room, closing the door behind him.

I faced the projector towards the white wall and started the movie. At first, I had no idea what I was looking at, but then I realized I'd seen something like this once before while peeking downstairs at my brother's bachelor party. The images of these movies looked the same. I remember all the people at my brother's party enjoying the movie and laughing about it, so it couldn't be a bad movie. I was very intrigued, and now I had the ability to watch the entire movie without my father sending me to bed. I was almost fifteen, and felt I was old enough to see what my brother was watching at his bachelor party.

The movie showed women—naked women—rubbing and licking and sucking. At some point, a man came into the picture wearing a workman's tool belt and little else. It was hardcore pornography and it was very exciting for me to see. I had zero sexual experience at this point, and I had never even masturbated. I still did not even have pubic hair, which I didn't think was unusual until my stepbrother, Steven, made it painfully obvious to me.

Thanks to Mr. Cuales, I was getting an X-rated education. For the first time in my life, I became sexually aroused. Mr. Cuales came back into the room after the projector had been running for a few minutes. Now that I think back on the incident, I bet he was just outside the door waiting for me to start the projector.

He looked at the small bulge in my pajamas and said, "I see you are enjoying the movie." He then sat on the bed next to me, but this time a little closer than I was comfortable with. I didn't know how to respond. "Have you ever done anything like that?"

"Um, no," I said, blushing.

"That's okay," Mr. Cuales said. "Someday you will."

"I wouldn't even know how to get a girl to do that stuff to me."

"Oh, don't worry about that," he replied. "I'll show you everything you need to know. Trust me."

I felt like a student in a sex education class and Mr. Cuales was my personal teacher. He started talking to me about the bulge he saw in my pajamas and something called masturbation. He asked if I ever had tried it, and of course I hadn't. He told me that my body wasn't developed because I was not doing certain things to it, and that he could help me and teach me what I should know to make my bulge as big as the other kids'.

Again, Mr. Cuales said, "I'll show you everything you need to know. Trust me."

He explained that if you rub your erect penis long enough, something very pleasurable happens. He explained that all the kids my age did it. Once more, I felt like I was left out of a big secret. All the kids knew about this and I never even heard of such a thing? He said this was something my father should have been teaching me, and that it was something that everyone did, ladies and men. He told me he could teach me what the kids did and walk me through the process. He said he helped other students in need as well.

Mr. Cuales then proceeded to remove my pajama bottoms and orally stimulate me while the pornographic movie was playing. The situation didn't feel right, but physically it felt good. Unfortunately, my body was not ready to be a man yet, and when I had my first orgasm, nothing happened. He told me it was perfectly fine and was not a big problem. As soon as something came out, my penis would get bigger and I would be just like the other guys at school. He promised to help me out until something finally came out of my penis.

He made me believe that everything we did was okay. He made it seem like he was doing me a favor by showing me how to force puberty so I could grow up and become like the rest of the kids in school. He told me that he always brought kids over to spend the weekend, that it was perfectly normal, and that I was perfectly normal.

And then after he was finished sexually molesting me, Mr. Cuales went upstairs and climbed in bed with his wife.

The next day we all sat at the breakfast table like everything was hunky-dory, like everything was normal. I now wonder how his wife could not have known what he was doing. How could she not question her husband bringing home so many of his male students? What did she think was going on in that tiny guest bedroom, or was she too scared to say anything to him about it? Was he physically abusing her while he was sexually molesting me?

He had me so brainwashed that I agreed to sleep over his house the next weekend, which was the last weekend before the Christmas holiday break. He mentioned that one of his other pet students, Ritchie, also used to spend the weekends. Sometimes Ritchie's twin sister would come over and stay at Mr. Cuales's house with her brother. Mr. Cuales told me what Ritchie's sister would allow him and Ritchie to do to her sexually. He told me he would talk to her and bring her out one weekend and let me do the same things to her after I knew what I was doing. Of course, being the sport that Mr. Cuales was, he would teach me what to do first.

After orally pleasing me, he said he didn't feel it was very fair that I kept taking from him, yet I didn't reciprocate. I told him I was not interested in orally doing that to him. Watching a movie and pretending in my mind that the girl in the movie was having sex with me was one thing, but doing it to another man was wrong in my eyes. If he was doing that to me strictly to help me mature, why did I need to do things to him since he was already mature? That is what he had a wife for.

Since I refused to orally please him, he pushed me face down on the bed and slowly climbed on top of me, saying he had a Christmas gift for me. It felt far from normal having a forty-year-old man on top of me, trying to enter me from behind.

"It's okay," Mr. Cuales said. "Everybody's doing it. Just relax."

He told me Floyd and all of the cool kids did it. But I remembered when my brother was married, everyone was making fun of two guys doing this. It meant they were gay like my cousin Mark. Now that he was on top of me, was I gay?

I tightened up and would not allow him to fully penetrate me, but the excitement of the situation caused him to have an orgasm anyway. He climbed off of me, said "Merry Christmas" and left the room.

I suddenly realized I had been "chiseled." It wasn't a short-term chisel where you get what you want on the spur of the moment. He actually chiseled me for many months. Not only did he get what he wanted, he took the chisel to the next level and made me feel like it was for me instead of for him.

Unexpectedly, I had an intuitive vision in bed that I would never return to that house. This vision was even stronger than the one I had with Tommy when he died. The next morning, I had breakfast with Mr. Cuales's wife and kids as I always did. I looked at them knowing I would never see them again. They were nice people and I felt a little guilty, but I knew what I needed to do. No matter how much I liked them, this was the last time I would set foot in that house.

I went home and started to wonder if this was my fault. Did I encourage this behavior on his part? Was this the vibe I was putting out there in the world? What was I thinking when I allowed this to happen? More importantly, what in the world was *he* thinking, and why did he select me?

The first semester of my sophomore year ended and Mr. Cuales gave me a 90 percent grade on my report card. Over the holiday break I started to doubt Mr. Cuales and his intentions regarding our friendship. I knew I needed to distance myself from him because I needed to think about what happened. The problem was that I could not discuss it with anyone. It seemed that whenever I talked to him about it, he had a way of mentally manipulating the situation to make it all seem right.

During the holiday break, Doug Henning had his second NBC television special on December 15, 1977. I really wanted to watch the show and study it, so I asked Stephen to tape the show on this new machine that he had called a VCR. Stephen invited me to sleep over at his house so I could watch Doug's show, and I remember being really paranoid. I was scared Stephen was going to try to do to me the same thing that Mr. Cuales did.

I never really knew if Stephen was gay or not, but he spoke in an effeminate way. I had a hunch he may have been gay, so as soon as I arrived at his house, I started playing my mind games with him. I quickly made him very uncomfortable in his own house by talking about my father being a New York City police officer. I also bragged about how much I liked taking karate class almost as much as I enjoyed doing magic. I told him I was excited because in two weeks I was taking my black belt exam. I knew I was safe because I defused the situation before it could happen. Stephen said goodnight and went to bed while I watched the Doug Henning videocassette on his VCR over and over, taking notes and learning from Doug's television special.

Chapter 15

Escaping the Abuse

During my time away from Mr. Cuales over the holiday break, I realized how wrong everything was. The only way I felt I was able to escape him was by not being near him, which meant not attending school. So when the January 1978 semester began, I started to cut class excessively. I couldn't take the sexual abuse anymore. My grades were bad, and my insides were screaming whenever I thought about how he was mentally manipulating me and physically molesting me.

The only classes I attended were Play Production and TV Studio. On the days I decided to attend school, I would make it my business to avoid Mr. Cuales in the halls.

Since I was cutting school so often, I was eventually called into the guidance counselor's office. Somehow Mr. Cuales heard I had an appointment. He stopped me in the hall and asked me if I requested the appointment or if they contacted me on their own. He also asked if I'd said anything to anyone about our secret friendship. He seemed to be really worried about the appointment.

The guidance counselor wanted to know why I wasn't attending any of my classes. I couldn't tell her it was because one of her teachers was repeatedly sexually molesting me. Instead, I told her I did not feel I needed a diploma to be a magician. I asked her about getting school credit for the things I was doing outside the school with my magic shows.

I felt that the school should encourage me to continue down the theatrical path. I knew some students in Mr. Cuales's printing class were getting extra credit for interning with a real printing shop outside of school. I was getting paid handsomely and making money in my field, so I felt I should be getting school credit, just like they were.

"Magic is what I want to do for a career," I said. "I want to be a professional magician. I even have a personal manager! This is my goal, and I am achieving it slowly. How can you and the school help me?"

"We're not designed to help you with your chosen profession," she said, and suggested that I attend the High School of Performing Arts in New York City. Since my parents' divorce, Mom didn't have much money. Sending me to that school would have been financially out of the question. It seemed to me like Bayside High School was designed to help students who wanted to be printers, not performers.

The guidance counselor said I was absent thirty-five days during the second semester, but I could not tell her it was because I was avoiding Mr. Cuales. She also informed me that I was failing everything. I told her I was fifteen years old, and the following October when I turned sixteen I planned to drop out of school. I explained the only thing I cared about was being in the school play and attending TV Studio. After our meeting ended, I headed to my Play Production class where Mr. Cuales was patiently waiting in his office in the projection booth in the back of the theater. He got on the theater PA system during my rehearsal and asked me to stop by his office when I had a moment. After my Play Production class I didn't go to the projection booth to see him. I left the school immediately to avoid him.

The next day, Mr. Cuales was eagerly waiting for me at Play Production class. He questioned me and insisted I tell him about every detail of the meeting. I told him only parts of the meeting, thinking that if I kept him worried, he might stop the molestation. Towards the end of April 1978, I started seeing Mr. Cuales with other boys, so I figured he had moved on. My only lingering thought was: Why did this happen to me? Was I gay, and did not know it? Did I attract this behavior from him because he knew something I did not know?

When the second semester of my sophomore year ended in June of 1978, I failed all of my classes due to excessive absence.

My personal hell with Mr. Cuales was over, but I wanted to understand what actually happened, how it happened, and how to prevent it from ever happening to me again in the future. I needed to know how I wound up in that situation. How was he able to mentally manipulate me into thinking he was helping me, when in reality, he was only satisfying his sick sexual perversion? How had he gotten me to the point of feeling so ashamed that I would never tell anyone what he really did to me?

I wanted to learn to deconstruct how Mr. Cuales mentally manipulated me. If he used this ability with bad intentions on me, and possibly many others, imagine what someone could do with this kind of mind manipulating skill if they had nothing but good intentions in mind.

One summer day in 1978 while hanging out at Tannen's I noticed one of the salesmen behind the counter demonstrating a strange magic routine. The salesman seemed to be able to control the mind of the customer he was performing for.

Watching the spectator freak out got me thinking: What if I was able to control people's minds? Or better yet, what if I was able to control Mr. Cuales's mind and figure out what his intentions were before he had the ability to carry them out?

That started me investigating the routine I just witnessed. The salesman said it was called mental magic, or "mentalism." He said mentalism is a hidden offshoot of magic, and magic is usually the training ground before someone becomes a mentalist. He explained a mentalist is a master manipulator of thoughts and behavior. I quickly discovered the secret to the mentalism trick he performed. The trick was designed to create the illusion that he was manipulating the spectator's mind and that he was doing something supernatural, but in reality was not. The average mentalist does not just decide one day to be a mentalist; it is usually something you slowly find yourself becoming involved in. I felt this was something I needed to learn immediately.

What if I learned mentalism? Would people think I really was reading their minds, or would they actually know I was just creating the illusion? Maybe it didn't really matter, as long as I had them wondering and feeling uncomfortable around me. The mental powers they thought I might have would keep them on their toes. If they were scared that I could read their minds, perhaps they would think twice about any inappropriate thoughts they were having around me. I needed control—control over my life, and control over others around me. I was spinning out of control and found I could use the art of mentalism as the rudder to straighten out my life.

Someone like Mr. Cuales, who had planned out from the beginning what he would do to me—someone who had done this to other young boys over and over again—might actually be afraid to approach someone like me if he thought I could read his mind. This idea was very appealing to me.

I asked the salesman how I could learn to be a mentalist, and he showed me a book called *13 Steps to Mentalism* by Corinda. He said this was the bible of mentalism, so I purchased it. Mentalism could open up a whole new world for me. *Let's keep them worried*, I thought, *and make them scared to think like that around me.* In my mind I compared it to *Star Wars*. Luke Skywalker was a simple farm boy until he met the master Jedi, Obi-Won Kenobi, who introduced him to the power of "the Force." Learning "the Force" gave Luke a new outlook on life and new control over people around him.

I tried a couple of the routines I learned from the book on some close friends and discovered people were incredibly freaked out by my newfound talent. I had found a new "superpower," and I liked it. What's more, I delighted in their discomfort and decided that I would not put someone at ease unless I felt comfortable with them. I thought possibly I could finally be in control. At the very least, with my newfound ability, there would be no more people like Mr. Cuales to contend with. There would never be another person who could manipulate me or my mind.

The more I studied mentalism, the more I realized it was not the trick itself as much as it was about the supposed mind manipulation and control you appeared to have over the spectator. If you acted confident enough, people would believe you had the power. If anyone purchased a magic trick in the magic shop, they could usually perform it as soon as they knew the secret, but with mentalism, knowing the secret was only part of its success. It would take a lot of practice, research, and understanding of the human mind to be totally convincing.

To be good at this, I was going to have to use a different type of practice. Most magicians practice their tricks alone in front of a mirror. I would need to practice my newfound mentalism skills on people.

When my report card arrived in the mail, my mother found out I was not going to school and told my father. As soon as I realized he knew I was cutting school, I took all of my magic stuff and divided it into two piles. One pile was full of the magic tricks that I did not really use that much anymore, while the other pile consisted of the mentalism tricks that I really, really liked. I created two separate boxes of magic so that if my father decided he was going to take away my magic as punishment for cutting school, I would just surrender the box full of old magic to him. My favorite mentalism tricks and books would be safe.

I couldn't tell my parents what really happened or why I was constantly cutting school. I played a little mind game with my father and told him that the African-American kids who were being bussed in from the other boroughs were picking on me. My father wasn't too fond of the African-Americans because of working in the Bronx, so I knew he would understand that excuse. He cut me some slack and I promised him I would go to school next semester.

Chapter 16

Here We Go Again

When the school year began in September 1978, I was still worried about running into Mr. Cuales in the halls. Also, since I failed all my classes during the previous semester, I now had to take the classes all over again. I figured it would be easier to skip classes for a month and drop out of high school when I turned sixteen in October. The only class I attended was TV Studio.

Again, my mother's pleas with me to return to school were falling on deaf ears. I could not tell my parents the real reason why I refused to return to school. My father really didn't care if I attended school or not. My mother told me since I was not going to school, she didn't want me hanging around the neighborhood doing nothing, so she gave me a job at her store. By now my mother had worked her way up and was managing the Madison Avenue cosmetic store. She knew I had no problem traveling into the city and she gave me a job in the basement stock room in February of 1979. I sat in the stockroom for hours, peeling the labels off other company's cosmetics and replacing them with labels reading *Boyd's of Madison Avenue* as if they manufactured the product themselves. I began to realize that you cannot trust anybody in this world. Everyone seems full of crap.

I was spending a lot of time working, but I still had time to hang out with my friends. One day I needed to get change for the bus to work and I went into Murray's Candy Store on 32nd Avenue. I discovered my childhood friend Brian was working there, so I began to visit him on a more frequent basis. We started to reconnect and hang out together again. Brian got me heavily into the rock band KISS. We played their albums all of the time, dressed up like them, and recreated their costumes. Brian and I even went to a KISS show, which was my first concert. Boy, did they rock the crowd!

The big movie out at the time was *Star Wars*. Besides purchasing new magic for my show, I also bought the entire *Star Wars* mask collection. On March 17, 1979, my sister Toni was a Jawa, my friend Billy Lynn was a Stormtrooper, Steve was Chewbacca and I was Darth Vader. We marched in a St. Patrick's Day parade. Our picture was in the Bayside Times. It was interesting to get press coverage for something not related to magic.

One day after I got off the bus and walked the rest of the way home from work, I noticed an older man building a strange structure in the backyard of the house across the street. I didn't know who he was, but I was intrigued by what he was building.

Eventually I approached him and introduced myself. His name was Frank Markie, and he told me he had moved from Kingston, New York to take care of his sister. She owned the house and had Parkinson's disease.

To keep himself busy, he was building a pigeon coop. He asked if I wanted to help him construct it, and I joined right in. Eventually we built a big coop that he filled with lots of birds. During this process, all the other kids in the neighborhood noticed I was spending time with Frank, and they started to migrate over to his house. It quickly became the place to hang out. We'd all sit around and chat, fly his birds, and the smokers in the group would smoke like chimneys.

One evening Frank and I were in his house watching TV. Before I knew it, he was kneeling in front of me while I sat on the couch, asking if he could see what was in my pants. I could not believe my ears! A sixty-five-year-old man wanted to see my private parts. Here we go again!

This time I was ready. I knew if I wanted to, I could have just kicked him in the face, knocked him over, and quickly left the house. But for some reason I felt that would be too easy. Frank and I sat there and we talked. I tried to figure out what was going on in his head. Why was he doing this to me? Was it me? Was I sending off a strange gay vibe? Was it just the inappropriate actions of an elder? When I asked him why he was doing this to me, he responded by merely saying, "A stiff prick has no conscience." I eventually left his house without anything happening to me.

I went home and started to think about what happened. Do I tell all the other guys? Did Frank try this on some of the other guys and they liked it—or was it just me? I finally decided to tell the guys what happened.

I let everybody know what type of person he was, and his reputation in the neighborhood was rapidly destroyed. Nobody was hanging around Frank's pigeon coop or with Frank anymore. Only one person decided to remain friends with Frank after I spilled the beans. His name was Joe, but we called him "Nine-day Joe" because he went camping at Brian's father's cabin, and didn't bathe for nine days. Over time we shortened his nickname to "Dirty Joe." We came to the conclusion Joe was having sex with Frank in exchange for cigarettes. We all distanced ourselves from both of them. Within three months Frank took apart his pigeon coop, packed his bags, and returned to Kingston.

Near the end of the summer, Floyd's mother asked us to perform at a flea market she was running at Fort Totton. Our show was actually a pretty big draw. After our performance, I was walking around the flea market and spotted a Lucite pad holder for a desk. It was clear, and the vendor would glue initials on it to personalize it. I fell in love with it and ordered one. When the vendor asked me what initials I wanted on it, I told him I would get back to him. I walked over in the corner and sat and thought hard.

Show business was all about being unique and not one of the many. I learned that lesson on my auditions. Most guys named Jerry spelled it with a 'J.' For some reason, I felt that whatever I told the Lucite guy was going to set my initials for the rest of my life. I went back over to him and told him my initials were G.M. It was decision I would never change. I was Gerry with a 'G,' and I was unique!

After the flea market performance, I realized I was hanging out less and less with Floyd. He seemed to be focusing all of his attention on a girl named Gina from Fort Totten. Floyd and I would only get together to perform. We had a repeat performance booked for Mr. Durney at Church on the Hill for an anniversary party and a show at Fort Totten.

All the routines Floyd and I worked on were designed for two people, and since he was so preoccupied with Gina, I needed to retool the act and come up with a solo routine. I started rehearsing the solo act, but I needed to audience test it. A benefit show was always a good place to break in new material; since I was donating my services, they had no room to complain if I was bad. On August 15th, I performed with my mother's boyfriend, Tommy, at the Brooklyn Veterans Hospital. I had a new name, a new solo act, and my new show was very well received. It gave me the encouragement to continue being a solo act.

Before the September 1979 semester began, my mother decided to reach out to family members to help turn around my academic failures and possibly change my mind. The person who was able to eventually talk me back into school was my father's brother, my Uncle Mike. A Senior Vice President working in the city for the Rockefeller Group, he told me how important a high school education was.

Uncle Mike was the successful brother in the family. Everyone, including my father, looked up to Mike. He told me if I buckled down and graduated, he would help me in any way he could after graduation. He would get me a job as an apprentice engineer in the building maintenance field, but only if I graduated. I thought Uncle Mike was a powerful man, and thought this might be worth a shot. I took his advice and decided to stay in school.

The school semester began, and as predicted, I did not know anybody in my classes. By now I was already a year behind all the students I originally started high school with. But I promised my Uncle Mike and his wife, my Aunt Irene that I would really give it a try.

Traveling into New York City every day for work became too time consuming, so I quit my job at the Madison Avenue cosmetic store in late August. In early September of 1979, my sister-in-law, Cindy, got me a job working at a Fotomat booth in the Garden World shopping center on Frances Lewis Boulevard. Fotomats were little drive-up film processing booths in shopping center parking lots.

Every day after school, I sat in the Fotomat booth for four hours, selling film to people and doing my schoolwork. I could not bring all of my magic props to work so I could practice, so I decided I wanted to learn to play guitar. Floyd played his acoustic guitar all the time and the girls swooned around him. Maybe that would be my ticket to getting a girlfriend. I asked my immediate supervisor, Nancy, and she said she didn't mind me bringing a guitar to work. I purchased my very first guitar and amp from a store called Consumer Distributors on Northern Boulevard. When my mother's boyfriend Tommy, who was a professional guitar player, found out how much I paid for the cheap guitar, he was upset with me. He said I should have asked him and he would have gotten me a much better guitar for the same price.

I had my friend Steve try to teach me how to play, but that did not work out too well. Since Tommy bragged about giving guitar lessons to José Feliciano, the famous blind guitar player and singer, I asked if he would teach me how to play. Tommy was a great player, but not a very patient teacher. My very first lesson contained a lot of homework. Instead of explaining to me things like the circle of fifths, he had me research them, figure it out for myself, and report back as to what I found.

Without my mother or Tommy knowing, I decided to take guitar lessons in a music store on Northern Boulevard called *Piano People*. My teacher's name was Rod, which was actually short for Gerard. He taught me bar chords and how to rock 'n roll. It was exactly what I wanted. Learning music theory was not something that really interested me. Eventually I stopped taking lessons with Tommy and only took lessons from Rod. After a few months, Rod left the music store and decided to give lessons on his own in his parent's house in Great Neck, New York.

I wasn't doing well in school because I was way too far behind, so I started cutting class again. The school year ended, and again I failed everything. This time I did not have Mr. Cuales to blame for not attending class—it was me. I realized I did not have the ability to focus and read for any length of time, as my mind gets very easily distracted. After reading the first paragraph, my mind is all over the place, and I have to start reading it over again to let the information sink in.

Fotomat opened a flagship store on Northern Boulevard, right off of Bell Boulevard. It wasn't a drive-up like all the rest of their locations—this one was a storefront. Nancy offered me a full-time job working at that location, which was so large a wall had to be constructed to divide the space. The store owners set up a bunch of filing cabinets in the back part of the store and used it as their unclaimed photo department. The main office transferred a guy named Jerry from another location to set up and organize the unclaimed photo department.

If someone dropped off film for developing in any drive-up booth in the Tri-State area and didn't pick it up, after ninety days it was sent to the unclaimed photo department in the back of my store. If the photos weren't claimed after one year, we threw them out. Before we threw them out we went through them. A lot of the pictures apparently went unclaimed because they contained questionable images.

We collected all of the unclaimed naked and pornographic photos and put them into albums. Our collection grew rapidly and became legendary within the company. Supervisors, managers, and district managers would all show up, pretending to check up on their flagship store. They'd tell me I was doing a great job and was an awesome employee, and then eventually they would ask to see the albums. These interactions revealed a new form of manipulation to me: If you had something that someone else wanted, you were the person in charge of the situation.

During that summer, puberty kicked in. At age sixteen, I grew in leaps and bounds and finally started becoming a man. The drastic change in my hormones caused me to have bad case of acne, so I was put on a brand new drug called Accutane. And the collection of unclaimed photos became my own personal pornographic image collection.

One day during the summer, a kid named Eric came into the store to buy some film. He remembered me from high school because we were in the same English class together, and he remembered that I performed magic. Since I cut school so much I really didn't remember him. We started to talk and we hit it off. He wound up staying in the store for more than three hours talking to me. He was a little older than me and already had his driver's license, and bragged that he could use his father's car any time he wanted. That one-time visit to the Fotomat quickly turned into a daily routine for Eric. He would come in the store and stay for hours until I closed for the night.

Eric began driving me home at night. We would often hang out and became buddies. But when I introduced Eric to Steve, Eric seemed to go into a panic. Steve told me he knew Eric already because Eric went to Steve's school before he transferred to my high school. Since Steve went to a school for special people, Eric knew his connection to Steve would indicate to me that he was not all mentally stable.

Chapter 17

The High School Sweetheart

One night Eric told me he wanted to stop at the Genovese Drug Store on Bell Boulevard to visit a female cashier he knew. He told me she was a model and said he knew her because her boyfriend Ritchie was in our English class, and the two of them kept in touch after classes had ended.

Eric introduced me to the cashier, Kathy. She was cute, with long blond hair and dressed in tight jeans, and Eric had a crush on her. During his conversation with her, she mentioned that she didn't have a ride home from work that night, so Eric happily volunteered to drive her home. We told her we would return when her shift ended. A few hours later, as promised, we returned and picked her up.

She sat in the front seat with Eric and I sat alone in the back seat. Eric did his best to flirt with her as he was driving her home. But the entire time, Kathy kept looking at me in the back, rolling her eyes, as if she was silently laughing at him and wanted me to know it. We did not say a word to each other, but it sure seemed like she was flirting with me.

I knew she had a steady boyfriend, and I knew Eric had a crush on her, but did she really want me? I seemed totally out of her league. It felt like Kathy and I seemed to have some type of chemistry between us right from the start. There was an unspoken attraction, but should I make advances towards her since she had a steady boyfriend? On the other hand, if Eric was trying to pick her up, why shouldn't I take a shot?

My brain went into overdrive and then it hit me. When Floyd and I performed together, I was the person who would squeeze inside of the illusions. Suddenly I had an excuse to talk to her. I told her I was a magician and I needed to find a sexy assistant, someone with model potential to levitate and dismember in front of my audience during my show. She instantly started asking details about the job, gave me her phone number, and said she was very interested in the job when I was ready to hire someone. We dropped her off at her house, and Eric tried to kiss her good night. She avoided his kiss, waved goodbye to me, and told me to call her. Eric failed and I scored.

My success was resulted from presenting a topic that was of interest to her, as well as a new confidence in myself. I'd grown five inches and had actually started to grow hair in all of the right places. My voice had changed and I was starting to fill out.

I began to feel the normal things boys my age were supposed to feel towards girls.

School began that week. At the end of the day, Eric and I were leaving school when we saw Kathy walking out holding hands with her boyfriend, Ritchie. He remembered me from the English class we all took together a year earlier, but I really didn't remember him. I just kept wondering, *What does she see in him?* I felt she deserved so much better. She asked me when I was going to call her, and again she seemed to be flirting with me. Ritchie noticed this and quickly made an excuse for the two of them to depart.

I decided I had questions about myself that I needed to answer. I needed to know that my experiences with Mr. Cuales, Stephen, and Frank did not define me or my sexuality. I needed to know that I was not gay. If Ritchie could get a girl like that, why couldn't I get one as well? Why couldn't I have Kathy? I decided that I was going to pursue Kathy under the guise of having her be my assistant, with the secret intention of eventually making her my girlfriend by using my mental persuasion skills on her.

I started having Eric pick her up at work more often. It gave me time with her so I could start to lay the groundwork for my plan. When I felt the time was right, I decided to ask Kathy out on a date even though she still had a steady boyfriend, and she said yes to my advances. For my birthday in October, we went out as friends to catch a movie at the UA Quartet movie theater on Northern Boulevard. She asked me to get a large Coke from the concession stand and an extra cup. She dumped half the Coke into the empty cup, took a bottle of rum from her purse, and added it to both drinks. We drank while watching the movie, but the alcohol sat in my stomach and did not affect me very much. After the movie ended, however, it hit me like a ton of bricks. We walked outside and I collapsed twenty feet from the theater, puking my brains out. She knelt next to me and rubbed my head. We took a taxi to my house, where she dropped me off at my basement door and then took her bike home.

I sat in the basement with all my magic props around me and my head was spinning. I felt so sick; I couldn't make it up the stairs to go to bed. The next day my mother knew something was up.

"Have you been drinking?" Her expression indicated it was a rhetorical question.

"No," I lied. "Some people were smoking marijuana behind us in the theater and I got sick from the smoke."

"You'd better not be lying to me. And if you are, and you're doing it to impress that new girl, dump her. She's not worth it."

I didn't listen and kept going out with Kathy. But I decided not to drink any more alcohol for a while.

My mental techniques worked so well that Kathy broke up with Ritchie, and on November 27, 1979 she agreed to be my girlfriend. I started working my magic again and quickly persuaded her into my bed after only seventeen days. Since her previous boyfriend was dating her for over two years and was never able to close the deal, seventeen days seemed like a miracle to me.

Having sex with a female felt wonderful—unlike the awkward way I felt when I was with Mr. Cuales. In my mind, the sex validated my manhood. I had overcome my fears of being gay. When I touched her body, it felt like electricity exploded up my spine and shot into my brain. It was like an instant high. Dating Kathy opened a whole new world for me.

Kathy lived with her parents and two of her three siblings. Her older brother Mike did not like me when we met. No one was ever good enough for his sister. He also hated the fact that I was a magician and a guitar player. If I performed a trick for him and the family, he would get annoyed that I fooled him but never admitted it. He'd always tell me he had a magic kit as a kid and knew all my tricks, even as he walked away pissed because he secretly was baffled by my performance.

Kathy and I were cutting school together and having sex on a regular basis, so now it was time to get back to show business. I had her try on the costumes I'd obtained and they fit! Her body type was small enough to fit the illusions, so I started to rehearse with her.

My Fotomat co-worker, Jerry, was an amateur photographer. I asked him if he would take photos for me to use as promotional photos for my show. I set up my *Super X Suspension Illusion* and took some promo shots of me levitating Kathy. Our boss, Nancy, stopped by during the photo shoot and I took a shot of her floating in the air just for fun. I cropped out the background and inserted the logo I created in Mr. Cuales's printing class. Then I had Fotomat print up a bunch of eight by tens of me levitating Kathy. I left the photos in the store and didn't pay for them. Since I never claimed them, they all would end up in the unclaimed photo department only to be tossed in the trash. That meant that I had a stack of free promotional shots thanks to Fotomat.

I continued working at Fotomat for money to fund the act, but I needed more money to fund my show. Eric got me a job working at a flea market on Saturdays loading and unloading a van for a guy selling jackets. I earned fifty dollars for a day's work.

Eventually, Jerry quit and Nancy hired her boyfriend, Rick, to run the unclaimed photo department. Rick used to smoke pot and blast Pink Floyd music while doing his work. His favorite album was *The Wall*.

Nancy would come by to check up on me, and inevitably she'd wind up in the back room with Rick. He'd come up to the front of the store and tell me not to come into the back of the store for any reason until he gave me the all clear. It was obvious he and Nancy were back there fooling around. Knowing what they were doing in the back room, and how wrong it was, caused me to have a huge crush on Nancy.

Floyd and I booked our last show on March 14, 1980. We were rehearsing for the performance with Gina, and Kathy was always very jealous of her. I was interested in Gina's younger sister, Cathy, and now that I knew what to do with women, I felt I should spread my wings. But Kathy kept me on a short leash and insisted she be a part of the show to keep me away from her. We were four months into our relationship, and I was already bored with her and wanted to move on.

Kathy and I dated for a few months before I learned that she wasn't what I thought she was. She was not a model; she simply posed for one professional photo to attempt to get modeling work, which never really happened. The one photo she showed off as a modeling photo was far from a modeling career.

Kathy's allure quickly faded in my eyes. I realized I was not in love with her; I was in love with the feeling that sex gave me. Unfortunately, that feeling faded, the firecracker type explosions vanished, and sex wasn't great anymore. Making love to her was more like a sexual stress reliever than an intimate act between passionate lovers. I could not take any more of Kathy's restrictive, jealous behavior and my eyes started wandering.

I decided I was going to break up with her. One night after a date with her, I dropped her off at her home and returned to my mother's where I was still living. No sooner did I walk in the door than my phone was ringing. It was Kathy, and she was crying hysterically. Her mother, who was babysitting for a client, went out to her car and had a massive heart attack. She died instantly while sitting behind the wheel before starting the car.

I was now in a no-win situation. Breaking up with Kathy would have painted me as an unsympathetic monster. So I decided to remain with Kathy and see other girls secretly on the side without her knowing. She did not realize I wasn't around much because between magic shows, school, and work, our time together was limited. So I had plenty of free time to hang out with other girls.

Eventually I broke up with Kathy at the beginning of the summer in 1980. Soon after our breakup, Kathy started dating her brother's friend, Frank.

Chapter 18

From a Double to a Single

The summer of 1980 was a game changer for me. I was seventeen years old and I started seeing many different girls. I soon realized the sensation of electricity running through my spine always occurred when I was sexually active with a girl for the first time. That exciting jolt quickly disappeared the more I was with a girl, unless I *really* liked her. Initially I thought Kathy was special, but I learned she was not. I started figuring out the different qualities I wanted in a girlfriend when I finally would decide to settle down and commit to a relationship.

That summer, I told my mother I was not going to go to college if I graduated high school. In show business, you are never asked if you graduated high school. The casting director or agent only cares to see your resume of where you performed. I thought college would be a waste of my time.

I no longer had a female assistant in the act, and Floyd and I had hardly performed together since I started using Kathy as my assistant. When I contacted him to see if he was still interested in performing together, he told me his family was about to move to Minnesota. I knew I needed to hire a new assistant if I wanted to perform the illusion show again. My *Sword Suspension Illusion* needed a female assistant to lie on the swords, as well as another assistant to place the girl on the swords. Since Floyd was moving, I would have no use for the illusion, especially since I'd purchased a *Super X Suspension Illusion*. Floyd told me he'd built a *Metamorphosis Illusion,* so he traded it with me for the *Sword Suspension Illusion* just before he moved out of state.

When it was getting close to my eighteenth birthday, it was time to get my driver's license. I needed a van like the one Charles Merrill had in order to travel with my illusions, so I scraped together all available funds and started shopping for a used one. Since I was not going to college, my mother said that I may as well cash in all of my savings bonds that she had been collecting for my college education and use them towards the purchase of my van.

Since I did not have a driver's license yet, I spent my free time fixing up the van while it remained parked in front of my house. I bought the van for two reasons: One was to transport my illusion act, and the second was to have a place to spend quality time with the ladies, which is why I built a bed in the back of the van.

On my birthday, the doorbell rang all day long with trick-or-treaters in their Halloween costumes. Later in the evening, when I answered the door, I was totally surprised to see Kathy standing there. She gave me a card with a little handwritten note explaining she missed me. We wound up talking for a few hours and decided to get back together.

Kathy told me her cousin, Jimmy, was in a program for people who cut class excessively. Bayside High School offered a program they called "the mini school" for the "troubled" kids. As a student in the program, you rotated between one of two classrooms hidden in the back of the school. The program was comprised mostly of drug addicts and derelicts. Kathy was trying unsuccessfully to enter the program but it had a waiting list.

Since I had been in the guidance counselor's office, I was given an open door invitation to talk to her. I told her I was interested in the class and I was admitted into the program. I seemed to flourish in that environment; in fact, I even made the honor roll in 1981. That wasn't a huge feat considering my competition. If you showed up with a pulse, they passed you.

On November 21, 1980, at the age of eighteen, I finally received my driver's license. Getting to and from school now became a little easier with a vehicle. I told Eric and my childhood friend, Brian, about the program and was able to get them both into it as well.

A week after receiving my driver's license, I was hanging out in my van with one of our neighborhood friends and was almost arrested. We were cruising around on 35th Avenue when Billy asked me to pull over. In his efforts to impress a girl, he took out his BB gun and started to twirl it around his finger while laying his verbal rap on her.

While I was talking on my CB radio, he continued his conversation with her as he openly played with his toy gun. The gun looked like the real thing, and it must have scared one of the neighbors because they called the police on us. The next thing we knew, there were three patrol cars and several police officers surrounding my van with their (real) guns drawn, yelling for us to exit the van with our hands in the air.

We got out with our hands up. The officers slapped cuffs on us and threw us in the back seat of one of the patrol cars while they searched my van. We tried to explain that the gun was not real, but the police were not really in the mood to hear our story. They told us they were going to take us down to the station house and book us. They had us sitting in the back of the patrol car for what seemed like an eternity. I guess they wanted to make us "think about our foolish actions" while they took their time searching my van. Finally, I got the nerve to speak. I knew my father would be furious with me if he found out what was happening, so I needed to figure out a way to get out of this situation without him finding out about it.

"These cuffs are kind of tight," I said. "Would you mind taking them off or making them a little looser?"

"Shut up!" One of the officers barked at me from the front seat while filling out his report.

"Officer, these are cutting into my wrists."

He ignored my plea, so it was time to take matters into my own hands and get myself out of this mess.

I used one of the homemade lock picks that was concealed in my belt. I quietly removed the handcuffs and proudly dropped them in the front seat of the patrol car.

"If you are not going to take off the cuffs, I *will*," I announced.

Billy said, "Take mine off also, Gerry." The officer quickly told me not to make a move.

Needless to say, the officer was not as impressed as I thought he would be with my escape from his handcuffs. Like the Boy Scouts, I was always prepared. I always had something on me—tools of my trade, if you will—just in case I was challenged to display my ability to escape from handcuffs. I know it sounds crazy, but I was becoming well known for doing magic and escape tricks, and I was challenged by someone at least once a week. So, I always kept a lock-picking device and small rope cutting tool in my belt or somewhere hidden on me, just in case.

Now that I had the police officer's attention, I needed to bond with them, so I explained that my father was also a police officer "on the job."

I rolled the dice and told them I recently performed at a benefit for the policeman charity ball and asked them if they remembered me. They said they did not attend the fundraiser. I never attended the gala, but I remembered my father recently talking about it. I started using my persuasive verbal skills and described details about the function. I told them I was sorry they missed the party and offered to show the officers a few magic tricks. They stood in awe and loved watching me perform. Two other patrol cars pulled up, and the officers for whom I'd performed asked me to show their coworkers a few tricks.

Now that I had them on my side, I explained to them my buddy was only goofing around with his toy BB gun, and was able to convince the officers to release us with nothing more than a slap on the wrist. The officer kept Billy's BB gun and told Billy if he wanted the gun back, he would have to ask his father to go down to the station and get it for him. Billy never did.

A few weeks later Charles Merrill, the magician I'd once apprenticed for, contacted me and told me he had a booking in a traveling indoor circus from December 15th through the 20th. He asked if I would travel with him as his male assistant, along with his two female assistants. Since I wasn't going to school, I took the gig. The four of us traveled from town to town in his van, performing his illusion and dove act in the circus. All of us shared one dressing room, and when we got ready for the show, the girls changed outfits in front of me.

Since they were required to squeeze into the small magic boxes, they did stretching exercises before the show. One of the two girls did her stretching exercises topless. I pretended to prepare the props for the show while catching every peek I was able to. Every day of that tour, I made sure I was in the dressing room during her stretching exercises, as well as during each and every costume change.

While on that tour, I met another magician named Mario Manzini whose specialty was escapes. He would be locked in a straitjacket or tied up in ropes and locked in handcuffs before escaping. He also did a fire-breathing act and an Elvis impersonator act. His wife Dina acted as his assistant. I made friends with Mario because he was a nice guy, and because he was doing magic that I never saw before. He told me that in his full show, he also performed the *Milk Can Escape* like Harry Houdini, and he needed a male assistant on stage with his wife in order to perform the escape. We exchanged phone numbers.

Later, after the final show of the tour was over and Charles and I were in the hotel room, he started questioning me about why I was talking to Mario. He seemed annoyed and jealous. I replied that I wanted to learn as many different forms of magic as possible, and performing as an escape artist was next on my list. I also mentioned that I had an opportunity to possibly work with Mario and make extra money. Charles became more agitated. Without warning, he jumped from his bed across to mine and pinned me down. He said he had been waiting a long time to do this, and before he lost me to Mario, it was time. He then started to open my belt and pants and tried to slide them off of me.

I immediately fought back. I was thin enough to be able to squirm out from under him and get away. "What the hell are you doing?!" I shouted.

Charles urged me to keep my voice down because he didn't want his female assistants in the next room to hear me. He started to apologize profusely. I realized I was in a position of power at this point. I told him I was going tell everybody what happened unless he gave me a raise. He immediately jumped at the opportunity and offered me a few extra dollars to keep my mouth shut.

I was able to get him to pay me double what he had promised me in exchange for my silence. When I insisted he pay me right there on the spot, in cash, he paid up immediately. Then I said I would not permit him to sleep in the hotel room with me that night. I told him to pack his bag and to go sleep in the back of his van. He quickly gathered his belongings and retired to the front seat of his van, which is where he stayed for the rest of the night.

During the drive home the next day, he was completely silent. The girls knew something was wrong but were too scared to ask. Charles decided to drop me off first. When I was exiting his van, I said goodbye to the girls and, knowing that Charles was listening, asked for both of their phone numbers. I said I had to give them a call later because there was something I wanted to discuss with them.

I then turned to Charles and said, "It's been a pleasure working with you again, and thanks for the big tip!" I knew that by saying it in front of the girls, it would force him to tip them as well when he dropped them off. I walked away knowing I just played an awesome mind game on someone I no longer respected.

I felt I was getting stronger mentally because I was able to prevent an attack with Stephen before it happened, and I was able to stop an attack after it started with Charles. But once more, my head was spinning with questions. Why did this happen to me again? What did these guys see in me that I might not be seeing in myself? Between Charles, Stephen, and Mr. Cuales, I was still very confused. When I was around girls, or when I was talking to girls, I really liked it. So why was I attracting all these guys? I was getting a handle on my mental manipulation skills, but my sexuality still had me so baffled.

Soon after severing ties with Charles, I started to work with Mario, who made his living working at colleges, private functions, and state fairs. The very first time I worked for him, we had to rehearse his *Milk Can Escape*. He was very proud of the milk can and asked me to thoroughly inspect it to see if I could figure out the secret before we started rehearsing. He also told me it was a one of a kind illusion that he purchased from the prestigious Tannen's Magic in New York City.

131

I quickly realized it was the very same *Houdini Milk Can Escape* that I was asked to repair when Mr. Cuales and I were in the Illusion Room.

While apprenticing with Charles, I learned about auditioning for jobs and maintaining a relationship with an agent. But with Mario I was learning what *not* to do. Mario did a lot of speaking during his performance, while Charles never spoke a word during his dove act or his illusion show. Mario's act was cheesy and his script was unrehearsed. He spoke like an uneducated Brooklyn thug who never knew in advance what he was going to say during his show.

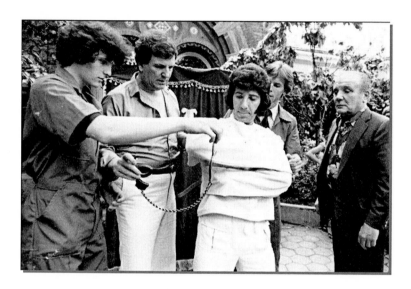

Gerry, Danny Aiello, Mario and Jake LaMotta

The most memorable show I ever did with Mario was on June 10, 1981, when he performed at the New York-New York Hotel in New York City at the premiere party for the John Carpenter movie *Escape from New York* with Kurt Russell, Isaac Hayes, Ernest Borgnine, and Adrienne Barbeau. I had to lock

Mario in a cage with Kurt Russell. Mario escaped, but Kurt did not.

Soon after, I did my final performance with Mario at the Westchester County Fair. He hired me to be his assistant for nine days straight, performing three shows a day. I remember the water in the milk can started getting full of mildew. It was disgusting and Mario got sick from climbing into the dirty water three times a day.

One of the other acts hired to perform there for the kids was *Presto the Magician*. When Presto wasn't performing his comedy magic act with his rubber chicken, we spent a lot of time together. We became friends and he taught me all about performing for kids and breathing fire. He claimed he was the magician who taught Gene Simmons from KISS how to spit fire. If this was the guy who taught Gene Simmons, then for sure he was going to be the one to teach me.

Gerry blowing fire

I watched everything Mario did with the escapes, and the closer I looked, the madder he got. He hated anyone knowing his secrets and had a major attitude problem. He was always yelling at Dina, screaming and shouting, "Leave! Get the hell out of here!"

On the seventh day after Mario and I finished performing at the fair, a kid came up to the stage and said he wanted to tell me how much he loved the show. He asked if I knew how Mario escaped from the milk can. I told the kid I had been Mario's apprentice for a long time and I still had no idea how he did it. I thought that was a compliment. I didn't realize that Mario was backstage and listening to what I said to the kid.

Later that night, Mario started screaming and yelling at me. "You are not my apprentice!" he shouted. "Who are you to tell anybody that I am teaching you any of my tricks?" He was furious with me.

I tried to explain that I meant it as a compliment. I made it seem like I was studying and working with him for years and I still had no idea how it was done, which actually impressed the kid who was speaking to me after the show. But Mario didn't see it that way. He was outraged that I would say such a thing and challenged me to a fistfight. Then he challenged me to a duel of magical talents.

For the next two days, Mario didn't say anything to me. He wouldn't accept my apology, and he was acting like a school kid sulking in the corner. At that point I decided this was not the person I wanted to work for or learn from anymore. When the gig was over, I said goodbye and drove myself home in my own van. He still owed me a hundred dollars, but getting away from him was more important to me than the money.

Later that night, I called Mario's answering service and left a message for him saying that I no longer wanted to work for him. I felt I gave him enough notice to find another assistant for the rest of the shows he'd booked me to do. As soon as he got my message, he called and left a message on my machine. He told me I was unprofessional, that I made a commitment to him, and I had to be there for him.

He added that if I wanted to learn anything from him, this was my first lesson: "The show must go on." I never returned his call. That frustrated him so much he kept leaving messages on my machine.

He said the promoters of the shows he booked wouldn't pay him unless he did the *Milk Can Escape*, his wife couldn't do it alone, and he really needed me. He would even give me the hundred dollars that he owed me and would never talk about what happened again. He was begging my mother to have me return his call.

My mother said, "The man was just about to cry on the phone. Please call him back."

I refused. "I want to work for a professional, not a child," I told her. My silence was mentally screwing with him. As far as I was concerned, Mario was dead.

Since his calls were going unanswered and he was extremely frustrated, he decided to type me a full-page letter. In it he repeated that I was unprofessional, but I didn't have to worry because he found a replacement for me. I was thinking that if he found a replacement for me, why did he need to type me a letter and think he was browbeating me even further? Because he always felt he had to win an argument. That letter was the last time I ever heard from Mario Manzini. The one main thing he did teach me was about mass mailing. He said you always receive a two percent positive answer to all your mail.

Mario called me about a year later. He pretended like nothing ever happened, like we were long time pals, and said he wanted to use me in some upcoming shows. I told him I would get back to him. I never did. I had a lot of fun traveling with

Manzini and his wife, but it was not worth putting up with his temper.

Kathy and I were able to earn our high school diplomas thanks to the mini-school program. In June 1981, a year later than I was scheduled to, I finally graduated Bayside High School. My overall GPA while I was in high school was horrible with a five-year average of just 60.5 percent. After graduating high school, I pursued a full-time career in magic.

Since I was now back with Kathy, I no longer needed to find a new assistant for my show. But it was time to put my magic career in high gear. School was finally over, I had a van to drive myself from show to show, and I wanted to hit the ground running immediately after graduation. I remembered Mario Manzini would book all of his shows from doing mass mailings, so I decided to follow in his success.

I needed money to print my promotional material and pay for the envelopes and postage to mass mail them, so I took a job delivering food for a Chinese takeout restaurant. I also started to rent my van out to young rock bands. They were too young to drive themselves to their gigs, so they would pay me fifty dollars to drive them to and from the clubs they were playing at. Many times the bands would work for the door. At the end of the night when they got paid, they didn't even make enough money to cover my van rental fee, so they would have to reach into their own pockets to cover my costs. They would play a four-hour gig, and I was the only one being paid that night.

I decided to try mass mail to local schools to solicit my show. Immediately, the mailing started to pay off because schools started to call. In early October 1981, P.S. 196 called and wanted to book me for three shows in one day. They said they wanted to send me a deposit. I typed up a simple contract outlining my deposit and balance payments, and sent it to the school. I quickly realized that deposits were good things. If they cancelled the show, I was allowed to keep the money. My first contract was typed on a portable typewriter. Since I knew it would be the first of many, I put blanks in the contract and had the contract duplicated so I could use the format over and over again. Soon after, P.S. 88 and P.S. 100 called and wanted to book me as well.

McCambridge Magic Ent.

Gerry McCambridge & Co. will be paid to perform at
P.S. 88 QUEENS on _April 5, 1983_. The time of
the shows will begin at _9 a.m.-11:30_. The payment for the
show(s) will be _$250.00_. A _$100.00_ deposit
for each show will be sent out as soon as possible to
insure the dates listed above. If the performance is
cancelled by the school or P.T.A. or anyone having to do
with the booking of the show, the deposit can be credited
toward future bookings. The deposit is non-returnable.

Gerry McCambridge & Co. will need at least 2 hours before
the performance to set props and sound. The school must
supply one microphone set back stage hooked up into the
schools sound system. No one will be permitted on stage
before or during the performance. If any of the above is
not followed correctly it might delay the starting of the
performance. The balance of the payment will be paid
before the start of the performance. Make all checks
payable to Gerard McCambridge.

Patricia A. Grayson   _Gerry McCambridge_
School Official   Gerry McCambridge

McCambridge Magic Ent.
P.O.Box 273
Bayside,N.Y. 11361

Gerry's first performance contract

Chapter 19

Looking Back and Moving Forward

In this chapter of my life, my brain was continually reinforced to learn not to trust anyone. I felt most people usually have an ulterior motive when they become your friend. It was easier to maintain a huge wall around me and my heart, and to keep people at an arm's length instead of letting them in and setting myself up for more pain. No matter how much I trusted someone, they would eventually betray me or hurt me. I learned how to protect my core self.

I learned how to create an artificial bond with someone by using my magic as the catalyst. I learned what mentalism was, and how it could be used to convince people I could read their minds. Using the mental intimidation aspects of mentalism also helped me to keep certain people away.

I discovered I had the skill to verbally manipulate my words and other people's words, and that using fear is good leverage when I am manipulating someone.

I learned the most effective way to manipulate someone's mind is to let them think they are getting what they want, while you are actually getting what you want.

When it came to learning more about my career, I was lucky enough to work with an illusionist, a close-up magician, a kids' show performer, a dove act, a fire act, and an escape artist. It all helped me to zero in on the type of magic I would eventually select as my livelihood.

Finding out that most of Mario Manzini's bookings came from his mass mailing efforts helped me continue to expand my business and move my career forward.

I witnessed the benefits of rehearsing my performance and having a script. I was taught how to produce a television show and how to communicate my needs with the television director when I am the one on camera.

I was educated in the business side of entertainment from spending time with and talking to different talent agents.

And I had the misfortune to have "sex education" taught to me by a pedophile male school teacher, who was able to brainwash me into thinking what he was doing to me was okay.

Using Mentalism

Chapter 20

Magic or Music?

While building a piece of my sound system for my illusion show, I drove down to the local Radio Shack for electronic supplies as I often did. The store was located in the Bay Terrace Shopping Center in Bayside, New York. I shopped there so much that the store manager, Richie, knew who I was. When I brought all my items up to the cash register to pay for them, he asked me what I was making.

"I'm a magician, and I'm making parts of my sound system for my show," I answered.

"By the looks of it, you obviously know a little about electronics," he said. "How would you like a job here?"

I considered it for a moment. "Thanks, but I'll pass. I just graduated high school and want to focus on my magic career."

Richie thought about it for a second, and then he offered me a deal. "You come work for me, and any time you need free time to perform a magic show, I promise I will give you the time off."

I still wasn't very interested until he mentioned that employees of Radio Shack received big discounts, so all of my future purchases would be a lot less expensive. That was enough to convince me to take the job.

After a short interview with his district manager, Ernie Hartman, I was now an official Radio Shack employee, working part-time nights. The night shift was usually slow, which allowed me to build things for my show while being paid an hourly rate by a large electronics company.

After receiving my first paycheck, I realized this was easy money. If I could secure a full-time position with the company, I could triple my paycheck and purchase so much more for my magic act. But Richie told me there were no full-time positions available. He said if I was a good salesman, he would eventually add my name to the long list of part-time employees who were waiting for a full-time opening, but I had to earn my way onto the list. I knew I didn't want to kiss his ass to eventually be added to the list, nor did I have the patience to wait that long. Once again, it was time to think outside the box and figure out a solution.

Soon after our discussion, I heard Richie on the phone trying to score brownie points with his district manager. He was talking to him about an offsite manager's meeting they would soon be attending. I could tell by the one-sided conversation that the district manager was asking Richie if he knew anybody he could borrow a van from because they needed supplies transported from the district office to the offsite meeting location at the Sheridan Hotel. I scribbled a note that said "I have a van and would like to volunteer to do it for him" and handed it to Richie. He crumpled the paper and tossed it in the trash.

At that point, our store became crowded and Richie asked his manager to call him back. When I asked why he did not offer my services to his boss, he said I needed to earn my way into the boss's good graces. After all the customers were taken care of, Richie went outside to have a cigarette.

When the manager called back, Richie was still outside, so I answered the phone and told him that I had a van I used for my illusion show and I would gladly transport the supplies for him. He was so relieved that I had solved his dilemma. He said the

144

company would pay me for my time, reimburse me for gas, and give me a hotel room to stay the night.

When Richie came back into the store, he asked me who was on the phone. I told him the district manager called back to continue their discussion, and he happened to ask me if I knew anyone he could borrow a van from for the day. I offered him mine. Richie was furious with me for going around his chain of command.

On October 26, 1981, my buddy Steve and I loaded up my van with the meeting supplies and took the long drive. When we arrived at the hotel, we unloaded the van, stayed for the night, and drove back home the next day. While I was there, the district manager approached me to personally express his appreciation for helping him out. He said he "owed me one." I told him if any full-time positions opened up, I was very interested in working under him.

A few months later, the district manager told me to report to a new store location they were opening. Two eighteen-wheeler trucks were arriving with showcases, store fixtures, and merchandise that needed to be unloaded. He said to report to the store manager, Doug, who was one of the up-and-coming "superstar" store managers. I thought this was the district manager's way of offering me a full-time position, but when I arrived, I noticed I was not the only salesman there to help unload the trucks. The district manager had asked three or four other salesman from other stores to assist as well. Doug and I seem to hit it off from the second we met, and we spent the whole day together unloading the truck and assembling showcases for the company's new flagship store.

I thought, *This is the store I would love to work in full time.* I asked Doug if he had hired any of his store employees yet and he said, "No." Since he obviously was a good enough salesman to become the manager of the store, I figured this was the man I wanted to learn sales from.

Doug and I worked side by side all day long, and it allowed me to bond with him. When we took a break for lunch, I showed him some magic. Soon after we finished building the store, Doug had a talk with the district manager and told him he wanted me as his full-time assistant store manager. The store manager I was currently working for in Bay Terrace was pissed when I told him I was transferring to this new store. Not only was this going to be the state-of-the-art flagship Radio Shack retail store, it would also have a full computer center. The basement would have the district offices and a computer school.

Most Radio Shack stores were pretty small, and each manager and sales force were responsible for cleaning and maintaining the stores. Since this flagship store was so big, the district manager wanted to hire an additional person to clean and maintain it. I suggested they hire Steve. After a quick interview, he became the official maintenance man for the flagship Radio Shack store in Fresh Meadows, Queens. Doug's only day off was on Sunday, and that was the day that Steve would come in and clean the store, the classroom, and the district offices from top to bottom. I worked on Sundays, so I could personally supervise Steve to make sure he did the job correctly.

He remained employed at Radio Shack for about eight years. He left the company because he landed a full-time porter position closer to his house.

Working together with Doug for eight to ten hours a day caused us to become close. To say we were best friends was an understatement. We were very close in age, and we had a lot of the same interests. After spending a ten-hour day together, I'd pick up my girlfriend, Kathy, and Doug would pick up his girlfriend, Christine, and we would all go out together. Doug lived with his parents and his younger brother, Cliff, who was attending college to become a chemical engineer.

One day in February 1982, my district manager told me that the Valley Stream store manager, George, had to go in for knee surgery. They needed a temporary store manager until he recovered, and he asked if I would be interested in the position on a temporary basis. A lot of salesmen in the district had more seniority over me, yet he decided to pick me to manage the store. I considered it an honor and accepted the position.

Doug and I still stayed close. Since we no longer saw each other every day at the store, I went to his house at night where we would hang out in his room and listen to Bruce Springsteen music and Doug's mix tapes. I played Doug's Stratocaster guitar, or sometimes I'd bring my guitar over and we would jam. Doug wasn't a great guitar player; the only reason I think he owned that guitar was because it was the same guitar Bruce Springsteen played.

When I suggested we start a band, Doug said his real interest was to play the drums, so we decided to form a rock band. Doug would buy a drum set, I already had a guitar, and Doug's brother Cliff was taking bass guitar lessons at the time.

Soon after deciding we would jam together, the three of us went to Sam Ashe Music Store on Queens Boulevard in Forest Hills and picked out a brand new drum set for Doug.

One night while hanging out in Doug's bedroom, I picked up a book off his dresser titled *Pink Floyd-The Wall*. It was a picture book from the movie of the same title. I knew about the album because I heard it all the time when I worked at Fotomat with Rick, but I never knew the album was turned into a movie. Noticing that the book fascinated me, Doug offered to take me to a midnight showing. While sitting in the theater, I was completely in awe with what I was watching on the screen. The next day Doug made me a cassette tape of the entire *The Wall* double album. Every night when I went to bed, I fell asleep with my headphones on, listening to one of two albums: Pink Floyd's *The Wall* or Meatloaf's *Bat Out of Hell*.

At first, the three of us held band practice in my mother's basement. The room was small, and since her house was semi-attached, the noise we made drove our neighbors crazy. We needed to find another place to rehearse. The Radio Shack store in Valley Stream that I was temporarily managing was very close to my brother Malcolm's house, so I asked his wife Cindy if we could use her garage for band practice once a week. She readily agreed.

So every week on Tuesday, the band would meet, and we'd pretend we knew what we were doing. My friend Perry from Bayside, was looking for a job, so I employed him as my part-time salesman. He was also a music student of Rod's and he was a really good lead guitar player. He occasionally enjoyed jamming with us in the garage. The music we created was horrible, but we all had a lot of fun.

One night after my guitar lesson, Rod and I went for a drive. We met up with Rod's friend, tennis player John McEnroe. (Rod and John belonged to the same country club.) They decided to smoke some marijuana together. I couldn't believe I was hanging out with a tennis legend while he was getting high! That night while we were hanging out, I decided to have a few drinks. Unfortunately, I drank way too much and had to pull over. I threw up out the window and all over the door, and ended up sleeping in my van on the side of the road. If that wasn't bad enough, I had to get up the next day and report to work. Perry worked the counter as I slept on my desk.

In the summer we practiced with the garage door open, and in the winter we practiced while bundled up in the ice cold. We used portable space heaters that kept blowing the garage circuit breakers; the heaters and our guitar amps were too much for the breaker to handle. During one jam session, Cliff showed up with gloves on his hands that had the fingertips cut off so he could stay warm while still playing his bass. Cliff also drank Jack Daniels to keep warm during rehearsals. Because of my last two drinking experiences, I refused to drink any, no matter how cold it was.

I didn't have enough money to buy a big amplifier for my guitar, so I made my own. I took a speaker, some insulation, a tweeter, a midrange, a crossover, and the wireless receiver all from the Radio Shack I was managing, and built my own amplifier. I plugged my amp into the wall and hit a switch a switch that activated a power car radio antenna to rise out of the back of the amplifier. The antenna was connected to the wireless receiver for my guitar. It was pretty high tech for its time!

I actually thought we were getting good and should have some type of gimmick like my favorite band, KISS. I wanted to combine my love for magic with my love for music and tried to figure out ways that the band could play music while I performed magic. We were also trying to figure out a name for the band.

The cosmetic store my mother managed was located in the lobby of a high-rise office building. Bill Acoin, the personal manager of KISS, was one of the tenants in the building. The band's lead singer, Gene Simmons, and his girlfriend, Cher, frequently shopped in my mother's store. My mother knew I was a big KISS fan, so she had Gene sign an autograph for me.

Since Gene shopped there so often, I figured if I wrote him a letter, eventually my mother would have the opportunity to personally hand it to him. In the letter I told Gene of my concept for performing magic while the band played music behind me. I then asked Gene if I could go on tour with KISS. I would be a roadie, his personal assistant, a guitar tuner, his personal gofer, or anything that he needed me to be, as long as I was able to learn the entertainment business firsthand touring with the band I loved.

One day Gene came into the store and my mother gave him my note. After reading it, Gene asked my mother for some paper and a pencil. He then took the time to write me back. Not an autograph, not a one or two sentence note, but a full-page letter. He gave it to my mom and left.

While my mother was on her break, she called me to tell me that Gene had just left the store and that he wrote a response to my letter! I asked her to read me his note over the phone, but she said she did not have enough time because her break was almost over. I'd have to wait until we both got home from work. From the moment I hung up the phone until I saw my mother later that night was the longest few hours of my life.

I waited anxiously out in front of our house for her to come home and finally saw her walking from the bus stop two blocks away. I ran over to meet her and asked, "Where's my note?"

She handed it to me and I eagerly opened it. I couldn't believe the length of Gene's response! He told me how honored he was that I wrote him and gave me some conceptual ideas for my band.

He also told me I needed to be the best at what I do if I want to succeed. I could not be part of just another rock band—I had to be the master of what I was doing. We had to be the "Masters of Magic" when we performed. There it was, right in front of me, the name of the band! We would now be called the *Masters of Magic*! And we also had bragging rights about who named our band. During the day we were Radio Shack store managers, and once a week at band practice, we were rock stars. We even had black satin embroidered jackets made up for the band members.

One of the benefits of being a Radio Shack store manager was being able to attend the annual Managers' Meeting, where all the managers got together and discussed sales strategy. That year the meeting was in Atlantic City.

Doug and I arrived early, so we decided to take a walk on the Atlantic City Boardwalk. A shuttle bus went by with an advertisement for magician David Copperfield on the side of it. I wanted to see if tickets were available because once Doug Henning disappeared from the magic world, I started admiring David's success and performance style. When we arrived at the box office, though, the first show was just ending and the second show was already sold out.

Since the time I started sneaking into Broadway shows, I loved to look at different types of theaters and I wanted to see the one that David was performing in. As everybody exited the theater, Doug and I entered. I noticed a bunch of people gathered around the doorway next to the stage; it looked like David's "meet and greet" area. We walked over and just blended in with the group. A few minutes later, a security guard escorted the entire group into David's dressing room. David was sitting in the corner on the couch, legs crossed, looking like a king about to hold his court.

David's manager asked who each of us were and decided who he'd take over next to meet David. Eventually Doug and I were selected and introduced to David. I briefly explained to him who we were and why we were in Atlantic City. I also explained my idea for having a rock band that also performed magic while playing music. David was very nice and cordial and said the concept sounded very interesting.

When I asked if he had any advice for a young magician, he said, "You need to be the best at what you do if you want to succeed." Before he greeted his next guest, he offered us each a signed poster from his television special—the one in which he made the Statue of Liberty vanish. While he was signing the posters, David asked if we had just seen his show. I told him we just arrived in Atlantic City and the show was already sold out by the time we made it to the box office. I noticed he looked up at his manager and gave him a little nod before we were escorted away.

The manager took us aside and told us when we finally got the band together, he would love to come and see us perform. He also asked if we were interested in seeing the next show and told us to meet him outside the theater five minutes before show time. When we returned to the showroom an hour later, his manager was waiting out front to escort us into the theater and seat us at David's personal table. It was the first time I ever got to see David's performance live, and what better way to see it than from his own private table!

One of David's tricks was to disappear from the stage and reappear in the audience. When I saw him disappear during the illusion, I knew what was coming next. Seconds later, David was standing right next to our table in the audience. He looked at me and whispered, "How are you enjoying the show?" as he climbed up onto the tabletop. Seconds later, the spotlight hit our table and revealed David's reappearance. He looked down at me, gave me a wink, and ran back up onto the stage to receive a well-deserved standing ovation.

I loved the casino environment and the showrooms in Atlantic City. One of the other Radio Shack managers asked if I had ever been to Las Vegas and told me it was a hundred times better than Atlantic City. I had never been there, but I knew it was a place I wanted to see.

The managers' convention ended a day later and we all returned home. After the excitement of meeting David Copperfield wore off, I thought about what he said and realized it was exactly the same advice Doug Henning, Gene Simmons, and Harry Blackstone, Jr. had given me. Around that time, Doug Henning pulled a disappearing act from the public eye, and I had not heard from him in a while. David Copperfield became my new magic hero to look up to.

At this point in time, my mother's boyfriend, Tommy, was living at the house with us. I watched Tommy practice guitar every day. For hours and hours he sat in front of the television playing scales on his guitar. I realized the dedication that was required to become a musician. This was a man who had perfect pitch, and was one of the best in his business, yet he still needed to practice for hours every day.

After taking lessons from Tommy and Rod, I came to the realization I did not have what it took to be a good musician. I could play the chords, and I could play the notes, but I could never hear the music in a way that somebody like Tommy heard it. The consistent advice from the people I looked up to made me realize that no matter how well I played guitar, I could never be the best, so I would never really succeed at it.

That day I loaded all of my guitars, sound effect boxes, electronic tuners, and anything else related to the music business into my van, and took a drive to the Sam Ashe Music Store in Forest Hills. At the age of eighteen, I was making one of the biggest decisions in my life: I was completely giving up music and putting all of my efforts back into magic. I sold all of my guitars; in my mind, my music career was officially over. I knew deep down in my heart that the goals I would make about being a professional musician were goals that were unattainable. If I had the chance to be the best at anything, it was going to be performing magic.

I decided I wanted to have an act that didn't require a van to transport it around the country. I wanted an act that was small enough to fit in one suitcase that would allow me easy traveling from gig to gig using commercial airlines. My illusion show was way too big for this. I wasn't sure how I was going to entertain without a van full of props, but I knew I no longer wanted any of my illusions. I sold them all, including my birds, to a friend who had a dove act. Once again, I had to use my imagination and come up with a solution.

Chapter 21

The Magic of Love

All of my friends were getting engaged around this time. It seemed like the thing to do, and since everyone else was doing it, Kathy started pressuring me to get married. I really did not want to get married just for the sake of it. I was comfortable with the way things were in our relationship. I managed a Radio Shack during the day, practiced my magic at night, and hung out with my friends in my spare time. But Kathy wanted more.

I actually considered getting married, but for the wrong reason. I really wanted to know if being blood-related to someone intensified the feeling of love one had for another person. I figured having children would be the only way I would ever feel that connection, so after some thought, I decided to give marriage a try. What was the worst that could happen? I would have children and then get divorced like my parents did. It really did not seem that marriage was "'til death do us part" anymore.

I took the money from selling my guitars and illusions and went to the diamond district in New York City to pick out an engagement ring. I also sold my van and bought a black Z28 Camaro. To me, the engagement was a joke, so on April Fools' Day 1983, I asked Kathy to marry me and presented her with the ring. At first, Kathy's family did not like the fact that I wanted to be a full-time magician because they didn't think that was a way to support a family. But now that I was a full-time retail store manager, making a good salary, they were happy with our engagement.

My father and my family, on the other hand, were not happy for me. They told me to get in my car and drive to Las Vegas with my magic act. They said I should follow my dreams while I was still young. They knew I wasn't in love, but no one knew my true intentions for getting married. After I told them I was going through with it anyway, my father offered to throw us an engagement party at a restaurant near his house in Forest Hills on May 27, 1983. All of our friends and family were invited to attend.

Gerry McCambridge (left) is congratulated on his recent promotion to manager of Store 2643-Bayside, N.Y. by District 0348 Manager Ernie Hartman. "I'm looking for a big turnaround," says Hartman, "and the way Gerry has accepted the challenge, I won't be disappointed."

Eventually George, the Radio Shack store manager who I was covering for, returned from his knee surgery and I had to give him back his store manager title. As things worked out, another store manager at the Springfield Boulevard store was being promoted, so our district manager offered me the permanent position as manager of that store.

In November 1983, the district manager called a meeting with all the top earning store managers informing them that their pay scales were about to be drastically cut. A store manager who was with the company for twenty years making $120,000 a year would have his pay cut to around $90,000 a year. Since everyone in the company made a percentage of the person below them, the district managers would get a bigger chunk of the pie if the store managers made less.

The company also knew that none of the managers would walk away from a job paying them $90,000 a year. I didn't think that was a fair way to treat employees and decided this was not the company I wanted to work for. Since I was being pressured into getting married, working for an unstable company like this didn't give me a good sense of security. I asked my Uncle Mike if I could still take him up on his job offer as an apprentice in the building engineering field. He offered to make some calls for me.

Not long after our discussion, my uncle secured an interview for me to work at EAB Plaza in Uniondale, New York. It was a new two-story office building that was being constructed across the street from the Nassau Coliseum. The interview was not for the job, but with the union. Local 30, the International Union of Operating Engineers, would be responsible for running all the heating and refrigeration equipment in the complex. My interview was nothing more than a formality since I was already hired due to the political connections my uncle had.

I was hired as an apprentice engineer. When I received the seal of approval from the union, and my boss gave me a starting date, I gave Radio Shack my two-week notice. The district manager said they were short on salesman and asked me to stay on as a part-time salesman, so I agreed to stay for a short time.

I had no idea that Local 30 was a father-son union consisting mostly of Irish men. The fact that I was being given a job because of my political connections did not sit well with the other employees on the job. When I showed up at the job site, the other workers weren't too happy with me. They hired a skeleton crew consisting of a chief engineer, a lead engineer, two stationary engineers, a mechanic, and an apprentice (I was hired as the apprentice). The mechanic's name was Danny, and he was also the union shop steward. He disliked me the most because he knew there were other young men sitting in the union hall, unemployed, who should have had my job.

The building was funded by European-American Bank. EAB had an engineer named John who worked at the EAB office located on Old Country Road. When the new complex opened, John's building would be sold and all the EAB employees would move to the new building. John was also given a position at the new complex. Danny didn't like him much, either, because he was not in the union. Danny felt he was taking a union job away from an unemployed engineer at the union hall. So, needless to say, John and I bonded and became good friends, and we both stayed away from Danny.

Since the office complex was still being built, for the first few months the company paid us just to walk around and observe the construction process. We documented where pipes were located before the ceilings were sealed up. John and I spent many hours together roaming the halls and socializing with other union construction workers. When the building eventually opened, they would hire a much bigger crew to operate the refrigeration and heating equipment. If I went to school to get my engineering license, John said I would have a very good chance of being hired as an engineer when the building was fully opened, and my salary would triple.

That seemed like a good "Plan B" to me. If my magic career did not work out, I would be a licensed refrigeration engineer, with medical insurance for my family and a pension for my retirement. In order to get "Plan B" in place, I put my magic career on hold and channeled all of my efforts into passing the two-part stationary engineering test.

A few weeks before my wedding, I took the written part of the engineering test. On May 28, 1984, at twenty-one years old, I married Kathy. When we returned home from our honeymoon, I took the practical part of the engineering test. I passed both parts with flying colors. In less than a year, I went from being a single entertainer to a married stationary engineer.

Kathy and I got our first apartment in Whitestone, New York, and she landed a job at a janitorial supply office. When I was a kid, I always loved birds, especially sulphur-crested cockatoos. As a kid, one of the television shows I loved to watch was *Baretta* with Robert Blake. In that series, he had a pet cockatoo named Fred. So as soon as I moved into my own apartment, I purchased a cockatoo and named him Monty.

Since my goal for getting married was to have a child, we tried to conceive immediately. Unfortunately, I was no longer in love with Kathy; she was nothing more than a means to an end. That addictive, magical feeling of electricity up and down my spine no longer existed at all in my life because I wasn't sexually attracted to her, and I was no longer performing on stage. Kathy soon became pregnant, which excited me beyond belief, but she miscarried the baby.

When we went to the doctor to see what was going on, he asked if it was her first pregnancy and she told him, "No." I was in total shock. Later she revealed that soon after we broke up the first time we dated, she discovered she was pregnant with my child. She told me her boyfriend, Frank, was there for her and took her to get an abortion. I felt totally horrible for not being there for her and not being able to take responsibility for what I did.

The doctor suggested we wait a few months and try again. Eventually Kathy would become pregnant, and I would finally feel what it was like to love someone I was blood-related to.

In less than four months after I was married, though, I knew I had made a big mistake. Getting married just to have a child was not a good idea. The explosive electrical sensation I hoped would eventually return was not coming back. Kathy and her family had brainwashed me into thinking that being a magician was an impractical idea. I completely resented them all for talking me out of pursuing my dream. I knew I should have listened to my father and my sister-in law Cindy. I should have hit the road with my magic act and headed out to Las Vegas and never gotten married.

Instead of hearing the applause of an audience, I spent my evenings listening to the whine of a commercial-sized centrifugal refrigeration machine, an air compressor, a few boilers and a dozen circulating pumps. I was working from four in the afternoon to midnight, five days a week. Every day that I reported to work, I resented my new wife more and more.

In August of 1985, Kathy became pregnant again. I immediately told her to quit her job since we didn't know why she lost the first baby, and we did not want work stress or job travel to be a factor in her losing another baby. And as soon as it was confirmed that she was pregnant, our sex life came to an abrupt halt.

In May of 1986, my first child was born. Out of respect for Kathy's deceased mother, we took her mother's name and used it as the baby's middle name. Kristina Marie was born late in the night after a long day of intense labor. She was not fitting down the birth canal, so the doctor decided to perform a Caesarean section. Immediately after the baby was cut from the umbilical cord, they gave Kathy drugs that knocked her out. I stood there holding this little bundle of joy, instantly falling in love with her the moment I saw her. We bonded in the delivery room for a while before they took her into the nursery. Kathy remained sleeping and I finally went home.

The next day I woke to a phone call from Kathy, who was crying her eyes out. She explained that baby was severely jaundiced and they were talking about transferring Kristina to another hospital. When I arrived, the nurses were getting Kristina ready for transport to a hospital with a more specialized neonatal intensive care unit. They explained to me that jaundice, a common condition in newborns, refers to the yellow color of the skin and whites of the eyes caused by excess bilirubin in the blood. Bilirubin is produced by the normal breakdown of red blood cells. Normally, bilirubin passes through the liver and is excreted as bile through the intestines. Treatment for jaundiced babies involves phototherapy, where the doctors use light to eliminate the bilirubin in the blood. Kristina did not react to the phototherapy during the night, and she was being transferred as a safety precaution.

In 1986, if a mother had a Caesarean section, she would be required to spend three or four days in the hospital recovering. I spent most of my day in the ICU with Kristina, bonding with her and feeding her. When she went to sleep, I drove to Kathy's hospital to spend time with her, and to show her photos of the baby and me.

Kristina's condition worsened, and the doctors were talking about giving her a blood transfusion. They asked me to find out how many family members had the same blood type as Kristina because the blood banks were running low.

But before a transfusion was needed, her condition took a turn for the better and the phototherapy cleared up her condition. That experience inspired me to start giving blood. I was allowed to donate to the blood banks once every fifty-six days. I made it a point to give as often as I could, and eventually donated gallons to the blood bank.

Chapter 22

Is He That Funny?

Between studying for the engineering exam, learning a new trade, preparing for my wedding, and learning how to be a new dad, I totally forgot about my magic career. I had sold all of my illusions to purchase an engagement ring. My remaining magic props were packed up when we moved into our apartment, stored in a trunk in the back of the closet, and I never unpacked them. I was a full-time father, husband, and an operating engineer. All of those things would have seemed great to the average person, but there was something I was missing. I missed the applause, the attention. I had a need to entertain an audience and feel their energy.

At this time I was on the graveyard shift at EAB Plaza. I sat in an office for eight hours watching gauges and listening to the machinery operate. If something sounded wrong, I investigated the problem and either made the necessary repairs to the equipment, or switched over to the auxiliary equipment and let the dayshift make the necessary repairs.

Every night at 12:30 a.m., I watched *The Late Show* with David Letterman. It was one of the highlights of my shift. I really enjoyed David's sense of humor. He was dry, sharp, sarcastic, and fast. No matter who was sitting on the couch next to David, his guests were never able to get the best of him. He had total control over the situation. He could ask any question he wanted and somehow get away with it. If any opportunity to make a joke presented itself, David would be right in there making it. It got me wondering: Was he really this good and this fast, or was the crowd being prompted to laugh and applaud by a stage manager or a blinking applause sign?

What if I could mix his fast, dry sense of humor along with some of my magic tricks? That could be a unique way of performing. I needed to see if David was really that fast-witted, and I wanted to see what it was like to be in his presence and feel his energy. I also wanted to know what it was like sitting in the studio audience watching the show being taped. I contacted NBC and requested a ticket to attend one of the tapings of his show. Much to my surprise, I was told that there was a year and a half waiting list to be in the audience for David's show. A year and a half? I didn't want to wait that long just to attend the taping. There had to be another way to get into that studio and watch David work his magic. Time to start thinking outside the box for a faster solution.

One of my favorite segments on the show was called "Stupid Pet Tricks." David made jokes while people showed him the unique talents of their pets. I thought I could get on the show by pretending my pet cockatoo, Monty, had some type of exceptional gift. I was a magician, so I could use my magic skills and make it seem like the bird was doing something really amazing. That day I went home and pulled out my box of parlor and close-up magic from storage, and my brain went into creative mode. I was thrilled to be putting my hands on the magic props again.

My creative process usually involves laying out all of my props around me on the floor. I reach out and touch them and hold them; I play with them and ideas come to my head. I eventually decided to do a card trick with the bird, making him seem amazing when in fact he was doing absolutely nothing at all. I took the bird out of his cage and tried the trick with him. He

164

was a natural! When I fanned the deck in front of his face he reached out and yanked one of the cards out of the deck. That's all I needed him to do because I could do the rest.

I called the NBC studios and was transferred to the *Late Night* offices. I told them that I wanted to audition for the "Stupid Pet Tricks" segment, and they told me to submit a videotape of my pet and me performing the trick, which I did. On July 15, 1986, Sue Hall, the producer of the "Stupid Pet Tricks" segment, called me and asked me to report to the Amity Arts Center on West 15th Street at 7:00 p.m. to audition with Monty, the bird. After we auditioned for her, she said the producer, Barry Sand, didn't care much for magic tricks, but she would get back to me because she thought we were really good.

She called me back on Friday and told me to report at 3:00 p.m. on Wednesday, July 23, 1986, to be a standby for that day's taping. My plan worked, because I was going to see the show with only a one-month wait, not a year. I didn't care if I was a standby or if I got to be on the show; all I wanted to do was to attend a taping to see if David was really that funny. Since I did not think we were going to be on the show, I didn't let anybody know except for my close family.

Early that day, Monty the Bird and I showed up for rehearsals. The "Stupid Pet Tricks" segment always highlighted three pet tricks, but five of us were rehearsing. One at a time, each of went on to the set and performed our trick with a person who was standing in for David Letterman. They told me that David did not want to see the tricks because he wanted all of his true reactions caught on camera live. After all five of us rehearsed, we were placed in a holding room. A few minutes later, Sue came in and read the lineup for that evening's show. I had been bumped up from a standby to an act and I was going to be on the show!

165

While sitting in the dressing room waiting for the show to begin, I heard the audience coming into the studio. The excitement of being in a professional TV studio, with all the cameras, the audience, the crew, the bright lights, and the knowledge that I would soon be entertaining millions, was exhilarating. I felt that old familiar surge of current in my spine.

I remember standing backstage with Monty, watching the act before me on the monitor, knowing I was up next. I wasn't shaking because I was scared; I was just really excited. I was going to be walking out on stage, performing for an audience, while meeting David Letterman for the very first time. I had to soak it all in while staying calm and cool. I had to make it seem as if Monty the Bird was the star, and I was just his owner. I could not mention how much I wanted to be a comedian like David, or how many magic shows I performed over the years. I had to step back and play the straight man, while Monty took center stage.

David's show ran for sixty minutes, and the "Stupid Pet Tricks" segment usually followed David's opening monologue. When David introduced me, and I walked out in front of the cameras and the live audience, the feeling of electricity racing through my spinal cord happened again! It reminded me of what I was destined to do.

After Monty and I were done performing, we sat backstage watching the rest of the show being taped. My brain was going a mile a minute. I decided right then that I needed to get back into performing. I needed to be on stage. I needed to entertain people. I needed to make people laugh and smile. Sitting in a boiler room watching gauges was not what I was meant to do. I really wanted to be a professional entertainer.

And by the way, David Letterman really is as funny as he appears on TV.

The next day I called a local newspaper to see if they wanted to write a story about my bird and I appearing on the Letterman show. They said since the show already aired, it was old news. If I'd called them before the show aired, they would have run a story about me.

Even though I could not get any local publicity out of my appearance, brainstorming for the show forced me to take all of my magic equipment out of storage, which in turn ignited the performing spark in me again and put me back on the magical path I was destined to follow.

Working the night shift totally turns your life around since you are on the opposite schedule as the rest of the world. Reviving my performing career would take all of my efforts, and working the night shift would not allow me to do the things I needed to do. Since none of the engineers at EAB Plaza had any plans on retiring in the near future, I knew there wouldn't be any openings on the day shift, and I would be stuck on the night shift for a long time. So I asked my union representative Jack for a transfer to the South Oaks Psychiatric Hospital, which was located very close to my house in Massapequa. He told me there were no openings in the engineering department, but I could have a job in the maintenance department. At that point I really did not care about the money; I just needed to be back on the day shift so I could work on my performing career. I knew that if an opening eventually occurred in the engineering department, I would be the first one considered for the position.

Jack set up an interview with the Human Resources Department at South Oaks Hospital, and before I was able to drive home from the interview, there was a phone message from the engineering department head. I passed the first interview and now he wanted to interview me himself. I made an appointment and went to meet with Bob. One of the things that disturbed Bob during the interview was the fact that I was a licensed engineer, and he wondered why I was taking a lower paying job as a mechanic. I told him I wanted to be a professional magician and I was working on my magic act, and as soon as the act was together, I would be quitting. He said he wanted to hire me, but made me promise I would do a good job as a mechanic until my big break in show business came along. I agreed, and he hired me right there on the spot.

Soon after I was hired at South Oaks Hospital, Sue Hall from the Letterman show called again to inform me that the show I appeared on was being re-aired on June 3, 1987. I called the *Amityville Post* newspaper again. This time they were eager to do a story and sent reporter Lance Ulanoff to my house to interview me. I had decided I wanted to perform comedy magic, but I didn't have an act yet so I was not going to let Lance know that. I followed the old expression, "Fake it 'til you make it."

I told him that at the age of twenty-four, I'd already spent quite a few years performing in comedy magic and I was going to be appearing at some of the local comedy clubs on Long Island soon. In reality, I didn't have a comedy magic act nor did I have any comedy club dates booked. He said it sounded very interesting and would consider doing a follow up story on me after seeing me perform.

The Human Resources Department at South Oaks Hospital also sent out an employee bulletin to the entire hospital announcing I was going to be on the Letterman show. Then on Wednesday, June 10, 1987 the story broke in the *Massapequa Post*, and I instantly became a local celebrity at the hospital and in my town.

Chapter 23

My Magical Rebirth

Immediately after the newspaper article ran, a secretary from a local school bus company called the newspaper and asked for my phone number. She then contacted me to ask if I could stroll from table to table at their annual company dinner and perform magic for the bus drivers. I never did close-up strolling magic before, but I decided to accept the challenge and take the job. I felt I was ready to perform again.

When I arrived, the restaurant was running very late with the food service, and I had to stand around for a long time while the company presented awards to their employees. It was a very poorly planned function, and my contract only detailed the deposit they had to send me and the balance due at the end of the performance. It didn't specify what time I would start to perform, so I had to sit around and wait to perform if I wanted to be paid the balance.

At the end of June, South Oaks Hospital was having their annual block party for all of the families of the employees. Liz, who was in charge of the activities department, asked me to perform magic for all of the children attending. After spending a lot of time with my buddy Presto the Magician, I knew I did not want to be a kids' show magician. I told Liz I wanted to perform my comedy magic for the adults, but she had already lined up another magician to perform for the adults, so she only needed a kids' performer. I turned down the job.

Next I was asked to perform a magic show for three hundred kids and adults at the Local 30 annual picnic on July 29, 1987 at Eisenhower Park. They promised to rent a trailer that opened up to a large stage where I could perform my show. Since I never performed my new adult comedy routines in front of an audience, I figured a non-paying show like this would be perfect to record on video and learn from.

When I arrived at the park, however, there was no stage as promised. I had to stand in the dirt and perform for a small group of people. Before my show, someone walked around with a bullhorn and announced all the children should gather in the open area for the magic show. An audience consisting only of kids caused me to eliminate more than half of my act. The show was a disgrace and I immediately deleted the video.

I realized it was now time to draft a contract for any future performances, preventing things like performing in the dirt or standing around for hours because the restaurant staff was running late. I did not want things like this happening to me again in the future.

As the summer came to an end, the buzz from the newspaper article died down and the job offers for me to perform stopped, but I kept working on my adult comedy routine as much as possible. I was researching all my old books that I had in storage for routine ideas I could use in the act. One of the books I came across was the *13 Steps to Mentalism* by Corinda. I remembered how potent mentalism was when I needed it to convince people I could read their minds, and keep sexual attackers away from me.

What if I combined a quick-witted, sarcastic, David Letterman delivery style of comedy with my verbal manipulation skills and these amazing mentalism routines? This concept might be something new and unique, so I figured I'd give it a shot. For the next five months, I focused all my studies on my new comedy and mentalism ideas. Eventually I felt I had some good routines ready to go, but I needed to try them out on a live audience to see their reactions.

A nursing home called Broadlawn Manor was on the same campus as South Oaks Hospital. I approached Liz and asked if I could perform for the residents. She loved the idea but told me their entertainment schedule was already prepared for the holidays. Her January events calendar was also filled up, so the soonest I could perform would be Sunday, February 22, 1988 in the main activities room after the residents ate their lunch. I agreed to the date because it gave me time to contact the newspaper reporter so he could make arrangements to attend my performance and write another article about me.

I contacted the reporter and asked him to save the date for my upcoming performance, but he didn't seem too enthusiastic about attending. He said it was too far in advance for him to commit. If nothing else newsworthy was going on that day, he would try his best to attend my show.

That did not sit well with me. I needed him to see how good I was so that he would be bursting at the seams to write another article about me. But how could I ensure that he attended this performance? Once more, I found myself having to get creative and come up with a way to make certain he showed up—and with enthusiasm!

One of the routines I remember reading about in the mentalism book would allow me to predict the headlines of a newspaper days, weeks, or months in advance. I could give the prediction envelope to someone to hold in advance, and then have that person open it at the proper time to reveal the accuracy of my prediction. What if I gave the reporter the envelope to hold, weeks before the show date? That would force him to show up to the performance to check the accuracy of my prediction. That should pique his interest enough to generate a commitment from him.

I wasn't happy with all of the methods I read about for accomplishing the prediction. I checked my *Tannen's Magic Catalogue* to see if there was another way I could do it. I found a routine I felt I could pull off, so I ordered it. When it arrived, I put a lot of practice into perfecting it. But the question remained: Would I be able to do it in front of a live audience, under the close scrutiny of a newspaper reporter?

The Local 30 business manager's wife called and asked if I would perform again, this time for the Union Christmas party in early December. I said I would only do it if the show was for the adults as well as children. I decided I could use the performance to try out my new mentalism routines, including the newspaper prediction effect. If it went over well, I would perform it again at the nursing home with the reporter present.

I wanted to see how it looked, so I asked my friend Richard to videotape the performance for me. Richard was an occupational therapist who also worked in the nursing home. Once a week, I held a wheelchair clinic at the nursing home using Richard's office as my workshop. Any residents who had problems with their wheelchairs could come down to see me, and I would make the necessary repairs for them. Over time, Richard and I became good friends. We'd eat lunch together and occasionally play racquetball after work. I also asked my sister's boyfriend, Jerry, to take still photos for me at the performance.

On December 5, 1987, for the first time ever, I tried performing two comedy mentalism routines during my comedy magic act for a large audience. I performed a trick called "Room Service" and also the newspaper headline prediction. I was really stressed before the show because performing mentalism was nothing like performing magic. Both of the mentalism routines went over well, and I was never so relieved after a performance. I really enjoyed performing the two mental effects sandwiched in the middle of my comedy magic routines, and I loved the fact that the mentalism routines were prop-less. I did not need any silks, magic boxes, or magic tubes to amaze the audience. All I used to entertain the crowd were a newspaper and a room key, both items the audience could easily relate to.

Reading the headline prediction

After the show, people came up to me to congratulate me on my performance. They didn't talk about the magic tricks I performed, only about the mentalism routines and how they never knew I was a psychic. They asked me for advice on their lives and wanted me to answer personal questions for them. When I saw all the excitement my performance created, it was like a light bulb went off in my head.

When we are children, we believe in magical things and magical places. We believe in Santa Claus, the Easter Bunny, the Tooth Fairy, elves, leprechauns, and flying reindeer. But when we get old, we get wiser and realize these magical things do not exist. We become disenchanted, and the magic leaves our lives. We wake up to reality.

When an audience member watches a magician perform, they pay close attention in hopes of figuring out the trick. A magic act is more of a challenge to an audience. A typical person won't look at a girl floating and wonder how the magician figured out how to defy the laws of gravity. Instead, he or she will look for the wires or invisible support or the secret behind how the floatation is being accomplished.

I wanted to create a show that brought the magic back into people's lives. If only for a moment during my performance, I didn't want an audience member to wonder *how* I did it; I wanted them to wonder *if* I was really doing it. I wanted them to question if what they were seeing was actually possible.

I immediately knew I was truly meant to perform mentalism, and that was where I needed to focus all my efforts from now on. After years of researching the different types of magic, I'd finally found my calling. I was not to become an illusionist like my mentor Doug Henning, nor was I going to become a close-up strolling performer or a children's magician. I wasn't going to become a comedy magician or an escape artist, and I was definitely not going to become a rock musician. I was destined to become *The Mentalist*!

I realized I had just rediscovered the type of magic that really interested me. The first time I discovered mentalism, I needed it as a form of self-defense. Now I could use it to allow my personality to shine on stage and keep the audience talking about me long after my performance is over.

Immediately I started selling all of my magic tricks and ordering every mentalism effect I could afford from Tannen's. Packages started arriving daily at my house. Ordering all these new mentalism routines used up all of the money I received from selling off my magic props. Since I was working as a mechanic and not as an engineer, and Kathy refused to work, we didn't have extra money to support my mentalism once all of my magic props were sold off. So until an opening occurred in the engineering department, I decided to take a second job to earn some extra money.

My Uncle Joe told me he occasionally worked with his brother-in-law, Gene, as a security guard in the show business industry. Gene was a retired police officer who started his own private security company called Star Watch Security. They would do all the security for top celebrities as well as all the security for the Beacon Theater in New York City. Uncle Joe contacted Gene on my behalf, and Gene gave me a job.

I worked my first job on January 26, 1988 at the Beacon Theater: the after-show party for the Broadway show *Phantom of the Opera*. It was their opening night party and it was great! There were a lot of celebrities in attendance, and I felt like I was in my element. Molly Ringwald, Audrey Meadows, Mary Hart from the show *Entertainment Tonight*, Beverly Sills, Carrie Fisher, Barbara Walters, Michael Crawford, Andrew Lloyd Webber, and of course the entire original cast from the Broadway show itself. There were a lot of rich people with plastic smiles. Most of them looked bored with the party, as if they wish they had been somewhere else—possibly *with* someone else!

I became friends with the rest of the security staff, along with the ushers and the other theater employees. I always had a mentalism trick or two in my pocket to perform for them. I quickly became known as *Gerry the Mentalist*. I noticed every time I performed a mentalism routine, the reaction was so much stronger than if I'd performed a magic trick. People loved to ask me questions about their personal lives because they thought I had psychic abilities. Every time I performed a mentalism routine, it reinforced my decision that giving up magic and focusing on mentalism was the career path I was meant to take.

The gas and toll money I had to pay to drive from Long Island into New York City made the security job not very profitable. After about six months, I stopped working for Star Watch Security.

One slow day in the nursing home, during my wheelchair clinic, I was reading the newspaper and noticed a story about a schoolteacher who was arrested for allegedly molesting young children and receiving child pornography magazines from the Netherlands in the mail. The picture in the newspaper showed a man and his son being escorted out of their Long Island home in handcuffs. When I looked at the picture, I almost fell off of my chair. It was my old high school TV Studio teacher, Mr. Arnie Friedman! The article said he had a computer classroom set up in the basement of his home where he taught computer classes to children. My favorite schoolteacher and his son, Jesse, were accused of playing bizarre sex games with the children during computer class. The authorities caught up with them during a federal sting operation and arrested them both.

After being found guilty, while Mr. Friedman was waiting to be sentenced, he reached out to me from jail. In a handwritten letter, he asked me to write to the judge and explain what a good schoolteacher he was, and how much he influenced my future. He also wanted me to tell the judge how he never sexually abused me or ever laid an inappropriate finger on me.

I felt really bad for him because he was nothing but nice to me while he was my teacher. Did he and Mr. Cuales have a gentleman's agreement not to hit on each other's conquests, or was he just a polite teacher to me? Maybe I was not his type, who knows... All that I knew is that I felt more of a sympathetic bond with the children he molested than with him as my former teacher. I did a lot of soul searching and deliberation with friends and family. However, I was not able to reach out to the judge on his behalf because he did plead guilty to multiple charges of sodomy and sexual abuse. Years later, in 1995, I learned he committed suicide while in prison.

In 2003, my friend Seth told me I should see a really good movie that was receiving a lot of attention at the film festivals. It was titled *Capturing the Friedmans*, and it was about a mutual friend of ours, David, who performed using the name "Silly Billy." At the time, Silly Billy was the most popular kids' show magician in New York City.

Seth said that a filmmaker named Andrew Jarscki was making a movie about birthday party entertainers, and was including our friend David in the movie. During his research, Jarscki learned that David's brother, Jesse, and his father, Arnold, had been convicted of child sexual abuse. Jarscki interviewed some of the children involved and ended up making a film focusing on the Friedmans.

It turned out that the movie contained a lot of footage taken by Mr. Friedman himself. All of the times I packed up the portable camera after my TV Studio class, Mr. Friedman was actually taking the camera home to shoot home videos. While he awaited trial, he was allowed to stay at home in order to prepare for court and continued to shoot videos of his family for years. The pictures were not made for the purpose of making a movie, but as a way to record what was happening in their lives. The movie showed family dinners, conversations, and even family arguments. Arnold's wife quickly decided that her husband was indeed guilty and advised him to confess and protect their son.

I was shocked when Seth told me about the film and our friend. I never knew David had changed his name, or that his father was my TV Studio teacher. Because of the name change, I never made the connection in my head.

Chapter 24

Newsday

To help pay for all the new mentalism tricks I was ordering, I tried to work as much overtime at the hospital as I could. During the day I worked as a mechanic, and at night I worked diligently on my act. I tried to read as many books as I could on performing comedy and mentalism. I started going to the local comedy clubs just to watch the comics perform and take notes on their style, delivery, and timing. I was learning what it took to make an audience laugh. Kathy was very unhappy with the fact that I was constantly going to comedy clubs to do research and hang out with my new friends. She was content with me being a nine to five mechanic making an okay living. Her resistance to my pursuit of my dream started to create more friction in our marriage.

As part of my self-education, I would write a comedy routine for my mentalism show and read it into a tape recorder as if I were delivering it before an audience. I then took notes on my delivery and tweaked the jokes. I repeated the process over and over again. I wanted a script that made people laugh from start to finish, and I wanted it to be well thought out.

On January 13, 1988, when I was twenty-five, I walked into the *Amityville Post* office with a locked wooden box that I had constructed in my spare time at the hospital. I asked to see the main editor, told him who I was, and thanked him for doing a story on me. I mentioned to him that Lance, the writer of the

181

story, wanted to come and see me perform. To make the story interesting for them, I handed him the wooden box and I explained that in forty days I would be performing at the Broadlawn Manor Nursing Home. In the box I just handed him was the headline for that day's newspaper.

I did not want to limit my publicity to the local paper, so I told him the headline was for the *Long Island Newsday* newspaper. I asked him to hold the box and keep it secure for the next forty days, and have Lance bring the box with him if he came to the show. He called Lance out of his office, handed him the wooden box, and told him his next assignment was to do a follow up story on me.

While Lance was preparing for the story, he decided to contact the editor of *Newsday* and get his opinion on my prediction. The editor said he knew nothing about the prediction, never heard of me before, and assured Lance no one knew what the headline for the newspaper was until moments before they went to print. He said predicting the headlines would be absolutely impossible for anyone. The story Lance was working on intrigued the *Newsday* editor enough to want to cover the story for his newspaper as well.

On February 20, 1988, the day before the Broadlawn Manor Nursing Home show, Mr. Nick Goldberg, a reporter from *Newsday*, called me for more information about my show and to get details about my prediction of his newspaper's headline. I gave him some details concerning the show but was very vague concerning the prediction. He said he would do a little blurb about me the day of the show.

On Sunday morning, February 21, I rushed out to my local 7-11 convenience store and bought the *Newsday* newspaper. Standing in the store I opened the very first page and there was a story about me on page 2 questioning if I was really a man ahead of my time.

The story talked about what was going to happen a few hours later during my performance at the nursing home. *Newsday* decided to send a photographer and a reporter to the nursing home show to cover my performance. I'm sure they wanted to expose me as a fraud, and they took it as a personal insult that I claimed to be able to predict their headline before they even wrote it.

A Man Ahead of His Time

By Nicholas Goldberg

By the time you read this story, you will know what the headline is on Newsday's front page today.

But Gerry McCambridge, a self-proclaimed mentalist, says he knew it 40 days ago. And he says he's going to prove it today.

McCambridge says that 40 days ago, he predicted the headline, wrote it on a piece of paper and, in the presence of a notary public, sealed the paper in an envelope. He then put the envelope in a locked box and gave it to the news editor of the Amityville Record for safekeeping.

"I've been dying to know what's in it," said Lance Ulanoff, the editor, who said he had the box in his office. "I shook it, but I couldn't hear anything."

Today, at 2:30 p.m., Ulanoff is to open the envelope at a free performance given by McCambridge for residents of the Broadlawn Manor Nursing Home in Amityville.

"It's mentalism. Clairvoyance. Intuition. Whatever you want to call it," McCambridge said yesterday. At the show, he says, he'll do "the basic stuff" of mind-reading. For at least some portion of the show, McCambridge will be blindfolded, with half-dollars over his eyes, putty and tape around the coins, covered in gauze bandages.

"It's pretty unlikely that he'll guess it," said Doug Wolfson, a Newsday news editor. "I'd be willing to wager with the man that he can't get it right. We never know what will happen before the paper is published."

Page 2   NEWSDAY, SUNDAY, FEBRUARY 21, 1988

I returned home and the pre-show activities at the house were going as planned. We arrived at Broadlawn Manor Nursing Home at two o'clock. I went straight to the dressing room and Richard and Jerry took over show preparations. As I was preparing for my show, my boss, Fred, came into the dressing room to give me some encouragement. When he walked in, I was meditating, visualizing how I wanted the show to go and what I was going to say during my performance. I was mentally rehearsing each and every word and every movement of my show.

When I went out to be introduced, the wireless sound system was not properly hooked up so I had to wait in the hall until it was fixed. At that point, Lance and his younger brother approached me and started taking notes while talking to me. After a few minutes of talk, Susan Howard from *Newsday* came over and started interviewing me. I later found out that she had only been working for *Newsday* for about five weeks prior to covering my show. She talked to me right up to the minute I was introduced. The show finally started and it was going very well.

The hospital used a plastics company called United Plastics to fabricate miscellaneous things. I had them make me an opaque plastic blindfold for my first routine. It was a design duplication routine where I was able to duplicate a random audience member's drawing without actually seeing it. The audience really seemed to enjoy that segment of my performance. Next, I successfully predicted the random amount of change in a spectator's pocket. Finally, I was able to mentally synchronize my watch with a spectator's watch from across the room.

Then came the big newspaper headline prediction trick. I asked for the prediction box to be brought up on stage and opened. While Lance was opening the sealed box, a *Newsday* cameraman was getting in the way taking photos every fifteen seconds, trying to document the entire process in hopes of exposing my scam. I later found out that before the show, the photographer spent twenty-five minutes with the prediction box, probing it, trying to find a secret opening where he thought I could secretly insert the headlines. The box was not a trick box and it was very solid, so he did not discover anything. The box was finally opened, the headlines were read out loud, and everyone was amazed at my accuracy.

During my performance, someone paged me on the nursing home's PA system. The WALK 97.5 FM radio station was calling wanting to know the results of the prediction. After the show, I called them back and they interviewed me right then on the phone. They used the interview over the air during their hourly newscast.

After my show ended, the reporters from *Newsday* and the *Massapequa Post* interviewed me extensively. When the interviews finally ended, I went home with everyone and we all had a big pizza dinner. We heard the WALK 97.5 FM radio interview every hour. It was a big thrill to hear the newscaster talk about me and my performance, and to hear my voice on the radio! It seemed everyone was excited except for my wife. Kathy. I think she was able to see the writing on the wall.

After our pizza party ended, everyone eventually went home, not knowing that I was secretly worried what *Newsday* was going to print about me the next day. Would they issue a challenge, expose me as a hoax, call me a fraud, or something worse?

Reading Between the Lines

"Hoax Exposed: The Story Behind the Mentalist's Prediction"

If that headline ever appears in Newsday, someone may win $5,000.

But, in the meantime, self-proclaimed mentalist Gerry McCambridge of Massapequa claims to have proved he could get inside the minds of those who write the headlines for Newsday. And you can believe it or not.

On Jan. 12, McCambridge claims, after 15 hours of meditation over three days, he visualized two headlines that would appear on the front page on Feb. 21 — yesterday.

As he entertained resi-

Gerry McCambridge
Mind Reader

dents of the Broadlawn Manor Nursing Home in Amityville yesterday, McCambridge, 25, unlocked a box that contained an envelope that con-

tained another envelope that contained a piece of paper that bore what McCambridge said were the headlines he wrote down Jan. 12:

"High Tides, High Stakes, Weather Erodes L.I. Barrier"

"Wife Acquitted in Murder Plot, Oceanside woman cleared"

There were three main headlines on Newsday's front page yesterday. Two of them were:

"High Tide, High Stakes"

"Wife Acquitted in Murder Plot"

The outer envelope that sealed McCambridge's prediction bore the seal of notary public Dorothy Warren. Lance Ulanoff, news editor of the Amityville Record, said he had kept it in a locked wooden box since Jan. 13.

Ulanoff said he kept the box in his office and that McCambridge, who kept the keys to the box, never had access to it. "He doesn't have the keys to our office and no one has broken in, so there's no way for him to get to it," Ulanoff said.

McCambridge said he would pay $5,000 to anyone who can prove that he cheated his way into the headlines. —Susan Howard

Page 2   NEWSDAY, MONDAY, FEBRUARY 22, 1988

The next morning I woke up for work and put on the radio. The morning radio station was talking about my $5,000 offer. At that point I knew that *Newsday* printed something, so I ran out and bought a copy of the newspaper. I was so relieved to read it; it was actually a good article! Not great, but good. They didn't believe I really predicted the headlines, but they could not prove it to be a fraud or expose my trick. I had them all wondering if I was real or not. They were talking about the performance a day after it ended. That is exactly what I wanted and it was great publicity.

The next day, I went to work at the hospital and everyone was telling me they heard me on various local radio stations: WALK FM, WBAB, WBLI, WNYG and a few more. Everyone saw the newspaper article, and the opinions varied on what I did. Some people thought I was born with a great gift and wanted private readings, some thought it was a good publicity gimmick, and then there were the skeptics. But no matter what they thought, they were talking about me and my performance. That was all that mattered to me.

One of my co-workers told me that Mr. Bob Buchmann from WBAB 102.3 FM wanted me on his morning radio show. When I went home that afternoon, there were two messages from him on my answering machine. There was also a message from Joe Santiago, a reporter from WNYG 1440 AM. I spoke to Joe Santiago first and he questioned my predicting abilities. He said he was not a believer, but wanted to interview me on the air anyway. He booked me to tape his radio show on Tuesday, February 23, 1988 at 6:00 p.m. He said it was a half hour talk show, and the entire show would be dedicated to me. The show would air five days later.

When I spoke to Bob Buchmann, he wanted me on his show immediately, so we booked it for the same day as the WNYG interview, but at 7:30 a.m. It was a live broadcast, and he was very impressed with my talents. He mentioned that he was a true believer in people having psychic ability. I told him I was not psychic, I was a mentalist who used skills and intuition to entertain. To me, "psychic" implied some sort of supernatural power, which I did not want anyone to think I had. The title "Mentalist" seemed to confuse him a bit, but I was able to explain that I was not psychic. Richard videotaped the entire morning interview for me. If all this fame and publicity was going to be short-lived, I felt I wanted video memories of it for my kids. During our live interview, Bob challenged me on the air to predict the upcoming Academy Award winners. I did not know how I would do it, but saw it as a chance to return for more interviews, so I quickly agreed. I told Bob I would get back to him with the details of how my prediction would unfold.

During the interview with Santiago, he asked me what was next. I really enjoyed the response I received from the blindfold portion of my show so I started to describe my idea for a blindfolded drive as a possible future mentalist stunt. The interview went okay but he still didn't think I could predict the headlines. He said I was just one of New York's finer magicians who fooled everyone. Jerry videotaped the entire interview with Santiago.

That same day, *Newsday* called and informed me that a school teacher named Arthur Romita from the South Country School in Bay Shore, Long Island, had sent a letter to *Newsday* and was trying to claim my $5,000 offer. He was also pestering the newspapers and constantly calling the nursing home looking to expose me as a fraud. He claimed he knew my tricks, but everything he claimed I did was wrong. I wrote him a well-crafted letter in return, and played a few mind games with him. I sent a copy of the letter to Lance, the *Newsday* editor, and to Arthur's boss, the school principal. If he wanted to use his school's letterhead for personal financial gain, the principal should know what one of their teachers was up to. I immediately received a very soft apology letter back from him, gracefully backing down from his claim.

The reporter from *Newsday* told me that a bunch of magicians kept showing up to their offices trying to expose my prediction trick, looking for publicity for themselves. Instead of supporting a fellow magician, and keeping a secret, they were the first to open their mouths in hopes of having a story written about them. The reporter told them I did not use any of the methods they were describing.

Newsday was so inundated with magicians showing up at their office trying to cash in on my challenge that they were forced to put out a public statement saying they did not wish to interview any more magicians. The paper made it clear that these people should *not* come to their offices unless one of them had the $5,000 challenge check from me in hand, and only then would they write a story. But until then, they were exasperated with the whole prediction story and wanted no part of trying to expose it.

I used the publicity from the prediction and made copies of both the *Newsday* and the *Massapequa Post* articles to create a little media package about my show. I sent a bunch of them to local comedy clubs and booking agents to try to get some work. I started keeping a logbook of all the media contacts I was making from the prediction so that when my next stunt was announced, I would have a list of interested media contacts.

Around this time, Kathy found out she was pregnant with our second child. I was extremely worried about having a second child because I didn't think I would be able to love another child as much as I loved Kristina. I thought it would be unfair to the new baby if I had a favorite. It was a topic of many conversations between my mother and me. She tried to convince me that my heart would never run out of love, no matter how many children we had.

The hospital newsletter also ran a story on me, which included a photo of me levitating my boss in the shop.

On the "Lighter" Side

Engineering's **Gerry McCambridge,** "Master Mentalist", is shown here levitating Engineering Coordinator **Fred Strade**. Something new for Fred, no doubt, but not for Gerry.

"I've been doing magic since I was 12 years old," Gerry says. "I prefer working as a mentalist these days — it's more personal, and shows more of my personality."

Gerry has appeared on the Joe Franklin show and the David Letterman show. He's become a regular on the comedy club circuit. He has met the Amazing Kreskin's challenge and become his chief rival.

Gerry, you see, can predict what you are thinking. Or at least, he can sure make it seem that way. "How do I do it? Lots of study and years of developing abilites which we all have. I'm sure a lot of people have studied what I've studied — body language, expressions, key words that help you 'read' a person."

Gerry has worked in our Engineering Department for two and a half years, where he is responsible for what he calls "preventive maintenance": ongoing work such as testing every fire extinguisher in South Oaks and Broadlawn every month, maintaining residents' wheelchairs at Broadlawn every week, or maintaining the fitness equipment at Wilsey Hall.

Gerry appears at comedy clubs and colleges throughout the area regularly. He invites everyone to catch his act and try to figure out how he manages some of his "tricks."

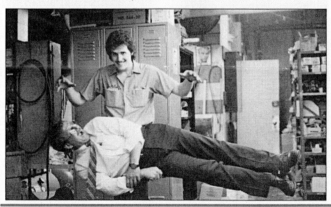

One of the talent agencies I contacted was Bill White Productions, which had a nice-sized ad in the Yellow Pages. After speaking to Bill for a while, it became obvious Bill was a kids' party magician who booked himself. When he wasn't available, he would book other performers in his place and take a small commission. He bragged to me that he was the Vice President of the local chapter of the International Brotherhood of Magicians Magic Club.

Bill told me the club had recently been contacted by *Newsday* after I predicted the headlines. He said *Newsday* was trying to get the club to spill the beans on how I was able to make my prediction. *Newsday* wanted five of the club's magicians to duplicate my prediction in their office, and the editor tried to tempt the club with my $5,000 offer. The club had a meeting and passed on having anything to do with *Newsday* since they were looking to expose a magician's secret. At that point I had total respect for Bill's club.

Bill invited me to attend his local I.B.M. Magic Meeting, which met once a month in the basement of a local library. He told me the club had only one member who was a mentalist and his name was Roy. Bill said Roy was a member of a few local magic clubs as well as a member of various mentalism clubs. I did not know there were any mentalism clubs in existence, so I decided to attend the I.B.M. Magic Meeting so I could meet Roy.

At that first meeting, I met a bunch of nice guys who, for the most part, were hobbyists that loved magic but did not make their living from performing. Eventually Roy showed up at the meeting and Bill introduced me to the grey-haired old gentleman. Roy told me he read all the newspaper articles that were being written about me, and was curious to meet the mentalist who was getting all the great media publicity. Soon after Roy and I met, the Magic Meeting began. Roy and I didn't have much more time together to discuss mentalism in private, but we exchanged phone numbers before the meeting was over.

A few days later, Roy came to my house and we talked about nothing but mentalism. I showed him all the props I built and the routines I created. He was in shock, because most of the routines I thought I created on my own had already been created by other mentalists. I was reinventing the wheel and did not even know it. He told me about two different mentalism clubs he belonged to. One was the Psychic Entertainers Association, which was the international organization of psychic entertainers and mentalists. The second club was called The Legendary Thirteen. It was an exclusive group of mentalists who met in New York City once a month. The club limited itself to thirteen members, and no one could join unless a member passed away. Both clubs intrigued me.

Roy wanted to see me perform, so I invited him to attend my next scheduled performance. Afterward, Roy and I went to a diner for a snack. He told me the execution of my mentalism was perfect, and that technically I was perfect when it came to performing the routines. He said I was very funny, but I needed to work on being more likable. The audience liked me as a performer, but he felt they should *love* me so much that they would want to invite me back to their house for dinner after my performance. I told Roy I was working on just that. I explained I was writing jokes and I wanted to be funny as well as amazing during my show. He said I should add "likable" to my persona, and I would be a star in the mentalism field.

Soon after Roy watched me perform, he gave me an application to the P.E.A. and told me I'd love the organization. My application was accepted and I was now a member of two magic clubs. But my secret, short-term goal was to become a member of the exclusive Legendary Thirteen.

I attended my first P.E.A. convention on June 9, 1988 and met a lot of mentalists from around the world. I noticed some of them used the title of Psychic Entertainer on their business cards. I was using the Mentalist title, and that seemed to confuse people; they were not really sure what that meant. I decided to try Psychic Entertainer to see if agents and potential clients would better understand what I did. I was asked to perform in the Friday night "New Members Show," which I gladly agreed to do. Without realizing it, I also met most of the members from The Legendary Thirteen at the P.E.A. convention. I was invited to attend the September Legendary Thirteen meeting as a guest. On October 7, 1989, Roy called and told me the membership of the Legendary Thirteen voted me in as a member. One of the members had disappeared and lost touch with everyone in the club, and his departure provided an opening for me to fill. Goal accomplished!

One of the members of The Legendary Thirteen was Charles Reynolds, who was Doug Henning's magical consultant from his Broadway show and his television shows. Becoming friends with Charles, and having him tell me all the inside scoop about Doug's rise to fame, was not only interesting, but invaluable to someone like me looking to recreate my mentor's success. During one of our many conversations about Doug, I told Charles about how I met Doug and how we became friends, and I showed Charles some photos I took of Doug at the Cort Theater. I was blown away when Charles told me he remembered Doug showing him copies of those photos after one of my visits to the theater.

Another member of The Legendary Thirteen was Ken, who was a hypnotist and a mentalist. When Ken heard I was doing a blindfold act, he told me that his close friend Gil did the best blindfold act he'd ever seen. After that conversation, I started to research Gil and study all the video footage I could find of his performances. Soon after, Ken introduced me to Gil and we became good friends. I used his success as a goal for me to emulate.

Chapter 25

Making Things Happen

In this chapter of my life I learned that if someone could not help me get to where I wanted to go in life, there was always someone else who could. I would not sit back and wait for my lucky break in show business—or in any other aspect of my life, for that matter.

I learned to set master goals, then break those goals down into mini-goals. I followed through with the plans and made any necessary corrections along the way. That's a requirement in order to be persistent and stay focused on the goal.

I came to the realization that I did not have any musical ability whatsoever, and no matter how much I wanted it, I could never be a great musician. I could set all the goals I wanted, but they would be unrealistic goals because I didn't have what it took to achieve them. That experience taught me that goals needed to be realistic to become attainable.

I did not want to be on the road, driving around from gig to gig in a van full of props for the rest of my life, either literally or figuratively. I needed to create an act that could easily be carried with me on a plane. I also learned the importance of requiring a signed performance contract outlining all the details of my show before I accepted a job.

I discovered the power of media promotion. Positive or controversial promotion is good, but negative promotion is bad.

Free media coverage was a much better form of advertising for my show than actual paid advertisements.

I liked performing live because of the immediate affirmation I received from the audience. The collective feedback was very satisfying. But performing on television has the ability to reach a much bigger audience, so I needed to be able to adapt to both venues.

I learned there is an art to delivering jokes, and comedic timing was crucial to be a good comic and performer. I learned I needed to be fast when it came to humor and, most importantly, the audience needed to like me as well as be entertained by me.

My understanding that people were never what they claimed to be, that they usually presented a facade, was reinforced. My emotional walls became bigger and stronger when it came to letting people into my life or trusting them. I adopted Pink Floyd's *The Wall* album as the soundtrack of my life.

The birth of my first child made me realize that whether I was blood related to someone or not, there was no difference when it came to love. But love out of guilt will never be stronger then true love.

Unfortunately I came to the conclusion that most magicians were jealous, backstabbing, self promoting, narcissistic people who I did not like associating with.

Finally, I realized that comedy mentalism was the type of magic that I would be able to excel at the most, because of my quick wit and verbal manipulation skills.

And Away We Go

Chapter 26

Academy Award Prediction

I knew I needed to hire someone who had some media savvy to come on board to assist with the next stunt I wanted to do. I asked Lance, the *Amityville Post* reporter, to join me and be my public relations director. I told him his first job was to get me permission from the Amityville Town Board and Mayor to allow me to drive blindfolded through the streets of Amityville. He accepted the position and created a new letterhead for me to use when we submitted the offer.

He then drafted a request on my behalf to the town board, asking permission to drive blindfolded through the town of Amityville to raise money for charity. Lance hand-delivered the letter to the Amityville Town Hall and was told the request would be brought up at the March 28, 1988 meeting. When I read the letter Lance sent to the Mayor, I noticed a bunch of mistakes. Since Lance was supposed to be a professional journalist, his typographical and grammatical errors came as a surprise to me.

Richard, Kathy, Lance, and I attended the town hall meeting. When my letter was being read aloud, everyone in the boardroom started laughing and joking. They did not take me or my publicity stunt proposal seriously. When the Mayor asked if I was in the courtroom, I was almost too embarrassed to stand, but I did. He briefly asked me about the stunt and immediately decided to take a vote. It was twelve against three—Kathy,

Richard, and some man who said he saw a stunt like this before, that it went very well, and it raised a lot of money.

The Mayor did not want to hear any positive responses so he closed the topic and didn't let me finish explaining my reasoning for wanting to perform the drive in the middle of the town. He said if I was truly psychic, I should have known he was going to reject my proposal, and I would not have wasted my time coming to the town hall meeting. Since I was going to perform it as a fundraiser for the new town park, I considered it their loss.

Since the blindfolded drive was turned down, I figured I'd put it on hold and focus on the Academy Award challenge. Bob Buchmann said he didn't want the prediction handwritten on a piece of paper. He wanted the prediction to be recorded on an audiotape that he could play on the radio, and he also wanted to hold the tape personally before the Academy Awards ceremony. After some research in *Tannen's Magic Catalogue*, I found the trick that would allow me to satisfy his challenge restrictions. I called Tony Spina, who was now the owner of Tannen's Magic, to question him about the seven hundred and seventy-five dollar prop. I was so proud to tell him that I had been challenged by a radio station to predict the Academy Awards, and thought I could rent the prop or make payments over time.

Tony responded by saying he was not going to rent me the prop. He went on to tell me I was too young to be a mentalist, and that mentalists were usually well-traveled and worldly performers with a touch of grey in their hair and wisdom in their minds. His lack of encouragement was rather disappointing and started to take the wind out of my sails. I quickly became annoyed and ended our call. His telling me that I could not do what I was already doing did not turn me off, however. Instead, it fueled the fire for me to prove him wrong, and to become a young, successful mentalist.

I didn't have the money to purchase the prop I needed to fulfill the challenge, so I called up the radio station and told Bob I could correctly predict the winners, but I needed a sponsor to help fund my prediction. I was hoping he would recommend somebody or volunteer to have the station front the money. Instead, he said that making the prediction work was not his problem, and that it was something I needed to solve on my own. He said I should call him only when I figured out a way to make it happen. It was time to put my thinking cap on and think outside the box.

I thought about how the entire routine would play out on the radio. I knew the cassette tape could not be given to Bob unless it was properly sealed in a box preventing him from prematurely playing the tape without my permission. What if the box was made entirely of clear plastic so people could see the tape inside at all times? And what if the box was on display somewhere people could always see it? That would generate publicity even before the prediction was revealed. And what if I was able to sell advertisement space inside the box? That would help me generate the money needed to fund the project.

United Plastics made the blindfold for me when I performed the newspaper prediction at the hospital and I really liked their work. I'd heard that a new owner recently purchased the company. My boss at the hospital, Fred, was dating a girl who worked as the receptionist in the plastic factory. What if the plastic factory made the box for free, and had their business card on display inside the box? That would be great publicity for them. And what if I asked Bob Buchmann to carry the box around when he made personal appearances for the radio station? Bob would generate interest in the radio promotion, and United Plastics would get publicity from the event.

I told Fred that I wanted to have a meeting with John, the new owner of United Plastics. When Fred mentioned the idea to

John, he expressed interest in sponsoring the event. The next day, Richard and I met with John at his shop. I told him it would cost eight hundred dollars to sponsor the entire event. Every time Bob mentioned my name on the radio, he would mention United Plastics as well. Every time Bob made a personal appearance, the box would be there with him, showing off John's work. John liked the idea and said he would finance the entire stunt. He then gave me an eight hundred dollar check. At the age of twenty-five, I was able to talk my first investor into putting money behind one of my performances. I took the next day off from the hospital and went into the city to Tannen's for my big purchase.

A few days later, I appeared on the morning radio show with John and explained the entire set-up to Bob on air. I had him sign the tape to prevent it from being switched before the prediction was played. The tape was then sealed in a beautiful clear plastic case that John crafted to look like a briefcase, complete with a handle so it was easy for Bob to carry around to all of his personal appearances. The amount of airtime and promotion John received from the box sealing alone made it well worth his eight hundred dollar investment.

Everything went as planned prior to the prediction being played. Bob carried the box around and mentioned it often on the air. Immediately after the Academy Awards ceremony was complete, John, Richard, and I met with a small group from the radio station. John had to use an electric saw to cut the prediction box open. I knew it would take a while, so I planned to perform a little routine to impress everyone there. I borrowed a cellular phone from a friend and used it to call someone on the West Coast. I then read that person's mind using a pocket watch. Everyone watching was impressed with the long distance routine. When the box was finally cut open, the cassette was played. Everyone watching was shocked that I correctly predicted all of the Academy Award winners. The radio station representative took the cassette tape with him and said it would be played the following morning live on the radio station.

Performing a pocket watch and cellular phone routine

The next morning, John and I appeared on the radio show. Bob started referring to me as the "Massapequa Mentalist" because I lived in the town of Massapequa. He played the tape over the air and did a recap of the entire stunt. He questioned me, asking if I was psychic. My performances were getting so strong and believable, some people were actually convinced I had supernatural powers.

Chapter 27

American Legion

After hearing all the publicity I received from the Academy Awards prediction, people were asking me which comedy club I would be performing at next because they wanted to see me perform. I replied that I was unsure of my schedule and would check with my agent and let them know. I couldn't tell them that the comedy clubs I'd mailed my media packet to were not interested in booking me without seeing a demo tape of my act. I knew I needed to get a demo tape really fast. Time for outside-the-box thinking again.

I considered renting a reception hall and financing a show myself. I could charge for tickets to pay for the hall rental and have Richard videotape the show at the same time. And if I planned a big enough stunt, I could also get more publicity from the radio station. After brainstorming other ideas on how to make a demo video for the comedy clubs, I decided renting a hall would be the fastest avenue.

So I went to the local VFW hall and proposed the show idea to the council. They insisted I put up a deposit for the rental of the hall and would not hold the date for me in hopes I would sell tickets. I knew the idea would work, but I didn't have the money for the deposit.

I continued to study comedy by going to as many comedy clubs as I could to study the audience and the comics. I enjoyed going to a club called Garvin's Roadside Attraction on Tuesday nights because it was magic and comedy night. Not only would I be able to study comedic timing and joke delivery, I would also get to see how other magicians perform in a comedy club environment.

Every Tuesday night as I got dressed to go to Garvin's Roadside Attraction, Kathy asked me if going to the show was more important than staying home with her. I told her that she would be in bed sleeping by nine-thirty, and the show didn't start until ten. I wasn't really taking time away from her; I was doing research and studying for my magic career. She told me I had a career and it was as a boiler room mechanic. Each and every week she made a major issue out of me going to Garvin's, along with any other decision I made in regards to becoming a full-time performer.

On April 16, 1988, I went to New Jersey to have dinner at my Uncle Mike's house. I told him about the idea of funding a show myself. He saw my enthusiasm and understood my business plan, but more importantly, he loved me and believed in me. The next day he called and said he wanted to lend me five hundred dollars to be used for the show. A few days later, his check showed up in the mail.

On Thursday, April 21, his funds allowed me to rent the hall for a July 30th performance. I was also able to order the tickets from a local printer, which I picked up on Friday, May 6th. Now I needed a publicity stunt so the radio station would promote the event for free, and I needed a place people could purchase the tickets.

I contacted Bob Buchmann with a promotions idea. I wanted to give him a stack of tickets to give away on his morning radio show. At the same time, I would also give him a list of the names of the people who would randomly win the tickets. In other words, I would actually be predicting the names of the winners before Bob even gave them away. I told him that he could give away two tickets every morning up until the day of the show. He loved the idea and wanted to start the promotion immediately. So the next day, I made another appearance on his radio show and explained to the radio audience what I was trying to do. I handed Bob a stack of tickets and a sealed cassette tape. I told him not to announce the names of the winners on the air, and to keep the entire list of winners a secret.

Since I wasn't a big enough name to sell tickets, I needed a reason for people to want to come to the show. I designed another publicity stunt where five random audience members would be given the opportunity to challenge my mental abilities, and if they beat me, they would win a brand new Porsche at the end of the performance.

I wanted the performance not only to benefit me, but also those in need. I thought this publicity stunt would be a perfect way to help a charitable organization, so I decided to use the performance as a way to gather canned goods for a local soup kitchen. Audience members were encouraged to bring sealed canned goods with their name written on the label. When they entered the hall, they would drop their can in a giant collection bin. During the show, the bin would be wheeled to the front of the stage and Bob Buchmann would randomly pick five cans. The people whose names appeared on the cans would be allowed to come up on stage to get a chance to outsmart the mentalist and possibly win the Porsche. If an audience member decided to bring ten cans of food instead of one, their chances of being selected increased.

The stunt sounded like something I could pull off, but for one small detail: I needed to get a Porsche! Fortunately, there was a Porsche dealer in Amityville whose ads I heard all the time on *The Howard Stern Show*. I contacted Wayne Siegel from Legend Autorama, used my mental persuasion skills on him, and convinced him to have one of his brand new vehicles parked at the show for me to use as publicity. He would be allowed to make a sign and place it on top of the car as a form of advertisement for his Porsche dealership.

Now how would I perform the routine and be absolutely certain I wouldn't have to give away the automobile? I remembered reading about a two hundred dollar trick that would allow me to perform the Porsche challenge, so I used my credit card and made the purchase. Now all I needed was a place to rehearse the effect.

In the meantime, Dolores from South Oaks Hospital wanted me to do a show on Friday, May 13, 1988 for her new growing retirement community called Waterways. I had Richard videotape the show so I could study my performance. There was no PA system, and ninety people over the age of fifty were in the audience. It was my best performance to date, but unfortunately the video camera broke so I couldn't study it later. I received two hundred dollars for the fifty-minute performance, which allowed me to pay off my credit card bill. The show also allowed me to perform the Porsche routine in front of a live audience, but I didn't use a car as the basis for the routine. I was able to disguise the presentation to look totally different, but still allow me to field test the routine to make the auto stunt work correctly. Dolores started spreading the word around work that my show was great, which helped with ticket sales.

The camera failure made me realize I might be putting a lot of time into planning this big performance on July 30th, and it might all be a total waste of time if the video camera broke again. I needed to find a professional video company to record the tape that would hopefully advance my career. South Shore Tele-Productions advertised a lot on the radio station, and their staff taped everything from weddings to TV commercials. I set up a meeting with owners Mike and Frank for July 7th. When I arrived, I saw that their offices were in their garage. They were not as big a company as their radio commercials made them seem to be. I told them I wanted them to shoot the show for me, and they would be allowed to sell the finished video to audience members who wanted a copy. They readily agreed to the terms of my deal.

On Monday, June 13th, I did a show at a Knights of Columbus meeting. Steve, from the pharmacy department at the hospital, hired me for the function. I received a hundred and fifty dollars for that performance that also went toward funding the July 30th show. Once again, I practiced the Porsche routine in front of a live audience but disguised the presentation to look totally different. Midway through that show, I realized that the men in the audience were more interested in the free food buffet than they were in me, so I cut my performance short.

Since reading a mind long-distance seemed to go over so well at the Academy Award tape unsealing, I decided to use it during the July 30th performance. I wanted to use a cell phone to accomplish this, so on June 29th I had an appointment with Rick Greenberg from a company called Car-Tunes. I told him I could generate some publicity for his stores if he sold the tickets to my event for me. Every time the radio station talked about the show, they would mention that tickets could be purchased at any one of his Long Island locations. I also asked him if I could borrow one of his cell phones on the night of the performance. He loved the idea and agreed.

Lance made up a flyer for the show, and it included the Car-Tunes and Legend Autorama logos on it. Steve and I went to all the radio station softball games and put the flyers on the cars in the parking lot. Richard frequently attended concerts at the Jones Beach Theater where he distributed some flyers as well.

The cost of all the new props for the show, the backdrop sign I ordered to hang on the stage, the flyers, the tickets, and everything else started adding up quickly. At the time I was still working the security job at the Beacon Theater, but it wasn't enough. I needed another way to make money so I answered an ad in the newspaper and took a job as a bartender in a yacht club. I started on Friday, June 24th, and I was scheduled to work there three nights a week. The elderly man who interviewed me was also a member of the club. He asked me if I had ever bartended before. I lied and told him I used to bartend at the Beacon Theater in New York City, and failed to mention I was really a security guard.

He told me I was hired with one stipulation: Money would never change hands at the yacht club. If a member ordered a drink, they would sign for it and be billed on their monthly statement. The yacht club was not going to pay me minimum wage and allow me to accept tips; instead, I would be paid ten dollars an hour, and would not solicit any tips.

Every week the men had a business meeting upstairs while the women sat at my bar. To prevent them from being bored, I performed mentalism tricks. They thought I was going over and above my bartending duties and would secretly tip me. The man who hired me found out and gave me a warning: "If you accept tips from these people, you will be fired. If they start to tip you, that means I have to do the same, and I don't want to tip anyone or look cheap because I'm not tipping you."

On July 4th the club had a huge party. Many members invited friends and relatives to the event. The guests were not aware of the no-tipping policy and were leaving tips every time they came to the bar. No matter how hard I tried to convince them that it wasn't necessary, they insisted on leaving the tips anyway. The day after that party, the man who hired me fired me because he didn't want to have to tip the staff due to the precedent I had inadvertently set.

During my time there, though, I was able to purchase an effect that I used to promote the show. On July 5th, I used the helicopter traffic reporter during my routine on the radio show. When I entered the studio, I had a briefcase with me. I told Bob it contained a prediction and that I was going to concentrate really hard and try to project a random time on a clock up to the traffic reporter. When she received my thought, she would announce what it was. Then Bob opened the briefcase and discovered a small digital alarm clock set to the exact same time the traffic reporter just called out. My appearance on the show went very well.

On July 14th, Richard and I went to the American Legion Hall to drop off my final payment and meet with the guys from South Shore Tele-Productions. They had a chance to look at the room and take notes. Afterward, we all went out for coffee at the Nautilus Diner. They told me they had connections at a local cable TV station and wanted me to buy six leased access time slots on the station. This way we could broadcast the show to everyone on Long Island in hopes of generating more videotape sales. They told me they would bring an entire production crew and tape my show with three cameras. In exchange, they wanted me to give them three commercial spots per TV show. After much talk and negotiations, we all reached an agreement.

So far, not only would I be able to sell tickets to my performance and make money, I would also be helping to raise food for a local charity, and my performance would be broadcast on a local TV station six times over a six-week period.

July 30th arrived and the day, for the most part, went very smoothly. At 11:00 a.m., Richard came to my house. We discussed the day's activities and proceeded to load my car with my props. When we arrived at the VFW hall at 12:10, South Shore Tele-Productions was already unloading their equipment. My buddy Andy Pope, who was also a mechanic at South Oaks hospital, was on location to help in any way he could. We pulled my car around to the stage door and unloaded my equipment.

The setup went until four-thirty when we finally stopped for lunch and had a verbal run-through of the show. They went back to setting up and Richard went to Car-Tunes to pick up our cell phone.

The Porsche arrived promptly at 5:30 p.m., and it was a gorgeous automobile. I promised myself that someday I was going to have a beautiful car like this one. I checked the keys to the car for the routine for the final time. I finally returned home at six-thirty to shower and shave. I played *Endless Summer Nights* by Richard Marks over and over while I mentally rehearsed my performance. I arrived back at the theater at 7:40 and it was already filling up with people. There was a slight delay with the start of the show due to some type of audio trouble with South Shore Tele-Productions. I wanted the audience laughing a lot on the final edit of the show, so I'd hired two comics to open for me. I did not pay them for their performance, but promised them a good quality video of their entire act to use for publicity. I told the cameramen to record a lot of audience laughter during the comics' routines. The first comedian went on at 8:30, the second around 9:00, and finally I began my performance at 9:35.

My performance lasted seventy minutes and included a routine where I was blindfolded and played a game of Russian Roulette with four hand guns. When I walked off the stage after the show was over, I was soaking wet. The stress of being the producer of the entire event, performing for television cameras, and possibly losing a car worth more than I could ever afford, made my body sweat profusely. I LOVED IT! The entire performance was going as planned so far. This would be the very first time I performed the actual Porsche routine, and if I happened to mess it up, it would cost me dearly.

I had a small wooden cigar box that contained six Porsche keys, each attached to a different colored key chain. Only one of the keys started the car; the other five keys would not.

Bob Buchmann came on stage and selected five cans from the food collection bin. The random audience members whose names were written on the cans came up onto the stage. They were each allowed to secretly select one of the keys from the cigar box, leaving one key in the box. If any of their keys started the car, that person could keep the car. If the key randomly left in the box started the car, no one won the car.

The car was parked right outside of the stage entrance. We'd set up a movie screen next to the stage and had a camera set up so the audience could watch each spectator walk out and try to start the car.

One at a time, the participants left the stage, exited the theater, and tried the keys. Right up to the point that the key wouldn't work, I did not know for certain if I would succeed or fail, but I found the pressure exciting. When the last audience member unsuccessfully tried their key, my stress ended because I didn't lose the Porsche to an audience member.

Following the performance, I quickly changed out of my wet clothing and went into the bar area of the VFW hall. When I walked in the door, everyone applauded and a crowd formed around me. Everyone was congratulating me on a great performance. I was introduced to Bob Buchmann's mother, who claimed to be one of my biggest fans. I slowly made the rounds from table to table greeting everyone. The bartender gave me free drinks—it was a great night all around! After loading up all our equipment, Richard and I took the crew from South Shore Tele-Productions out to dinner to thank them for their work.

The following Monday, Bob discussed the show on the air. He loved it and could not say enough nice things about my performance. I sent him a thank you note for his kind words.

On Monday, August 15th, I went to South Shore Tele-Productions with Richard and viewed the rough edit of the show for the very first time. The first edit was just okay. I told them how I wanted it to look and instructed them to fine tune the rough edit; they said it would take some more time.

I called Uncle Mike to see if he got my check, and he thanked me for returning his money so fast. He also said that when the final edit was complete, he wanted to take the video to his friends at NBC studios.

A week later I returned to South Shore Tele-Productions. The video was now edited down to a thirty-minute cable show. I sold all the commercial spots, and the show was scheduled to run for six weeks on the Viacom leased access cable channel. The very first week, the show started ninety minutes late. I called up Mike Rudy at the station to complain and he gave me a seventh week for free. He also gave me ten commercial spots of advertising per week for my TV show that aired during his other shows.

When it was all over, I had a professional demo video of my mentalism show to send to potential clients and comedy clubs. I was able to finance and build an entire mentalism show and made some money from ticket sales. I had my own TV show running for seven weeks, allowing me to add a TV credit to my resume. The St. Rose of Lima Church received a donation of a couple hundred cans of food, and my Uncle Mike was presenting a copy of my video to NBC for evaluation. In my eyes, the entire event was a huge success.

Chapter 28

The Comedy Club Years

In January of 1989, we had our second child and this time we used my mother's name as the baby's middle name. Jennifer Frances entered my life and I instantly fell in love all over again. I was worried there was not enough love in my heart for two children, but I quickly learned there's always enough love to go around for those that you love. My mother was right when she told me I had nothing to worry about. I bonded with Kristina because she was my first child, but I felt a very special bond with Jennifer from the moment she was born.

Now that my family was growing, I felt my demo video needed a variety of performance footage to make it really interesting for potential clients. I thought another TV performance would improve my chances of getting booked more, so I contacted the *Joe Franklin Show*, a local talk show that became famous when Billy Crystal did a parody of him on *Saturday Night Live*. After sending the producer my media kit and my current demo video, I was able to book a spot on his show.

When I was talking to Joe on the phone, he said he read my promo material and thought I was a younger, hipper version of "The Amazing Kreskin." I remember seeing Kreskin, who specialized in performing mentalism, featured in my *World's Greatest Magic Book* and on the *Mike Douglas Show*. A magician friend of mine, Howard Schwartzman, claimed he knew Kreskin personally and would forward anything on to him that I wrote. I sent Kreskin a letter and told him how much I admired his work and asked if he did any mentoring. On January 27, 1989, Kreskin responded by sending me a brief letter thanking me for my kind words and included an autographed eight by ten photo. He did not send any words of encouragement or guidance about my performing career like Gene Simmons from KISS did, just a signed photo.

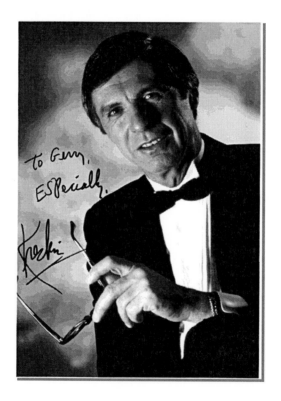

On February 4, 1989, when I was twenty-six years old, I taped a segment on the *Joe Franklin Show* in the New Jersey studios. Richard and Roy came with me to the taping. After all I learned from taking TV Studio class in Bayside High School, along with all I recently learned working with the TV crew at my VFW Hall show, telling the director of the *Joe Franklin Show* what shots I needed him to get came rather easily to me.

I added the Joe Franklin appearance to my promotional package and sent it out to the local comedy club bookers again. My persistence finally paid off because on February 27, 1989, I performed at the Rags to Riches Comedy Club during an open-mic night. I only did eighteen minutes consisting of my watch routine and my blindfold Russian Roulette routine, but I received a standing ovation after my performance.

The club manager, Roger Paul, who I knew when he was an agent for Spotlight Productions, told me he wanted to book me in a paid spot. But since the Amazing Kreskin was going to perform at the club in two weeks, he couldn't book me back as the opening act until June 5, 1989.

My new promotional package also landed me a booking on March 28, 1989 at Garvin's Roadside Attraction, the bar and restaurant in Huntington, Long Island where I often went to watch comedians perform. On Tuesday nights, a local magician named Vito hosted the "Comedy and Magic Night." I'd sent Vito a copy of my promotional video and he gave me a spot on the show. I really enjoyed performing in an environment where people wanted to laugh and be amazed at the same time. After the show, Vito told me my three-piece suit was a little over-dressed for a comedy club performance and said I needed to loosen up. He also told me I completely blew away a table full of magicians who were in the audience that night.

I took the money I was paid for the show and bought two seventeen-dollar tickets to the Amazing Kreskin show at Rags to Riches Comedy Club on Long Island on April 15, 1989. I took my old friend Steve with me. I felt that if I could meet Kreskin personally, and express my interest in the art of mentalism, he might have words of encouragement for me.

TICKET   66
SEC   ROW   SEAT
    1st SHOW

APR 15 1989
ADMIT ONE   THIS DATE
SHOWCASE OF
   COMEDY
  Presents
K R E S K I N

122 JERICHO
TPK, COMMACK
    MAYFAIR
SHOPPING CTR.
 SAT 8:30 PM
NO REFUNDS PRICE NO EXCHANGES
   $17.00
SEC   ROW   SEAT
TICKET   66

    1st SHOW

He had an early show and a late show, and our tickets were for the early show. As soon as Kreskin took the stage, he proudly announced to the audience that instead of doing two performances that night, he was able to convince management to let him combine both shows into one big show. He would start with his mentalism show, take an intermission, and then perform his hypnosis show. He called it his "full evening concert." The audience was impressed, thinking Kreskin just did them a huge favor.

During the intermission I spoke to Roger, the club manager, who said the real reason Kreskin combined his shows was because very few people bought tickets to the second show. The club paid him in advance for two shows, and the club owner wanted to sell drinks. I did not know it at the time, but Kreskin's stardom had been dwindling over the years, and the low number of tickets he sold for two shows was a good indicator it was getting close to retirement time for the aging mentalist.

I was hoping his live show would be exciting and entertaining, because he was so long-winded and boring every time I saw him perform on TV. He took five minutes to perform his average trick. He would bore the audience with his four and a half minute set up, while bragging about how famous he was and how many times he performed on *The Tonight Show*. Then he would finally get to the payoff and amaze the audience. He would always greet someone with a ridiculous, forceful handshake. He wore big horn-rimmed eyeglasses that he must have purchased from a clearance sale at his local optometrist office.

Unfortunately, I was wrong. The live show was twice as boring as one of his television appearances. During his show, I kept a running time sheet to see how long each effect lasted and how long he talked about himself. It took him about ten minutes to perform his first routine that night. What if he added comedy during his trick setups instead of bragging about himself? What if he was entertaining and funny for the entire time he performed? Now *that* would be a good show.

After the show I made my way over to his dressing room. I had a handwritten note ready to be delivered to the "amazing one." I gave the note and my program I just purchased at the show to his personal assistant, who quickly disappeared into Kreskin's dressing room. A few minutes later he came out and told me that Kreskin was too tired after his show. He did not want to see any guests after his performance, but Kreskin did take time to autograph my program. Moments later, his assistant took four other audience members into the dressing room to meet Kreskin. It wasn't that Kreskin did not see guests after his show—he just didn't want to see me.

Harry Blackstone, Jr. was a big celebrity who had his own Broadway show at the Majestic Theater. When I was seventeen years old, I attended the show and I waited by the stage door to get his autograph. When Harry found out I was a young magician, he told me to walk with him through the streets of

New York City. There I was, walking the streets with Harry Blackstone, Jr. and his wife, Gay, while he was giving me advice on how to be a better performer. When I met Doug Henning for the first time, he took time to talk to me, take photos with me, offer words of encouragement, and mentor me over the years. These were two huge celebrities in the magic world who took time to help a kid who might be one of the next generation of upcoming magicians.

But the Amazing Kreskin did not have time to give me a few words of encouragement or even a brief "hello." I decided I wanted nothing to do with *The (un)Amazing Kreskin* or his boring type of mentalism. Instead of befriending him, I decided I wanted to challenge him head-to-head.

Two days after I attended the Kreskin show, I finally received an answer from NBC. They thought my act was interesting, but I needed more work. I did not let the news discourage me; it only inspired me to work harder.

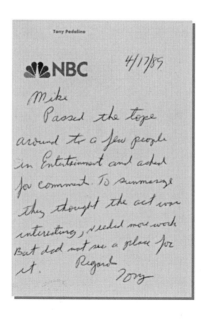

Soon after my first appearance on the *Joe Franklin Show* in February, Joe invited me back to tape another segment. I decided I was going to take my first poke at Kreskin during this appearance, using the opportunity to let Kreskin know there was another sheriff in town. Kreskin had a public challenge offering one million dollars to anyone who could suspend a pencil in a clear box, and make the pencil move and write with merely the power of their mind. I decided to take him up on his challenge, working on the routine until I figured out a way to accomplish it. On May 19, 1989, I returned to the Joe Franklin studio to tape my second appearance. During that appearance, I accepted and fulfilled the challenge on television with Joe Franklin as my witness.

Kreskin found out about my performance and had a transcript of it sent to him. He contacted Marchello Truzzi, who was a mutual friend of ours. Marchello and I spoke at the P.E.A. Convention and he asked if I was serious about claiming Kreskin's million-dollar challenge. I told him he could tell Kreskin to relax, and that I was not going to take his money…this time.

After the VFW hall performance, two appearances on the *Joe Franklin Show*, and a performance at Garvin's Roadside Attraction, I now had a pretty impressive promotional video. Once more I mailed it out to all the comedy clubs and agents in New York, and this time I started to receive a very positive response.

I started performing as the opening act in a few comedy clubs and was quickly moved to the middle spot, but I needed more material to fill that slot. Since audience members thought I was psychic and would always ask me to answer questions for them using my ability, I decided to use my blindfold routine and answer audience member questions. September 30, 1989 was the first time I ever performed the blindfold question and answer routine, and I performed for forty-five minutes on my own. Doing that act caused the headlining comic to start complaining to the club owner that he did not want to follow me. I knew I just struck gold! Soon afterward, I was moved up to the headliner spot. One of the agents who heard about my show, Craig told me he could book me in other venues including boutique high-end summer sleep-away camps.

I performed at Garvin's Roadside Attraction on a regular basis, as well as Fast Eddie's Comedy Club, Eastside Comedy Club, the Brokerage Comedy Club, The Boston Comedy Club, Mostly Magic, Topper's Comedy Club, Dangerfield's Comedy Club, The New York New York Comedy Club, Rascal's Comedy Club, Caroline's Comedy Club, Jimmie's Comedy Alley, Konkoma Komedy, Danford's Inn, and many other locations.

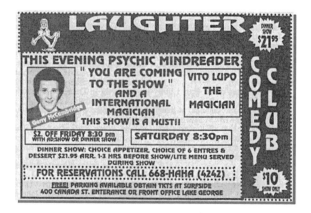

By the time 1989 ended, I was twenty-seven years old. I had performed fifty-two mentalism shows that year—and I was actually paid for thirty of them. I knew I made the right decision by selecting comedy mentalism as the form of magic to specialize in. The word about my performance was spreading like wildfire.

While performing at the Brokerage Comedy Club, I became friends with Linda and her assistant, Eileen. Linda owned a small talent agency that the two of them ran out of Linda's mother's basement. She booked the comedy acts in the Brokerage Comedy Club in Bellmore, Long Island, as well as Dangerfield's Comedy Club in New York City.

At the time, a soap opera star named Walt Willey was performing in comedy clubs at night. His fame as a soap star would draw his crowd, and his comedy routine would entertain them.

Linda decided she wanted to approach other soap stars and convince them they could also cash in on comedy club appearances. She approached John Callahan and Kelly Ripa from the soap *All My Children* with the offer and they accepted. Linda asked me to attend the performance to see what I thought. I wasn't impressed, and neither was the audience. The audience was mostly couples, and the men were there because their wives dragged them to the show. They were bored.

KELLY RIPA
CO-HOST
MUSIC SCOUPE

John and Kelly came out and the women in the audience went crazy. After the initial excitement wore off, John and Kelly took a shot at improvisational storytelling and comedy. When that quickly ended, they would do a question and answer segment. All the questions from the female audience members were based around the characters on the soap. "Why didn't Edmund marry Erica instead of Maria?" was typical of the questions they received. Why? Because the writers did not write that in the script. The audience thought the actors seemed to have a part of the decision-making process, and that made all the questions boring if you were not a fan of the show.

I approached Linda after the performance and offered to perform my show along with the soap stars. Let the soap stars draw in the crowd and appear on stage. Have them introduce me and I could entertain the ladies in the audience as well as the husbands, who were completely unimpressed with the actors themselves. Linda proposed the concept to the soap actors and they went for it. I figured riding on the coattails of the actors would help build my following.

Linda told me John Callahan's co-star, Eva LaRue, was throwing him a party in a private room in country western bar in New York City called Denim and Diamonds. She suggested I perform at the party so they could all see what I did. Afterward, we could approach them with the suggestion of having me join their comedy club shows. After my performance, they immediately went for the concept of mixing our shows together.

At the party, I met Eva's husband, actor John O'Hurley. During my performance, all the audience members were allowed to think of questions for me to figure out using my mentalism skills. John O'Hurley had two questions. First, he asked about his financial investments, and then he asked if he should move out to Los Angeles to look for acting work. I had a feeling his wife Eva was having an affair with her co-star John Callahan based on how I saw them interact together and the chemistry that was painfully obvious to the trained eye, so I told John that I felt the move would be good for his career. He made the move and quickly landed the role of J. Peterman on *Seinfeld* and became the host of *Family Feud*.

John Callahan, Kelly Ripa, and I started appearing in clubs together, and it was an instant success. I used the actors as assistants in my show. When I had an audience member stand so I could read his or her mind, we wanted to catch their excitement over the loudspeaker so John or Kelly took the microphone to them. The ladies in the audience would get so excited when they stood next to their favorite soap star, it was a win-win situation for everyone. Linda secured more bookings for us, the actors did not need to fill as much time during the show, and I was rapidly gaining a new following. More importantly, the *entire* audience was enjoying the show.

John Callahan and I quickly became good friends. He assumed with my mental ability that I would eventually discover he was having an affair with his soap costar, Eva LaRue, so he just came right out and told me about it.

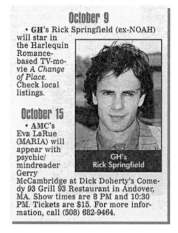

October 9

• **GH**'s Rick Springfield (ex-NOAH) will star in the Harlequin Romance-based TV-movie *A Change of Place*. Check local listings.

October 15

• **AMC**'s Eva LaRue (MARIA) will appear with psychic/mindreader Gerry McCambridge at Dick Doherty's Comedy 93 Grill 93 Restaurant in Andover, MA. Show times are 8 PM and 10:30 PM. Tickets are $15. For more information, call (508) 682-9464.

GH's Rick Springfield

I really knew my marriage was in deeper trouble after meeting Eva. I quickly developed a huge crush on her and knew I should not feel that way towards another woman if I truly loved my wife. I wanted to figure out a way to spend more time with her to see if it was just a physical attraction or if I truly had deeper feelings for her. I knew John wanted to get Eva in on the comedy club gigs, so I told John I wanted to work Eva into my act and we could title our show "The Psychic and the Soap." I felt that was catchier than the longer title of "The Psychic Entertainer and the Soap." John went for it, and Eva and I started spending a lot of time together rehearsing, performing, and traveling from show to show.

One night we were all hanging out at Denim and Diamonds when I spotted John with another woman. I realized Eva was really in love with John, and John was in love with everyone, including himself. The drama would be too much for me to take, so I aborted my attempt to possibly form a deeper relationship with Eva. We performed a few times together and enjoyed each other's company. Eva eventually divorced John O'Hurley in

1994 and married John Callahan in 1996. That marriage lasted for nine years before they finally divorced.

DAYTIME DATA ... DAYTIME DA

SCHEDULE OF EVENTS

PERSONAL APPEARANCES:

All My Children
Who: EVA LA RUE (Maria)
What: Psychic/Comedy performance with Gerry McCambridge
When: Wednesday, Aug. 10
Where: Rosebuds/Kahoots, West Point, N.Y.
Cost: $15
Info: (914) 565-6588

Another World
Who: DIEGO SERRANO (Tomas)

Beverly Hills, Calif.
Cost: $55; Send money orders (checks) with SASE to: Debbie Morris, 13518 Louisville St., Houston, Texas 77015.

Who: JOHN REILLY (Sean) and others
What: Roast to celebrate Reilly' 10th Anniversary on *GH*
When: Saturday, July 23
Where: Beverly Hills Ramada, Beverly Hills, Calif.
Cost: $65
Note: Send cashier's check/M.C with SASE to: Debbie Morris, 13

Eva went on to star in a TV show called *CSI: Miami* portraying Detective Natalia Boa Vista of the Miami-Dade Police Department. Kelly Ripa eventually moved on to co-host the morning show *Live with Regis and Kelly*. I lost touch with John Callahan.

In January of 1990, somewhere between my boiler room job and performing every weekend in local comedy clubs, Kathy became pregnant with our third child. We knew the sex of the child before he was born. Since I was not happy with my father for leaving his family, I felt that if I named my son after me, my father would think the baby was named after him. So we decided to use my birth name for the baby. Scott Thomas was born in October of 1990. He was my first son, and I was so proud of him.

During the birth of my three children from late 1988 to 1994, I was continually headlining in many of the East Coast comedy clubs. The final few years on the road, Vinnie Mark, a Long Island comic, became my opening act. He would split his time either opening for me or for Bob Nelson. Vinnie had been performing in comedy clubs for years as a part of an improv troupe that included Bob Nelson and Rosie O'Donnell. Vinnie had a lot of comedy club connections and was able to keep us pretty busy. In 1994, we were in such demand that I was able to buy myself a new car. We drove from show to show in my burgundy Jaguar XJS, and Vinnie and I had a blast on the road together.

In 1991, I also started working at country clubs and at corporate events such as business meetings, award banquets, closing dinners, and employee appreciation functions. Corporate events paid much better than comedy clubs, but most of the corporate shows were out of state.

One of the corporate shows I booked in late 1991 was in Las Vegas. I had never been to Las Vegas and always wanted to see the town. When I arrived, I instantly fell in love with the city. I walked the Strip from one end to the other. It had the same type of vibe as Times Square. At the age of twenty-eight, I knew I wanted to move to Las Vegas and have a steady show on the Strip. From the moment I stepped off the plane, I fell in love with the city, the lights, the Strip, the shows, and the sexy showgirls! I had found the place I wanted to call home.

Chapter 29

The Magic of Goal-Setting

When I returned home from Las Vegas, my goal was to get a steady job in "Sin City," so I needed to formulate a plan. My trip to Las Vegas made me realize that Linda and her company, Coastal Entertainment, were too small for my goals. I did a lot of shows for Craig while he worked for an agency, and now he was starting his own New Jersey agency. I liked Craig because he had a new agency, he was hungry, and he had the same desire to succeed as I did. I decided to take him on as my personal agent. We had a gentlemen's handshake agreement, and all my bookings would eventually go through his office.

Every night while watching *The David Letterman Show*, usually in the wee hours of the morning, I saw an infomercial by a young man named Tony Robbins. He talked about achieving one's goals, making dreams come true, and gaining financial independence. I had a feeling this program would be able to help me with my Las Vegas goal, but I couldn't afford the tape program. Without my wife knowing, I went out on a limb and ordered the cassette tape program anyway. It was almost two hundred dollars, but I figured since I was alone in the office all night long, I would be able to duplicate the books and tapes and return them before she even knew it was on the credit card bill.

My plan worked like a charm. She was at work when the package was delivered, and I immediately hid it in the trunk of my car. That night at work, I was able to duplicate all of the workbooks that came with the program. The next day I duplicated all the cassette tapes for the entire thirty-day course. I immediately returned it and received a credit on my statement on the very same month.

I began listening to one cassette tape per day, and followed all the instructions that Tony spoke about. One of the first things Tony suggested was to keep a personal journal, saying that a life worth living is a life worth documenting. So I purchased a journal and on March 9, 1981, I started documenting my life with daily entries. Tony also walked me through the goal setting process, which is exactly what I needed to get myself pointed in the right direction. Basically, he advised figuring out your master goals and breaking them down into mini-goals. Each night I enjoyed going into work knowing that I would be listening to another cassette tape, and defining my future and goals. I began to feel empowered. I was feeling hopeful and excited about my performing future. For the next eleven months, I wrote down my goals, my dreams, my hopes, and my disappointments. When I learned that Tony was going to be in town, I jumped at the chance to see him live.

On February 13, 1992, when I was twenty-nine years old, I attended a live Tony Robbins "Competitive Edge" seminar in New York City. More than 2,700 people attended, but I arrived early, was number six on the line, and had a front row seat! I was not going to let one word from Tony's mouth slip past me. The seminar was great and his talk was informative. It covered a lot of ground that I already knew from his tapes, but he also touched on a lot of new ideas. During the breaks, I went over and spoke to his wife, Becky.

I came home from the seminar pumped up with knowledge. I practically bounced off the walls with energy at work that night.

I started receiving catalogues from Guthy Ranker, the company who distributed Tony's tapes. They had an entire catalogue of tapes from Tony and others who seemed to be just as inspirational and motivational. Over the next few months I ordered different programs, copied them at work, and returned them. I would keep one out of every six sets I ordered to ensure I would stay on the customer mailing list. One of my favorites that I kept was *Psycho-Cybernetics* by Maxwell Maltz.

The first thing I wanted to try was purchasing a house for my family. We were renting a house in Whitestone and I was tired of paying someone else's mortgage. I made a list of all the things I needed to do to get a house and started working on achieving the list. On July 1, 1992, we moved into our house on Jordan Street. Using the power of positive visualization, it only took me five months to reach my goal and buy my first home.

It was a big house with an unfinished basement that had a separate entrance. I wanted to make the basement into a studio apartment so I could have some rental income to offset my bills. I spent all my spare time over the next two months building the apartment.

On September 11, 1992, while laying the tiles in the bathroom, I received a call from my mother. She told me my cousin, Mark, was in the hospital and he was dying from AIDS. She knew he had AIDS for more than a year, but Mark had sworn her to secrecy because he didn't want people knowing he was infected with the virus. In 1992, getting AIDS was pretty much a death sentence. I told my mother I wanted to see Mark. I did not feel I had been a good cousin or friend to him over the years because of his sexual preference. Subliminally, I associated Mark's sexual preference with my being sexually molested by a man.

Since Mark's mother and father were driving up from Maryland, Mom said I should let them spend time with him first, and then I could visit him after the weekend. She called me the morning of Monday, September 14, and told me Mark had passed away soon after his parents arrived.

Working on my basement apartment and in a boiler room on the night shift gave me a lot of time alone. It made me wonder: If I knew I only had a year to live, what would I do before I died at the age of thirty? Deep down I came to the conclusion that I wanted to be a full-time performer, and Kathy was not only going to be non-supportive, she was going to fight me every step of the way.

I loved Kathy, but I was not the type of husband she needed. I wasn't the nine-to-five type who would come home from work and have my housewife waiting with dinner, then watch television together while I smoked my pipe as she knitted a sweater. After seeing Las Vegas, I knew it was the place I really needed to be. Getting divorced was the only way I could pursue my dream of being an entertainer.

Chapter 30

Divorce

Soon after coming to my conclusion, I was speaking to my sister-in-law, Susan, who was married to Kathy's brother, Mike. She had called to express her condolences about my cousin Mark. I told her that Mark knew he had only a year to live and how odd that must have been for him. I also said it caused me to do some soul-searching of my own and to have thoughts about divorcing Kathy. Susan admitted she was also considering asking for a divorce from Mike.

Susan and I started to become closer due to our similar situations, and we began to speak more and more. During one of our conversations, I mentioned the guilt I carried for getting Kathy pregnant while we were dating, and for the fact that I could not be by her side during the abortion.

Susan could not believe what she was hearing. "Kathy told you that was your baby?"

I explained to her what I was told. She then enlightened me that it was Frank's baby, not mine. She went over the dates with me and the math seemed to work out. She also told me that Kathy never quit smoking. Since Kathy knew I didn't date smokers, Susan said she would hide it from me and always chew gum or have breath mints around to disguise the odor. Apparently she would secretly smoke in the bathroom. For years, Kathy had been lying to me about quitting smoking as well as about who was the father of her first baby.

Ever since Kathy had her first menstrual cycle, she kept a log of her periods. I found her logbook in her nightstand and tried to validate Susan's story. The page indicating whether the unborn child was mine or not was ripped out of the book. After a little searching, I located the missing page and it clearly indicated Kathy had a period after we broke up before getting pregnant. The baby was obviously not mine. We were married for ten years, and she allowed me to carry this guilt without ever confessing her lie. That was the straw that broke the camel's back. Out of anger towards Kathy and revenge towards Mike constantly making fun of my magic career, I started having an affair with Susan.

A month later, on Saturday, October 31, 1992, Kathy threw a surprise thirtieth birthday party for me. All of my friends and family were there, including Susan and Mike. I had to pretend I was so thankful to my *loving* wife for throwing me the party, when in reality I was totally disgusted with her. I also shot a few dirty looks Susan's way, because she knew about the party and never told me.

A few days later, I was visiting my friend Vito telling him how unhappy I was with my marriage and how I was now stuck in an affair. I just wanted to get back at my brother-in-law Mike for degrading my profession for all these years, and didn't expect to get into a relationship with Susan. At that moment, Kathy called. She confronted me on the phone, asking if I was having an affair with Susan. Vito frantically motioned to me not to say a thing and hang up the phone, but something came over me and I admitted it to her.

Soon after my admission, Mike and Kathy corralled Susan and me in a room and questioned us about our affair. Again, I openly admitted to Kathy that I was sleeping with Susan, and I wanted a divorce. She asked me if it was because I loved Susan, and I said no. Mike was devastated that Susan was cheating on

234

him and they filed for divorce a short time later. Kathy, however, tried to forgive me and wanted to attend marriage counseling. I stopped seeing Susan, but it was too late. Too much water had gone under the bridge, and after a few counseling sessions I knew it was over.

When I went into work the day after the confrontation, I asked my immediate supervisor, Jack, if he was happy with his divorce attorney. He indicated that Pete was a very fair lawyer, so I called him. When I went to his office to bring him a retainer, he asked if we had considered marriage counseling. I told him the details about how I could not forgive the abortion, and he said under the circumstances, a divorce would be the best solution. I said that we'd recently sunk all of our money into a house we bought two blocks from my mother's and I didn't have any money to move out. Pete instructed me to move into my basement rental apartment so it did not look like I abandoned my family. He also advised against getting into any committed relationship in the early stages of the divorce. To satisfy my sexual urges, I had one-night affairs with different women while I was on the road performing in comedy clubs during the beginning of the divorce process.

While living in the basement, I consolidated everything we owned. I cashed in the mutual fund college accounts for all three children and put the money in individual bank accounts for the kids. I did some research and was able to draft up a full set of divorce papers on my own. I offered to give Kathy the house, all the bank accounts, and all other assets we had. All I wanted to walk away with were my clothes, my car, and my computer. Her lawyer said he knew my game plan was to be a Las Vegas headliner, so he was going to fight for future income. He was going to fight me for money I hadn't even made yet!

My closest friend, Doug, was the first to turn his back on me and take Kathy's side in the divorce. Months earlier he'd confessed to me that he was in very serious trouble for theft and was fired from Radio Shack. I was there for him completely, for emotional support and to help my friend in any way that I could. But when I needed him, he turned against me.

It broke my heart that when my chips were down, he was so quick to take sides with Kathy, and our friendship rapidly disintegrated. Did he end it because he secretly had a crush on Kathy, and didn't want to end their friendship by having to choose sides? Or did he end our friendship because his wife turned him against me because of the bitter feelings she and I had towards each other?

Soon after I moved into the basement apartment, Kathy started dating her brother Robert's friend, Marty. He was also going through a divorce, so they had something in common. I eventually moved out of the basement and back into my mother's house. By this time her husband, Tommy, lived there, and I soon realized sharing the house with Tommy would be impossible.

Before I moved out, Kathy broke into my office and made copies of all of my personal and business files. It was at that point her lawyer decided to depose me to question the files. We all met in my lawyer's conference room: me, my lawyer Pete, Kathy, her lawyer, and a stenographer. After the formal introductions, her lawyer's questions started. Kathy sat there with a grin on her face like she was teaching me a lesson.

Ten minutes after the questioning started, I asked to take a short break. My lawyer and I went into his private office. I told him I had her lawyer figured out and I felt I could totally control the direction of the divorce using my mental skills. I asked Pete for paper, a pen, and an envelope, and then took a moment to jot down a few notes. I sealed them up in the envelope and told Pete to hide it somewhere in his office where no one would accidentally discover it.

I waited in the hallway while he hid the envelope. When the strange task was completed, he asked what that was all about. I laughed and told him to just be patient. He said we should continue the deposition, and I said I would do all of the talking so I could manipulate her lawyer and mentally play with him. I instructed him to be silent unless I asked for his advice. He said it was my dime and agreed with my wishes.

We returned to the conference room and the questioning continued for hours. Every time Kathy's lawyer asked my lawyer a question, I answered instead as my lawyer sat there silently. Eventually this irritated Kathy so much, she turned to her lawyer and said, "Why is he answering all the questions?"

I responded, "My lawyer answers when I need legal advice, and so far, I have been able to handle your lawyer's stupid questions without any legal guidance." That completely pissed off Kathy and her lawyer. The court stenographer held back a chuckle.

Her lawyer's questions were so ridiculous. "So, Mr. McCambridge, I see you had three mutual fund accounts that were mysteriously closed, and the money does not appear on your financial disclosure form that you recently filled out for the courts. Can you explain why the money is missing from your accounts? Are you trying to mislead the courts?"

"The mutual funds are college funds I opened for my children," I explained. "The money's automatically deducted from my checking account each week and direct deposited into the accounts. Since I don't think Kathy knows how to maintain a mutual fund, I cashed them out and deposited them into individual bank accounts in her name for the children's education." I then asked him if he could show me on Kathy's financial disclosure form where the three accounts were listed.

The lawyer looked at Kathy, and she was furious. "Why does he get to ask questions while his lawyer sits there silent?" she asked.

My attorney quickly responded, "Because he is doing just fine without my legal guidance."

After the long day of questioning was over, I mentioned to Kathy that her lawyer was trying to milk her for all she had and advised her to get another lawyer. She responded by saying her lawyer told her I would say that, so the fight continued. In an attempt to prove to the court that I was worth more than I indicated, he sent subpoenas to all the agents I'd worked for over the past few years asking them to supply every contract they ever executed with me. He was doing everything possible to spend every dime of her retainer.

On May 7, 1994, my lawyer met me at the Brokerage Comedy Club where I was performing two shows that night. He said he'd spoken with Kathy's lawyer as they passed in the courthouse hallway. Her lawyer indicated she used up her retainer and she now owed him money. He requested that we draft up a fair proposal and he would convince her to sign it. My lawyer congratulated me and told me it was finally over. He asked me to come by his office the following Monday and we would draft the proposal together.

When I arrived at his office, he informed me that my ex-wife and her boyfriend just deposited another $5,000 in their retainer account, so the fight was back on. I would eventually discover when it comes to a divorce, it is never truly a fight over what is fair for either party or the children. It is really a fight to use up all of the retainer.

Chapter 31

The Rebound

When I was thirty-one years old, I was setting up my props for the first show at the Brokerage Comedy Club. Linda, the agent who booked the talent for the club, arrived to check up on me before she went to a local bar for cocktails with her friends. Everything at the comedy club was going fine, so before she left she invited me to join them for a drink after my show.

She introduced me to her two friends. One was a buxom blond named Donna, who was typically my type. But as soon as Donna said she was a lawyer, I was turned off because of my current legal battle. Linda's second friend was Kim, a twenty-five-year-old massage therapist from Astoria who had known Linda since high school. Linda told me both of her friends would be with her at the local bar if I wanted to party with them after my shows.

After my two performances, I met Linda and her friends at the bar. I was very impressed when Kim told me she had her own massage therapy business, which she operated by renting one of the offices at a chiropractic practice. She offered me a complimentary massage and invited me to her house, which was a semi-attached two-family dwelling in Astoria. Her parents occupied the first level and her grandfather lived upstairs. Her grandfather also owned the house that shared the driveway. Renting that house gave him income while allowing them total access to the driveway and garage.

Kim had a massage table set up in the basement of her grandfather's rental property where she fulfilled her promise. When my massage ended, we started talking, and eventually started kissing. We were quickly interrupted when Kim's ex-fiancé, Lynn, started banging on the basement window. Kim had to call her father next door to calm down Lynn and persuade him to leave. Kim convinced me their relationship was over and he was just jealous, but she had moved on.

Kim lived with her mom and dad. Every morning, she and her father went upstairs to have breakfast with her paternal grandpa. On most nights, he came downstairs to have dinner with the family. Kim's aunt and maternal grandma lived right down the street, and also joined the family for dinner on a regular basis. The family togetherness they seemed to have was something I hadn't experienced for a long time, and I missed it.

The only member of Kim's family who moved away was her sister, Tammie. She moved to Virginia Beach with her husband, Mark, who wanted to open a chiropractic business. Mark always was a very driven person with a positive attitude, but Tammie used every available opportunity to boost her own self-esteem by knocking her sister Kim. Since Kim never had the nerve to tell her sister how hurtful her insults were, Tammie never stopped. But no matter what Tammie said, Kim always seemed to go back for more abuse.

For the most part, they seemed like a very close, old-fashioned Italian family. I quickly fell in love with the "family environment" that came along with dating Kim. When we started dating, Kim did not let her family know I had three children because she didn't think her parents would approve of her dating a separated man with kids.

Because of my past, my brain always needed to reassure itself that I was not gay by having sexual relations with a woman. As a result, sex in a relationship has always been very important to me. Kim and I did not have a very intimate relationship because she suffered from endometriosis pains. But the tradeoff of having a family while dating Kim was worth the lack of sex to me.

While we were dating, I discovered that Kim had gone to school to become a beautician. She worked in a beauty salon but her beauty career went nowhere fast. Then she went to school to be a massage therapist to be like her older sister, Tammie. Soon after getting her license, Kim went back to school to become certified in pregnancy massage. Then she returned to school for equine massage therapy. It was my opinion that Kim wasn't really interested in working, so she was a professional student. Kim rented a treatment room in her then-boyfriend's chiropractic office to see her human clients. She also doubled as his receptionist. Initially when we met, I was really impressed by her independence. But that quickly turned to disappointment when I found out all the real details behind Kim's business.

In my opinion, she felt guilty about constantly taking money from her parents for school, food, and car insurance, so she needed a sugar daddy. Since I was already a well-established performer making good money, it didn't take long for her to learn to enjoy the financial benefits of my hard work. She admired my goal-setting skills, and learned that when I put my mind to something, I was like a locomotive traveling full steam ahead. She did not fully love me, but she admired my persistence. Soon after we started dating, Kim decided to go back to school and become a registered nurse.

I loved telling the story about Las Vegas magician Lance Burton. I'd read in a magic magazine that Lance had just signed a thirteen-year deal with the Monte Carlo casino. He would make $100 million during the thirteen years he was contracted to perform there. I told everyone I wanted to pursue the same dream. Kim knew that hooking her caboose to my train could be financially beneficial for her in the long run.

After the divorce from Kathy finally ended, I went to my lawyer's office to deliver his final payment. "You did a great job representing me," I said, "but I knew the entire time how it would turn out."

He laughed. "There's no way you could have known the outcome of the settlement."

"If I can prove to you that I knew exactly how it would turn out, will you waive my two thousand dollar balance?"

He chuckled and said, "All right." He just knew there was no way I could prove it to him.

"Where did you hide the envelope I gave you? Let me see it."

He retrieved the envelope from the back of his lower desk drawer, where he'd totally forgotten about it.

"Go ahead and read what I put in there," I said.

He eagerly tore open the envelope and was incredulous. I had written down exactly how the divorce would finally settle. Moments after meeting Kathy's lawyer, I knew he would be easy to manipulate and control. I knew exactly what they would settle for and how I would be able control the situation.

I shook my lawyer's hand and said, "Now we're even." Then I told him to turn the paper over. In small print on the back were the following eight words: "You will also take my bet, and lose."

He stood up at his desk and started to applaud. He said that was the most amazing thing he had ever seen. He then asked me if I would like a job selecting a jury for one of his upcoming criminal cases. I laughed and wished him well. It was now time to pursue my Las Vegas career and take a trip out to the desert.

On February 5, 1997, when I was thirty-four, I flew out to Las Vegas again. This time I did not have any shows to perform.

I was there to learn as much as I could about the town, and to see shows to determine if my act had Las Vegas casino potential. I saw Lance Burton's show at the Monte Carlo Hotel and Siegfried and Roy at the Mirage. I heard there was magic in the EFX show at the MGM, so I saw it as well. I was intimidated by the size of the shows! My show was nowhere near that big, and a mentalist show would be. The final show I saw was an afternoon performance starring a comedy magician named Nick Lewin at the Maxim Hotel. The room was much smaller than all the other showrooms, with a much smaller stage. His show was based on his personality more than it was on big props. I loved how he connected with the audience, and as I sat there, I thought I could perform my show in this room without a problem.

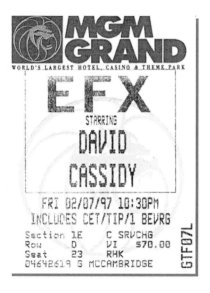

At the same time I was visiting Vegas, my agent Craig was there exhibiting a new game show called *The Rules of the Game*. Craig was the agent representing the show at the Super Show Convention along with the show's host, Scott, and his lovely female co-host, Renee. Craig left an exhibitor's pass for me at the check-in desk so I could come visit his setup.

When I arrived at his exhibit, he informed me he purchased tickets for the four of us to attend the Wayne Newton show later that evening at the Stardust Casino. I said I was not interested in seeing that show because I was in town to research magic shows, but he told me I should see a Las Vegas legend perform before he retired from show business. I eventually gave in to Craig's pleading and agreed to attend the Wayne Newton performance later that evening.

The four of us were staying at different hotels, so we agreed to meet at the show. I was the first to arrive at the Stardust Casino. I met Renee on the box office line and we went into the showroom together.

When I entered the theater, I instantly fell in love with the vibes in the room. This was an old school Las Vegas showroom. The usher seated us at one of the round-top tables, one table off of the center stage. We were seated with another couple and we all chatted. Craig and Scott had not yet arrived by the time the show began.

The show started with Wayne appearing in a cloud of smoke and wearing an astronaut suit. He removed the helmet and stood perfectly still as the entire outfit was suddenly ripped off his body, revealing a black tuxedo underneath. I wasn't sure what it was supposed to mean. Was he an alien from another planet put on this earth to entertain us mere mortals, or did he take a spaceship to the showroom to avoid the Vegas strip traffic?

Wayne started to sing, and as soon as he opened his mouth I realized why Craig said Wayne might be retiring soon. His voice was totally gone. He sounded like a bullfrog in heat when he sang. Every time he prepared to hit a high note, the audience cringed and prayed he would skip the note.

After singing a few painful verses of the first song, Wayne began to stroll along the catwalk and greeted all the audience members. One at a time, he shook hands with the guys and kissed the girls. If he found out it was someone's birthday or anniversary, he would spend extra time welcoming them to his show. He was like a slick politician working the room, one person at a time. It seemed to me that he was killing time, because each minute he was greeting the audience was another minute he did not have to sing.

Craig and Scott showed up more than twenty minutes late. When Craig sat down, he asked, "How much did I miss?"

"He's still on his first song," I replied.

"You're joking."

"He's greeting his audience one person at a time, but he's almost done."

Despite the fact that Wayne clearly could not sing anymore, it was a good lesson for me in showmanship. Wayne was a consummate showman who knew how to work an audience. I heard the percentage of audience members who walked out before the show ended (and asked for a refund) was pretty staggering. But those who decided to stay and listen to the frog crooner were clearly entertained by his showmanship.

When the show ended, I told Craig someday I would be performing in this showroom. I wanted to have a nightly Vegas show in this beautiful venue. After the show, we all went out for a sushi dinner at the MGM casino.

Before I left Las Vegas, I purchased a miniature replica of the famous "Welcome to Las Vegas" sign. I put it on the bookcase in my office so I could see it every day as a constant reminder of my goal and dream.

When I returned to New York, I began adding a little bling to my props and wardrobe. People started telling me my show belonged in Las Vegas. People also started telling me I looked like Wayne Newton. As a joke, a friend gave me a Wayne Newton t-shirt because of how much Las Vegas changed my performing style.

Gerry relaxing in his studio wearing his Wayne shirt.

The trip made me realize Las Vegas was an attainable dream. It was also very educational for me. I realized I needed more of a name before I tried to pitch my show to the casino entertainment directors. I needed marquee value to be able to compete with all the other shows in Las Vegas. I thought the best way for me to accomplish my goal was to have my own television special.

A few years earlier, when I joined the Psychic Entertainers Association, I had used that as my title: "Gerry McCambridge - Psychic Entertainer." During my Vegas trip, I also realized I no longer wanted to be known as a "Psychic Entertainer." I felt the word *psychic* implied supernatural abilities, and I did not want to send out a wrong message to my audience. I wanted a brand that would be simple and easy to remember, so I changed my title and purchased the mentalist.com domain name.

Kim graduated nursing school and took a job in a doctor's office. Her family finally accepted my three children and me. They taught me the meaning of family, something I had really missed since my parents had divorced when I was very young. During the divorce process from Kathy, I rented a house from a friend in Wantagh, Long Island. I asked Kim to move in with me, but her mother refused to allow it. However, Kim did travel with me to all of my shows. We would drive for hours to the summer camps and talk during the entire ride without having to put on the car radio. After the show, we would pull over on the drive home and lie on the hood of my car to enjoy the bright stars that seemed to blanket the sky.

At one point in our relationship, Kim and I broke up. She started seeing a chiropractor in Virginia Beach who was Kim's brother-in-law's best friend. After a few months apart, Kim and I decided try to revive our relationship.

We were very compatible because we were friends first, but were never very sexual because of endometriosis pain during intimacy. Even though she had a procedure to treat it many years ago, it seemed to have returned. She told me another operation would stop the pain, and our intimacy could possibly increase. However, she was no longer covered by her father's medical insurance and she didn't continue with a COBRA policy after he retired from the police force. That meant she would have to pay for the operation out of pocket. She didn't want to ask her parents for the money, so she suggested that getting married would allow her to use my union medical insurance.

She actually started planning the wedding before my divorce was complete. After both sides agreed and we signed the divorce papers, we had to wait for the judge to approve them. The wedding date was closing in and we started to worry. Kim's friend Pat, who worked for a lawyer, contacted the judge's secretary, pulled some strings, and got the papers signed just in time. My divorce was final on May 11, 1998, and twenty days later, on May 31, 1998, when I was thirty-five, I married Kim.

Many of my friends were shocked at how fast I jumped into a relationship and remarried. I really hated seeing my friend Kim in pain and wanted to get her medical relief, but I couldn't tell anyone why I was getting married so fast. Soon after the honeymoon, we traveled to Washington State so she could be treated by the best doctor she was able to find after much online research.

After the medical procedure, Kim implied the best way to insure her endometriosis would not return was to get pregnant. I told her that I didn't want any more children—I wanted to focus on my performing career. Since she married me, she was now the stepmother to three beautiful children. She assured me if we had a baby, she and her mother would take care of it, allowing me to pursue my dream.

This turned out to be a promise she would eventually use against me in court fifteen years later, when I would file for divorce and she would fight for sole custody, claiming I was narcissistic and not a very hands-on father. I should have read the writing on the wall when Kim and I needed couples therapy even before we were married. We saw a therapist for lack of intimacy and trust, as well as her inability to bond with my three children.

Chapter 32

Quitting the Day Job

As soon as Kim and I were married, I wanted to quit my day job at the hospital. The corporate shows were coming in on a regular basis and I was making more than enough to support us. I called the union hall to see what steps I needed to take to continue my medial insurance when I quit. They informed me if I continued to work until the end of the year, I would be fully vested in my pension.

When I joined the Local 30 Union in 1993, I needed to work ten years to become vested in the union's retirement plan, so I never considered staying until 2003 to become fully vested. But at the end of the year they said they were changing the vesting time to five years, so I decided to work another seven months to become fully vested.

In January 1999, after I was vested in the retirement plan, I contacted my accountant and told him I wanted to quit my hospital job. He knew I was renting a house and eventually wanted to purchase a home of my own. He said it would be a lot easier for me to apply for a mortgage if I had a steady full-time job and was able to document my income. As a full-time performer, getting approved for a mortgage might be quite a bit more difficult.

So I started looking for a house while I continued to work at the hospital. In August 1999, I finally found my dream house, but it was a little more expensive than I had budgeted for. I drained my bank account to put a deposit down on it. We closed on the house on December 1, 1999, when I was thirty-seven years old. The house was in Dix Hills, Long Island. It was a five thousand square foot house with an attached three-bedroom apartment. Immediately after closing on the house, I rented out the apartment to three college students who wanted to live off campus. One of the students was young man named Chris who was studying audio engineering at nearby Five Towns College.

I had a mutual agreement with another hospital engineer named Steve. Sometimes my shows would end late, causing me to show up an hour or two late to the hospital. Steve would cover my shift for me. Eventually he would accumulate eight hours and take a day off to go fishing. I would also give him cash bonuses and occasionally buy him beer when he worked for me. Having Steve cover for me with no questions asked allowed me to take every gig that came in. After the purchase of our house, my accountant gave me the green light to quit my day job. But things were going so smoothly working both jobs and having Steve cover for me, I was no longer in such a rush to quit the hospital job.

After we purchased the Dix Hills house, I had my weekly salary from the hospital, my performing income, and rental income. My next goal was to have at least one year's worth of living expenses in the bank before I quit my day job. I used most of our savings for the down payment on the house, so I needed to build up our bank account again. I decided to try to live off of my performing income and bank my entire hospital paycheck to get used to not having a steady weekly income. The bank account balance built up pretty fast with all of my hospital salary gong into it. As soon as I had saved a year's worth of living expenses, Kim gave me her blessing to quit my day job at the hospital and pursue my dream.

Kim had two dreams: she wanted a child and a pot-bellied pig. Since we now had a house with a large backyard, we started trying to have a baby. She also found a breeder and ordered a baby pig. For the first time in our relationship, I was intimate with my wife on a regular basis, but it was because she was trying to conceive, not because she desired me.

In February 2000, we went to the airport and picked up Charlotte Rose, the baby pig. In April, Kim discovered she was pregnant. At the time, I was making more than enough money as an entertainer to support the family, so I told Kim she could quit her job as a nurse. She said she really enjoyed her job and insisted on working at the doctor's office as long as possible.

As soon as Kim found out she was pregnant, our intimacy stopped, and to ensure I stayed away from her, she allowed the pig to sleep in bed with us—right between us. In my professional life, girls always wanted me, but the one woman I wanted most was shutting me out and wedging a pig between us. The average man might be able to live a life lacking intimacy, but my brain required it because of my past, and once more, I was growing more and more sexually frustrated.

Now that Kim had her pet pig and she was pregnant, it was time for me to pursue my Las Vegas dream. I knew I needed more of a name for myself before I returned to Las Vegas, so I figured I'd write a show and perform it Off Broadway in New York City. Then I would return to Vegas with an impressive credential under my belt.

The first thing I needed to do was to get an investor to back my show. My first thought was to approach my long time agent and friend, Craig, but I felt he became too diversified over the years. When I first met him, he started his own booking agency and he wanted to exclusively represent me. Soon afterward, he decided to buy a kids' summer sleep-away camp. Every summer, he lived upstate at the camp and I saw my bookings dwindle.

He left his assistant, Janet, in charge of the booking agency. Janet was great at doing all the administrative work for the office, but Craig basically did all the selling of the acts. She sent out my contracts to the clients, booked all of my flights, arranged my limo pick up, and took care of my hotel rooms. I was working so much that Janet and I were on the phone many times during the day. Sometimes it almost felt as if she was my personal assistant. But every year, Craig convinced me this summer would be different, and every year Janet and I watched my bookings take a dive. Then Craig decided to purchase the Catch a Rising Star comedy club organization. Now he was running his booking agency, recruiting kids and counselors for the summer camp, and running a chain of comedy clubs. I really admired his drive to succeed but felt his diversity took away from his focus on my career. I really wanted Craig to be my personal manager and handle everything in my career, but he kept getting sidetracked with different projects.

So instead of approaching Craig to invest in the show, I approached my friend Tom. He was a party planner in New York City who booked me to work a lot of the high-end Bar Mitzvahs and private parties. I had performed many times over the years for Tom and he was a big fan of my work. I told Tom I was looking for an investor and he immediately committed to the project. While I was in the planning stages of the show, a mentalist friend of mine named Marc Salem announced he was going to open his show Off Broadway.

I wanted to do something totally different than he did. Marc's approach to mentalism was academic and scientific. He was a college professor and that was the angle he used in his performance.

My approach was more comedic in nature. I was a New York wise-ass who was able to do cool mental tricks. But I felt the one-man mentalism similarity would still label me as a copycat, so I drafted an outline for a comedy show consisting of two mentalists performing as a team. It would be as if Abbott and Costello could read minds: one performer would be the straight man, and the other would be the comic. I told Tom about the two-man show I wanted to try. He said he wanted to produce my show as it was, but if I really wanted to try the two-person show, he would consider funding it.

In 1989, I attended a mentalist convention in Chicago and I met a fellow performer named Steve Shaw. He'd seen a copy of the demo video I sent to the Magic Island club in Texas. He said he really liked the ESP card routine I performed on *The Joe Franklin Show*. Steve was around my age and he was from Houston. He was very creative and we really seemed to hit it off, so we kept in touch over the years. Steve also bragged how good his wife was at getting him booked on television shows.

I knew he was the perfect performer to be the straight man in the two-person act. His wife could book us on television shows, which would add to my resume and, more importantly, add to my marquee value when I eventually returned to Las Vegas. I contacted Steve and told him about my idea for the Off Broadway show. I told him I already had the investor in place who wanted to produce the show. Steve was honored that I selected him and signed on to the project.

Soon after, I flew Steve to New York to meet Tom. I had two shows in one day around the same time, so I convinced Tom to hire Steve instead of me. I figured Tom would get a good report back from the client, and he would have faith in my decision to take on a partner.

When Steve arrived in New York, he told me he spoke to his wife and decided to change his stage name to "Banachek." I was not a big fan of naming himself after a TV show character, but he insisted it would be for the better. We titled our Off Broadway show *Mystical Minds with Gerry and Banachek*.

Whenever he was not performing at a college, he started spending as much time as he could at my house so that we could rehearse. He became a part of my family and I treated him like he was my brother. We booked a photo shoot and soon had promotional material to pitch the show.

Soon after the photo shoot, I had a booking for a summer camp's final weekend before the kids returned home. I was working so many hours that I began to doze at the wheel while driving. I needed Kim to make the drive with me, but she said she couldn't accompany me on the four-hour drive because she was feeling sick from being pregnant. After I made the long drive, I called home and discovered she had made plans with her parents while I was away. She did not seem concerned about my safety.

After the performance, I was very annoyed at Kim for lying to me, so I was in no rush to drive back home to be with her. I was also way too tired to make the four-hour drive back home, so I decided to sleep at the camp and drive home in the morning. The camp put me up in one of the spare counselor rooms that did not have air-conditioning. After lying in bed and sweating like a pig, I couldn't take it any longer, so I packed my bags and drove into the local town. I rented a hotel room for the night, but when I checked in, the air-conditioning in the room was off. I cranked it up to full blast and left the room to give it time to cool.

I remembered hearing loud music when I got out of my car, so I decided to investigate the source and discovered it was coming from a bar across the street from the hotel. I never took a drink since 1982 when I threw up all over my car door, but decided to take a look at the place anyway. When I entered the bar, someone instantly screamed out my name. Some camp counselors who were at my performance earlier that evening were celebrating their final weekend together at camp. They offered me drinks, and against my better judgment, I decided to have one. I figured I was safe since I knew I didn't have to drive, and my hotel room was right across the street.

I started talking to a tall blond girl from New Zealand. She flirted with me and made it known that she wanted to have some fun before returning to her country in a few days. After a few more cocktails, we wound up back in my hotel room. When I returned home to New York, I told Banachek what happened. I felt so guilty after sleeping with her that I decided to never accept another summer camp booking after that night. I realized that every time I drank alcohol, it did not turn out well. So I promised myself I would never take another alcoholic drink for the rest of my life.

Working on the Off Broadway show became a full-time job. We hired my tenant, Chris, as our sound and cameraman. The three of us rehearsed together and Banachek and I were writing routines all the time. In November 2000, the lead engineer at South Oaks Hospital was figuring out our December holiday work schedule. He informed me that this year I was going to work Thanksgiving *and* Christmas. I told him Kim was expecting our first baby soon and I wanted to spend the holidays with her. I asked him to please find somebody else to cover the shifts. He told me that nobody else would want the holiday shifts, because they would all want to be with their families as well.

Then I told him that spending time with my family was more important than making extra money working, and if he did not give me time off I was going to quit. Once again, he told me I couldn't take the days off. Soon after that discussion, I submitted my two-week notice. At thirty-eight years old, I took the plunge. I was about to become a full-time entertainer. It was one of the scariest times of my life, as well as one of the most exciting times of my life!

Gerry and South Oaks Hospital co-worker Andy

Chapter 33

Gerry and Banachek

Whenever I received a corporate booking, I tried to pitch the client on the *Mystical Minds* show instead of my solo show. I told the client it would not cost them any extra, and they would get two performers—plus a sound and lighting technician—for the price of one. I did not mind splitting my performance fee with Banachek because I felt we needed as much time as possible performing together.

Our first paid performance as a duo was on December 1st, 2000, for the Abstracts Corporate holiday party at the Vanderbilt on Long Island. The initial request was for my solo act, but I was able to sell them on the *Mystical Minds* show. I used the deposit check from the show to open a checking account. Since the deposit was made out in my name, I opened the checking account in my name. I asked for three Visa debit cards to draw off the account: one for me, one for Banachek, and one for Chris.

Two days after Gerry and Banachek's big debut, Kim quit her nursing job. A few days later Kim gave birth to a baby boy. Since Kim never had a brother, we honored her father, Ronny, by using his name as the baby's first name. We also honored Kim's grandfather, Louis, by taking his name as the baby's middle name. Ronny Louis was our beautiful baby boy. Since Kim never really cut the apron strings from her mother, whenever Banachek was not occupying the guest suite, Kim's parents would stay over to help her with the baby. It allowed me to put all my efforts into writing the *Mystical Minds* show.

Soon after the holidays in early 2001, he mentioned Penn and Teller purchased the performing rights to a bullet catch routine Banachek created. Since Penn and Teller had such a successful partnership I thought we should learn from them. Since Las Vegas was my final destination, I always looked for a reason to go back, so we started the New Year out with a short business trip to Las Vegas to spend some time with the duo.

The day we arrived, we attended the *Lance Burton Show* at the Monte Carlo. After the show, while we were waiting in Lance's dressing room to talk to him, we met Clint Holmes, a headliner from Harrah's Casino. We performed for Clint, his wife, and his mother, and Clint invited us to attend his show the next night. Immediately following Clint's show, we rushed over to the Rio to catch Penn and Teller's show. After the show, we spent some time with Penn and Teller talking about what makes a successful partnership. When we returned to New York we continued refining our script. Banachek and I tried out the new script changes every time we performed.

Gerry, Lance Burton and Banachek

One day Banachek told me he wanted to deliver more of the jokes. He didn't like being the straight man and felt it was unfair that I had the lion's share of the laughs. I tried to remind him that the reason I invited him into the two-person act to begin with was to be the straight man. I wasn't happy with his insistence on changing the format of the show, but was willing to give it a try. Unfortunately, I felt Banachek didn't have the same comedic timing as I did, and since I wrote my jokes for me, he messed up my punch lines when he tried to deliver them. I did not know how to tell him I thought he wasn't as funny as I was delivering the lines. I was starting to get irritated with him during our performances because he would steal my punch lines, and some of the time he would ruin the joke.

Tom, our investor, wanted to bring in another investor, Jeff, who owned a body powder and powder chocolate milk company. Jeff wanted to see what people thought of our act, so they arranged a backers' audition in the Rainbow Room at Rockefeller Center. After the performance was over, each of their guests was asked to fill out a questionnaire about the show. The feedback from the audience was mediocre at best.

With all the changes Banachek was trying to make to my original script, and with the investors' lack of confidence in the project, I knew I would have to end the partnership if I wanted to continue to work with Tom. I told Tom to start booking solo shows for me again, and to no longer pitch the *Mystical Minds* show to his clients. Banachek and I had one more show already booked, a charity fundraiser in Florida for The Donna Klein Jewish Academy on December 1, 2001. It was a commitment we could not get out of. We were getting $10,000 to perform, and we'd already reinvested the $5,000 deposit into the act. If I was going to let him go, I would have to wait until after that performance. I had some time and felt I did not need to rush my decision and possibly destroy our friendship.

Soon after the backers' audition, my grandmother passed away on August 20, 2001. A few days later, Kim's mother was admitted into the hospital with stomach pains. She was diagnosed with pancreatic cancer and given four to six months to live.

On September 10th, I flew into Virginia for a corporate performance I'd booked without Banachek. Kim was staying at my Uncle Joe's house in Maryland while her mom was in a local hospital for cancer treatment. My tenant, Chris, was taking care of the pig for us and it was making Kim feel a little uneasy.

The morning of September 11th, I was awakened by a phone call from Kim.

"Are you all right?" she asked, sounding anxious.

"Yeah, I'm fine. What's wrong?"

"Don't you know what happened?'

"How could I?" I retorted. "I was sleeping."

"Turn on the news on TV. A plane hit the World Trade Center." She didn't know what flight I was on, which caused her to worry. I put on the news and told her they must be filming a movie in New York City, because when I turned on the broadcast, I watched a plane come into view and strike the tower again. It must have been a second take on the shot.

I soon realized it was for real. I didn't know what to think. Then I heard about the Pentagon plane crash and reality started to sink in. We were at war. I told Kim I would call her back.

I knew it would only be a matter of time before they closed all the airports, so I started calling rental car agencies to reserve a car for a one-way trip that allowed me to drive the car to New York and leave it there. I found one and made the reservation. I then asked if they'd have the car ready if I came right down. I learned from renting so many cars over the years that having a reservation does not always mean you have a car when you get there. They assured me that once I arrived, they would call over to the storage area in the airport and have the car delivered in minutes. I told them that I was in a rush and needed a car waiting for me, and that I would pay extra if they went and retrieved it from the storage yard inside the airport before I got there.

Since I had this strange feeling the airports would be closed, I needed them to get the car out of there. I quickly packed all my clothes and went to the front desk. I gave my room key to the front desk clerk and asked him to hold it and check me out in two hours. If I returned, I wanted the key back. If two hours passed, he had my permission to check me out of my room. I asked the concierge if he had a road map and a highlighter pen I could borrow.

I hailed a cab, gave him the rental car depot address, and asked him to turn the radio to a local news station. Since I had to drive past Washington, D.C. to get home to New York, I had a hunch some of the roads would be closed for security reasons.

As the newscaster announced all the closures, I marked them with the highlighter on the road map.

When I got to the rental car depot, they told me the airport was closed and my car was the last one they were able to get out of the holding area. I took the keys and hit the road, avoiding all the highlighted roads as I drove home. Little did I realize, my cellular phone died soon after I started my journey.

The drive home took about ten hours. It was smooth sailing until I approached New York. I could not find a bridge that was open to traffic to let me onto Long Island. I was able to see the smoke from the burning towers when I was on the New Jersey side of the river. In shock, I pulled over and watched for a few minutes. I wondered how many of my friends who worked in the Trade Center were in there when they came crashing down. Hearing about it on TV and on the radio was one thing, but seeing the smoke and the void in the skyline where the towers used to stand was enough to bring me to tears. I started to remember all the times I performed in the Windows on the World restaurant located on the top floor. I also recalled all the shows I performed in many of the corporate office conference rooms over the years. It took me a while to regain my composure and continue my drive.

The long drive home was very strange because all the roads were empty and I was able to drive as fast as I wanted. I was alone with my thoughts for hours. I thought of Kim's mom and the chances of her getting better. I thought about my last moments with my grandma just two weeks earlier. I thought about how worried Kim must be since my cell phone was dead and I couldn't call her, and she had no idea I had rented a car or was on the way home.

The isolation also caused me to think long and hard about my partnership with Banachek. I recalled him telling me his wife could book him on any TV show and was great at selling his act.

Now a year later, she didn't get us on any TV shows, nor did she get us any bookings. I felt she was a very manipulative, phony person who would always get in the middle of our creativity and cause friction between Banachek and myself. All but one of our bookings were from inquiries that came in for my show, and I'd sold the *Mystical Minds Show* instead. As far as bringing in business to the partnership, they did not even come close to pulling their weight. I felt until he divorced her, we could no longer be partners.

A few weeks after the terrorist attack, Kim's mother passed away on September 28, 2001. Kim immediately slipped into a deep depression and started to smoke even though she knew I hated smoking. Banachek attended the wake and I had to pretend like everything was okay between us.

On November 30th, Chris, Banachek, and I flew into Boca Raton. Two of the ladies in charge of the function picked us up at the airport. Since we wouldn't have access to the theater for at least two hours, they offered to take us out for lunch at a local Hooters Restaurant that was on the way. Afterward, we were let into the theater and rehearsals began. Everything seemed to be going well and all indications were that the show was going to be a sellout success.

After the show, I told Banachek that Tom and Jeff called. They were worried about investing in a new show after 9/11, so they pulled their money from the project. I told him it was now his turn to pitch our show and book our act while I sought another investor for our show. He told me he couldn't book the act, and if that was the way it was going to be, then the *Mystical Minds Show* was finished. I was thirty-nine years old when I ended our partnership. We mutually split up the stage routines we created together and he returned home to his wife in Texas.

When I asked him to return his company Visa debit card, Banachek asked if I needed him to be present when I closed the company bank account. I told him the checking account was never under his name, he only had a Visa card that drew from the account, and I could close it without him since it was only under my name. I reminded him that when I was going through my divorce, my wife's attorney subpoenaed all the financial records he could. Since Banachek told me he may be getting divorced, I didn't want to be forced to turn over our company records, so I never added his name to the checking account. He was annoyed at that answer and wanted to know what would happen to all the money that was still in the account. I informed him there wasn't much of a balance, but he thought I was ripping him off. I knew our friendship would come to an end because his wife would turn him against me, but I secretly hoped we would eventually reunite as friends after he finally divorced her.

All of the promotional material we had created together, along with our website, was now useless since I dissolved the partnership. It was time to rethink my approach toward my television goals. I needed a new marketing strategy, so I started to redesign my website. Over the years I had performed for many different celebrities at various private functions. What if I became the "Mentalist to the Stars" and used celebrity names and quotes in my promotional material? If a celebrity who had millions of dollars could hire anyone in the world they wanted, and they hired me, that would be instant creditability. The celebrity's name might carry enough clout to convince potential clients and casino entertainment directors to hire me. So I redesigned the website to include quotes I had collected over the years along with photos of me with the various celebrities. Within a week, the redesign was complete and I launched my new "Mentalist to the Stars" website.

Chapter 34

Mentalist to the Stars

Two days after the launch of my new website, an agent called and wanted to hire me to perform at radio personality Howard Stern's New Year's Eve Party at his New York City penthouse on December 31, 2001. I told the agent I would only take the job if I could bring my wife with me. Since her mother just passed away, I did not want her to be alone when the clock struck midnight.

Gerry and Howard Stern

The agent called me back and said Howard did not want me to bring a guest to his party, so I turned down the booking. I told the agent I was a little insulted that he was treating me like a child. After a few phone calls back and forth he said I could bring Kim with me, but we had to leave immediately after my performance was finished. We were not allowed to stay at the party and socialize. I agreed to the terms and performed the show. Afterward, Howard invited Kim and me to stay and have a bite to eat. He was a gracious host and a very nice guy.

When we returned home, I attempted to continue the New Year's Eve celebration and tried to be intimate with Kim. We had not been intimate at all since her mother passed away. For months she used the same excuse. "You are asking me for sex when my mother just died," was all I ever heard.

Soon after her mother's death, Kim and her father attended a bereavement support group to learn to cope with the loss. Kim's father apparently learned to cope pretty fast and he bounced back quickly, because he hooked up with someone from the support group and secretly started dating her. Kim's recovery from the death was taking a lot longer. She refused to have sex with me and she was taking her time when it came to quitting smoking. She knew I did not kiss smokers, and she used it as a way to keep me away from her. For comfort, she went to see a priest and he made the mistake of telling her that her mother was watching over her at all times. That became her newest excuse to avoid me because she thought her mother would be watching us if we had sex. Between her smoking, the lack of intimacy, and her constant depression, I was now regretting ever remarrying.

On January 7, 2002, I received a call from Karyn Zucker, but she didn't tell me who she was when she called. All she said was, "Five years ago, on August 7, 1998, my husband and I saw you at a private party in the Hamptons. It was at the *20/20* news correspondent Perry Pelz's house. My husband was so impressed by your show, he took your business card and kept your phone number all this time. I was wondering if you traveled out of New York and if you could perform at a party in California?"

That was not a problem since I did events and parties in California all the time for celebrities. But then she told me the date was Saturday, January 19, 2002, and that is where our conversation came to a complete halt.

"I'm sorry, I'm not available on that date," I said. I had another performance already booked that evening at a theater in Connecticut that I could not cancel because I was the star attraction. It was a charity fundraiser billed as *An Evening with The Mentalist, Gerry McCambridge*. Tickets were sold with my name attached to them; people were paying to see me, not just any magic act. I told her to keep my name on file and if another event came up to let me know.

"You don't understand," she said. "There will be a lot of celebrities at the party, including Arnold Schwarzenegger, Lisa Kudrow and David Schwimmer from the cast of the TV show *Friends*, Rob Lowe, too, as well as some very important people in the television business. We've already sent out invitations." She proceeded to tell me her husband, Jeff Zucker, was a very influential man in the entertainment business. When he saw me perform five years ago, he was the executive producer of *The Today Show*, and now was the president of NBC Entertainment.

"You're making it sound terrific," I said. "But I gave my word."

"Okay," she said. "I understand."

I really wanted to perform for her and her husband because he had the connections to get me on TV, and that would make pitching my show in Las Vegas so much easier.

The following day, Mrs. Zucker called again. "What are you doing the day before on Friday the eighteenth?" she asked.

"If I can do your party and get a red-eye back to the East Coast to do my contracted show on the nineteenth, I will do it for you," I said. "But I thought you said everyone was invited already?"

"Well, they are," she said. "But we'll call them up and change the date." I agreed to do the show after checking with the airline and finding out I could take a red-eye flight home.

That night, I was lying in bed with my wife and we were watching a rerun of *Friends*. As I was watching Lisa Kudrow and David Schwimmer, two people Mrs. Zucker said would be at the party, I thought, *They just changed their social plans because of me. How cool is that?*

A few weeks later, I flew to California and performed on Friday, January 18, 2002, at the party at the Zucker home in Beverly Hills. There were about forty people there, including Lisa Kudrow, Rob Lowe, Jerry O'Connell, and Jeff Gaspin, who ran the Bravo Network at the time. There were a lot of Hollywood agents, producers, and writers in attendance as well. I performed flawlessly as I did a thousand times in the past preparing for this moment, and I was a big hit.

The show ended and I was in heaven. As a kid, I would stand outside Broadway show stage doors to get a minute or so of face-time with the shows' stars as they exited the theater. And now the television stars were all lined up after the show at Zucker's house to talk to me! With the help of this performance, the list of celebrities I performed for almost doubled overnight. I made sure to memorize every bit of praise the celebrities bestowed upon me so I could quote them on my new website.

Two weeks later, Mrs. Zucker called back and asked me to do another performance for them on April 6, 2002. This would be a more intimate gathering of about fifteen people that would include *Forrest Gump* producer Steve Tisch, *Seinfeld's* Julia Louis-Dreyfus, David Spade, and Larry David. When I arrived for the party I asked her if any of the cast from *Friends* would be in attendance. She said no because it was their final taping night of the season and they had a wrap party when they were done taping. Much to my surprise, Lisa Kudrow showed up to watch my performance a second time. I asked her why she wasn't attending the wrap party, and she said, "I wanted to bring my husband to watch your show instead."

At this point in time, I was now on a first name basis with Jeff Zucker. Before the party began, I wanted to tell him some of the ideas I had for a television special, and he quickly stopped me. He said to be able to listen to my ideas, I would either need to go through an agency or a lawyer.

After my performance, all the celebrities came over to tell me how much they enjoyed it. Larry David questioned the heck out of me because he was worried I could get into his head, and Steven Tisch, the producer of *Forrest Gump*, asked for my business card. Jeff made it a point to introduce me to his friend Scott Sassa, the president of the NBC Television stations division.

A few days later, Steven Tisch called and asked me to perform on May 18, 2002 in Florida at a family function. A few weeks after that, Scott Sassa called me directly and asked me to perform at his house for a private party on June 20, 2002. Scott lived in an old house once owned by Boris Karloff. When I arrived at the party, I noticed Courteney Cox, David Arquette, and Carrie Fisher in the audience. After my performance, Steven Tisch came up to me and said that Lisa Kudrow sent her regards. I asked him when he saw her, and he told me she was babysitting his kids so he could attend the party. At this point, my name was spreading around Hollywood like wildfire.

On June 17, 2002, I received an email from Richard Pine, who was a literary agent in New York City. He told me that he attended one of my shows a few years earlier and really enjoyed my performance. He thought there was a book in me and wanted to discuss the opportunity of working with me. I was patiently waiting for something to happen with Jeff Zucker from NBC, but he really did not seem too motivated to get me on television. I thought having a book published would give me the notoriety I needed to land a steady gig in Las Vegas.

I told Richard I was interested to hear what he had to say and we made an appointment to meet at his office in New York City. We had a nice long chat. The one thing I really liked about him was the fact that he was also Wayne Dyer's literary agent. Wayne was a best-selling self-help author and motivational speaker who influenced me so much on my path to a better life. Richard said he would make the appropriate appointments with the big publishing houses in New York City and we could pitch a book. I agreed, and on June 24, 2002, we had our first meeting with Warner Books.

Within the next few days, we had more appointments with different publishers. Each time pitched the book, Richard had me perform for the executive we were meeting with. I was not totally comfortable with the book idea that Richard was pitching. He was trying to sell a book based on intuition and teaching people how to use their intuition to better their lives, how to have better relationships with their partners, how to close business deals, using intuition to help raise children, and also how to read people's minds.

A little of what I do in my show is based on intuition and gut feelings, but a lot of what I do is based on magic principles. Deep down I felt like a snake oil salesman trying to sell a book on intuition, when in reality I was nothing more than a glorified magician with a tiny bit of intuition. After four pitch meetings without getting a publishing deal, Richard was confused. He told me at this point we had two options. One was to hire a ghostwriter and draft a sample of the book to show to the publishers. The second was to make me a celebrity and then re-pitch the book to the publishers. Since my goal was to be a celebrity and wind up in Las Vegas, I told him the celebrity option was the way I wanted to pursue selling my book.

Richard placed a call to his friend Brian, who was a literary agent for Creative Artists Agency, also known as CAA, one of the largest and most powerful agencies in Hollywood. He told Brian about my show, how popular I was in Hollywood, and the situation that had unfolded with the publishers. He asked Brian if he would represent me and help get me on TV. Brian said he would get back to him because he was in his car on his way to a basketball game with his son. While at the basketball game, Brian sent out a mass text message to all the agents in the CAA office asking if any of them knew who I was. Much to his surprise, quite a few of his coworkers responded in the affirmative. It turned out that many of them had attended Jeff Zucker's parties and had seen me perform. Brian was intrigued enough with the response he received to give me a call back.

Brian asked if I was going to be in California in the near future. I told him on Sunday, June 30, 2002 I was going to be in Los Angeles having dinner at the home of Courteney Cox. I also told him I had an evening corporate function to perform on July 2, 2002. He asked me to come by the office the morning of July 2nd when the agents had their weekly staff meeting. He asked if I would perform for the agents and the owner of the agency in the boardroom during the meeting and I readily agreed.

A few weeks later my wife, my son Ronny, my daughter Jennifer, and my niece, Paige, all traveled out to California. Jennifer and Paige were babysitting for Ronny while Kim and I drove to Courteney Cox's house. Every Sunday, Courteney had a family dinner, with different family members and friends gathering for a relaxing social. I rang the doorbell and Courtney answered. She invited us into her house and was very sweet and cordial. She introduced my wife to her husband, David Arquette, who was at the kitchen table working on a piece of artwork while Courteney was using odd pieces of kitchenware to prepare dinner with her personal chef.

A few minutes later the doorbell rang, and Courteney asked if I would answer the door for her. When I opened the door, Tim Burton stuck his hand out and introduced himself to me. I was a huge Batman fan and was honored to be meeting the director of the film, but I stayed cool when I shook his hand. Tim entered the soiree with his beautiful girlfriend, Helena Bonham Carter. A few more guests showed up including David's sister, Rosanna Arquette, and we all sat down to dinner. Here I was, Gerry McCambridge, a thirty-nine-year-old small-time magician from New York, as a guest at a private Hollywood dinner party with some of Hollywood's most influential people. I felt my master goal becoming closer than ever!

I wanted to show my appreciation to my gracious hosts, so when dinner was over and everyone was relaxing in the living room, I performed for everyone. I'd brought a little bag with me that allowed me to perform for about an hour. They all sat there in total amazement since they were not expecting me to entertain that evening.

During my performance, I gave all the guests the opportunity to think of questions they wanted me to answer using my mentalism skills. I systematically went around the room, read their minds, and not only told them the questions they were thinking of, I was able to give them very detailed answers.

I was in shock when I figured out some of the questions. For instance, Courteney was wondering what her next job was going to be. Here she was, one of the stars of the hit television show *Friends*, reportedly making one million dollars per episode, and she was worried about employment.

The next day, Kim and I took Courteney and David to dinner at *The Magic Castle*, a private club in Hollywood. We were able to see a few performances while we were there. One of the performers was a mentalist, and he was horrible. Courteney turned and told me that she saw why CAA was interested in signing me.

The next day I showed up at the CAA offices, and Brian and I chatted in his office for a little while. He left me alone to set up my props while he attended the start of the agency's weekly staff meeting. When he came to get me a few minutes later, he asked me if I was nervous. I chuckled at his question and said, "Never."

I entered the conference room and stood at the end of the room. I introduced myself and went into my dog and pony show. When I finished, the applause was exactly what I thought it would be from a room full of suits. I left the conference room and returned to Brian's office to pack away my props. A few minutes later, Brian returned and said the owner of the agency had one thing to say after I left. He asked the room full of agents, "Why haven't we signed this guy yet?"

Chapter 35

Life's Learning Curve

In this chapter of my life, I learned the power of media promotion, the power of negotiations, and the benefit of creating win-win scenarios for people I dealt with.

I learned the art of goal-setting and using the power of positive thinking. I aligned myself with people who were in the business I wanted to be in, and learned from their successes and failures.

The betrayal by my best friend Doug, the ten years of lying from my wife Kathy, and the mistrust from my partner Banachek reinforced my brain not to let anyone close to me or to trust anyone. No matter how much I trusted someone, they would eventually betray me or hurt me.

I do not think human beings are created to be monogamous; it's something we enforce on ourselves. I think it is hard-wired into the male DNA code to want to mate with many. We do not look at other women as a sign of disrespect for our partner; it is nature that causes the desire and clouds a male's better judgment.

I also realized that if a relationship is not good during the courting process, most likely it will not improve after marriage. I learned divorce lawyers had a bad reputation as being scum-sucking sharks, because most of them are.

I was shocked to learn that no matter how rich and successful you are, we all seem to have the same core desires and worries in life.

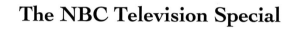

The NBC Television Special

Chapter 36

Preparing for the Pitches

When I returned from Los Angeles, Richard Pine, who was now acting as my manager, informed me that CAA loved my mini-performance and my idea for a TV show. They wanted to sign me before we had any further conversations. On July 11, 2002, Richard told me he received the contracts from CAA and advised me to get an entertainment lawyer to help with the negotiations. He suggested I hire Richard from Frankfurt Garbus Kurnit Klein & Selz to be my personal lawyer. But before Richard would look at the contracts, I needed to sign a contract with his firm to represent me, so on July 18, 2002, I signed the contract with the law firm.

Now that I had a personal lawyer, Richard Pine wanted a contract between us; it was signed on August 26, 2002. And now that I was signed with a lawyer and a manager, we all negotiated with CAA and eventually signed them on as my agency on September 9, 2002. It basically took two months to sign with all three players before we could start to focus on anything, like pitching the TV show.

Brian, who was my official agent from CAA, told me they wanted to partner me with a production company and sell our package to the networks. They wanted me to perform a showcase for all the production companies they had on their roster, then I would interview them and see how they envisioned making my TV show. From there, I would pick the production company I was most comfortable with. Two weeks after signing with CAA,

I flew back to L.A. and performed in their theater, which was located in their office complex.

After the performance, Brian started collecting the names of all the producers who wanted to work with me on my television special. He followed up with the production companies and made appointments with each of them. For the next week, I interviewed a few productions companies each day and ultimately selected Triage Entertainment operating out of Sherman Oaks, California.

We took the month of November to develop the pitch for the networks. The pitch had to be timed perfectly. We had to stay under a certain time while making sure we hit all the highlights of the show. We were not going to go in with a five-minute sizzle reel; instead, I was going to perform during the pitch so the network executive would get a firsthand feel of what my performance was like.

All of a sudden, the entire project came to a sudden halt. During December, Hollywood pretty much shuts down. No one is in town, and no one takes any meetings. I was afraid the momentum we had was going to come to a complete stop, and the show would fade into obscurity.

But the break in the schedule came at a good time because Kim gave birth to our second child in December of 2002. There were complications with her birth and we had to spend quite some time in the hospital taking care of our new baby. In honor of Kim's mother and my grandmother who both passed away, we named the baby after them both: JoAnn Concetta.

By mid-January, Hollywood was back in full swing. Triage Entertainment and I created an outline of the routines we planned on taping for the show, and how the final product would look on the screen. While we were creating the format, Brian was busy juggling network executive schedules. He wanted to pitch all four of the major networks around the same time.

I told Brian that I felt NBC was going to license my show, so why not pitch them first? He told me if Jeff Zucker wanted the show that badly, he would have already showed some type of interest. Knowing that my childhood dream and goal was to have a special on NBC just like my mentor Doug Henning, my agent also said not to be disappointed if my show was not on NBC.

I thought Jeff Zucker wanted me to take the standard route when it came to pitching the network, so I told Brian that I wanted him to contact Jeff first and get his input before we made any appointments. Jeff told him to pitch all the other networks first, and pitch NBC last. Jeff wanted us to give him the right of last refusal and did not want us to sign with any network until after we pitched my show to NBC.

Brian set up four pitch meetings over a two-day period. Each network was given the same exact instructions: We needed a conference room to present our pitch, and we needed at least ten people in the room that I did not know for whom I could perform. A few days before the pitch, I flew out to L.A. and we rehearsed it. Brian would speak first, followed by the Executive Producers from Triage Entertainment, Stu Schreiberg and Stephen Kroopnick. Finally, I would explain how I was a magician as a kid, my father was a New York City Detective, and that I learned how to merge his detective skills with my magic skills. Then I would perform a few mentalism routines for them. We had to rehearse it so the entire pitch was under fifty-five minutes. When we had it down, my agent invited his friends to come over to his house and watch as we did the complete pitch from start to finish. Our timing was perfect.

A few days before our first pitch meeting, Scott Sassa, the president of the NBC television stations division, heard from Jeff Zucker that I was going to be pitching the networks. Scott called to tell me that he thought my show would be perfect on the FOX network. He mentioned that in a few days he was having lunch with Mike Darnell, the FOX executive who we were going to be pitching my show to. Scott was going to talk to Mike about my show and stress that he should buy the show for the FOX network. I wasn't sure why Scott felt I was a perfect fit on another network, and not his, but I was new to this Hollywood negotiation game, so I just let him do what he thought was right.

After I hung up the phone with Scott, I was so excited. I had Jeff Zucker from NBC, who hired me privately three times and loved my show, interested in buying the show. And now we would have Mike Darnell from FOX also interested in buying the show! I asked Brian what would happen if *both* networks wanted the show. He told me there would be a bidding war, but again he reminded me he didn't think Jeff Zucker knew what to do with me, or he would have already done it.

On April 2, 2003, I woke up in a Los Angeles five-star hotel room, excited that the big day had finally arrived. I was not nervous at all, just very excited. Brian picked me up after breakfast. We met the two producers from Triage Entertainment and their agent, Alex Hartly, at the ABC Studios for the first pitch of the day.

Our first pitch meeting at the ABC studios was for Susan Lyne. It was an informal pitch with a handful of office staff relaxing on couches while watching me perform. Everything went just as we rehearsed it. We were told the network was very happy with the David Blaine magic specials they recently aired and wanted to follow up his success with another magician. They enjoyed my performance during the pitch meeting, but wanted to see how it would translate to television. They asked for a five-minute sizzle reel so they could get a better understanding of what the show would look like. When we left the pitch meeting, Brian said that was a good sign. They did not pass on the show— they actually wanted to see *more* of me. He took me back to my hotel room to rest until our second meeting.

Later that afternoon, Brian picked me up for the meeting at CBS Studios with Leslie Moonves. They had a nice conference room with theater seating located in the lower level of the CBS building. We were told that we had to finish on time because Mr. Moonves had to catch a flight to Las Vegas. We were scheduled to start the pitch at 4:00 p.m. and end it before 5:00.

After I set up my table and a few props, the audience started to file in. By 3:55, the room was full of eager CBS employees waiting for the big boss to arrive. But every minute he was delayed was a minute we had to cut off of the pitch to end it on time. I anxiously waited in the hall with the rest of my group. Eventually an entourage of people stepped off the elevator, and Mr. Moonves was in the center of the storm. He walked past us and entered the room without any type of apology for being twenty minutes late.

While he was greeting the other employees and getting settled in his seat, we had a quick discussion in the hall. Should we cut the pitch so we ended at five? Or should we do it as we rehearsed it and end twenty minutes late, knowing Mr. Moonves would most likely leave before we were finished with the pitch so he could catch his flight? We decided to do our pitch in its entirety as we'd rehearsed it.

First Brian spoke to the group, then the producers addressed the audience, and then I took to the platform. I performed the first part of the presentation without a blindfold and the remainder with my blindfold. It was at that point I realized I wouldn't know how much of my routine Mr. Moonves was going to see before he walked out of the meeting to catch his flight. But the plan was to continue, knowing we would run late.

When I was done and removed my blindfold, I was shocked and relieved to see he was still sitting in his seat, applauding along with everyone else. He was so intrigued by my performance that he had his assistant delay his flight's departure.

I did not realize he had his own jet, so ordering a delayed takeoff was much easier for him than for those of us who travel on commercial airlines.

When the pitch was over, he congratulated me on a great performance and turned to my agent. "I love him! The premise of a person using detective skills and mentalism skills is fascinating. I'll have one of my guys contact you about working with him."

While he was standing next to me, all the other CBS employees quickly exited the room since it was now time to go home for the day. As they filed past me, they told me how much they enjoyed the show.

Brian and the production company's agent shook hands and expressed how excited they were with the outcome of our pitch. I was then driven back to my hotel room because I had dinner plans with my friend, Kristi Vannatter. When Kim and I first started dating, we broke up quite a few times. Once when we broke up for a few months, Kristi attended one of my performances at *Monday Night Magic*, a weekly show in New York City run by another of my friends, Michael Chaut. Kristi was moving from Florida to New York and became my roommate in my Wantagh apartment while Kim and I were not seeing each other.

Now Kristi lived in L.A. and she was a real mover and shaker. During dinner, she gave me a magazine that had an extensive article about Mike Darnell, the FOX executive I would be pitching the next morning. She thought I would like to read about him before meeting with him. By the time dinner ended and she dropped me off at my hotel room, it was too late to read the article. I removed all of my props from my travel case and reset them all for the next day's big pitch meetings.

I called home to tell Kim about the exciting day I had. I was very confident we would get picked up by one of the four networks! Scott Sassa put the word in for me with the FOX executive, and Jeff Zucker already knew how amazing my performance was. CBS was also very interested after our pitch meeting, and ABC wanted to take our pitch to the next level and see a five-minute demo of the show!

Kim proceeded to tell me about her day with the children, almost as if I hadn't said a word about my exciting news. I felt as if she wasn't even paying attention to me as I was speaking. She was washing the dishes in the sink while I talked to her, and I had to ask her to shut off the water because it was loud like a jackhammer in my ear and very distracting.

I felt Kim was very jealous of my show business career because secretly she always wanted to be in show business. It was probably part of the ongoing competition with her sister. Tammie became a massage therapist, and eventually so did Kim. Her sister married a chiropractor, and Kim dated a few of them as well. Tammie thought she had talent and got involved in local community theater, so this was Kim's way to copy her. I thought she was also a very insecure person, so I could not tell her about having dinner with Kristi. I had to be very selective about what I shared with her during our entire relationship. Sparing her feelings and withholding the truth from her was something I became very good at doing.

Chapter 37

Sleeping with the Enemy

I woke up before the alarm clock went off on the second day of our pitches. I was looking forward to seeing Jeff Zucker again, and to proving my CAA agent wrong. I still had faith Jeff wanted my show, but he wanted me to go through the pitching process and get the best offer I possibly could.

Since I was awake nice and early, I figured I might as well read the magazine that Kristi gave me. The article about Mike Darnell was very interesting and lengthy, and I was shocked to see the list of shows he was responsible for bringing to television. Many of them were shows I watched and enjoyed over the years like *American Idol*, *Joe Millionaire*, *Temptation Island*, and *Who Wants to Marry a Multi-Millionaire*. But my heart sank when I read that he was responsible for *Magic's Biggest Secrets Revealed*, the show that exposed magicians' secrets to anyone who watched.

I felt like I was going to puke! If I worked for Mike Darnell, I would be sleeping with the enemy. It was something I was very uncomfortable even considering. I immediately called Brian. I told him to cancel the pitch meeting with FOX and that I wanted nothing to do with Mike Darnell because of his connection with the shows that exposed magic secrets to the public. I said I would refuse to sign, no matter what type of deal they offered me.

Brian told me that he had to pull a lot of strings to get all four of our pitch meetings with the top network executives in two days just to accommodate me. He also said that Alex Hartly, the agent for my production company, was also the agent for the *American Idol* television show.

American Idol just had a huge first year, and Alex was in negotiations with Mike Darnell to continue the show. Canceling my pitch meeting could possibly put Alex in an uncomfortable position with Mike during *American Idol* negotiations. Brian asked me to perform the pitch as planned, and promised me he would get me out of any offer they might make. I would not be forced to do business with the FOX Network.

Our appointment with Mike Darnell was for 11:00 a.m. He was given the same instructions as the other three networks: We needed a conference room and at least ten people in the room that I had never met before.

We arrived at ten-thirty and asked his secretary if we could set up our pitch in the conference room. She suggested we go down to the commissary and have some breakfast since another man sitting in the waiting room was there for Mike Darnell's 9:00 a.m. meeting, and that had not even started yet. We complied with her request and went to the lower level cafeteria to enjoy some coffee and muffins, killing time until they were ready for us.

Brian expressed my feelings to the Triage Entertainment producers about not wanting to do business with the FOX Network. They weren't happy with my decision to not do business with Mike Darnell and said that I shouldn't take it personally—it was just show business. I replied that I had integrity when it came to my profession, and anyone revealing my trade secrets, or a fellow magician's secrets, was someone I would avoid doing business with at all costs.

We reported back to Mike's secretary at 10:45 a.m. and again asked to set up in the conference room. She knew nothing about using the conference room and said that we would have to discuss it with Mike.

At 11:30, Mike finally emerged from his office. I was actually surprised how short he was. Even in his huge platform shoes, he barely made it over five feet tall. He briefly said hello to Brian and Alex, my CAA agents, took his phone messages from his secretary, and said he would be with us in a minute. He then went back into his office to return a phone call. Ten minutes later, he came out of his office and suggested we start our 11:00 meeting at 11:45.

Brian said he requested the meeting to happen in a conference room with ten strangers for me to perform with. Mike looked puzzled and, like his secretary, said he knew nothing about these arrangements. He looked around and noticed the office was pretty much empty since most of the employees had already left for lunch. My agent insisted that the pitch needed to occur with a couple of strangers so Mike could see how I was able to get into people's heads. Mike then looked at his secretary with an annoyed expression and asked her to round up some employees and bring them into his office.

My agent instructed me to go into Mike's office and set up my pitch. I was surprised at how small it was. But then again, Mike was so tiny I bet it seemed like a big office to him. Mike's desk sat at one end, and a small couch fronted by a coffee table were situated along the wall. I had to position myself facing the table and couch with my back up against a bookcase. The office was so small that neither of my producers nor our CAA agents could fit in the room with us. They had to stand outside of the office, staying close to the door so they could hear what was going on.

A few minutes later, Mike's secretary returned with three people to watch my pitch. They were clearly young interns who had no clue why they were asked to sit in on the meeting. They sat on the couch. Mike sat behind his desk and said, "You may begin."

I introduced myself to the four people in the room and started to perform my first routine. The interns were not sure why they were there, but seem to be enjoying themselves as I began. About sixty seconds into my performance, I noticed Mike motioning at his secretary through the office door. She was indicating to him that he had a phone call on hold, so he stood up from his desk and left the office, leaving me alone with three interns.

At this point Brian was fed up with Mike's rudeness. He stuck his head into the office and told me to pack up my props because we were leaving. Mike put his hand over the mouthpiece of the phone and, looking surprised, asked what the problem was. Brian retorted that we had scheduled an eleven o'clock meeting that Mike was very late for, we were supposed to have a conference room available to present our pitch that no one knew anything about, and we were promised ten employees as an audience, which never happened.

"And now, one minute into the pitch you leave the meeting to take a phone call?!" Brian's voice started getting louder. "You totally embarrassed me in front of my client!"

Mike shouted, "If you leave now, this show will *never* be on the FOX Network!"

Meanwhile I was standing in his office, frozen in front of three interns, while listening to the shouting match happening a few feet away from us in the hall. Once again, Brian stuck his head into the office and barked at me. "Let's go! We are getting out of here immediately!"

Inside, I was very happy because I was getting out of a meeting that was a total waste of my time. But outside, I felt very awkward with the situation as it was unraveling. Very quickly the f-bombs started to fly back and forth between my agent and Mike Darnell.

I quickly gathered my props and exited the office, embarrassed to look Mike in the eyes or even to say goodbye and thank you. When the five of us got into the elevator, Brian was still wound up and agitated. It seems Mike Darnell was known for being a rude jerk to many people in the past. Having a Napoleon complex seemed to be his reputation in Hollywood.

Brian told me I should not let what just happened bother me. He was going to take me back to my hotel and let me rest before our meeting with Jeff Zucker from NBC later in the day. Then he informed me that he was going to return to his office and send Mike Darnell's boss an email explaining what just occurred.

Chapter 38

The NBC Pitch

Before we entered the NBC office building, I asked Brian to take a picture of me standing out front. I knew deep in my heart this was the network where I wanted to be. This was the network that hosted my mentor Doug Henning's first one-hour television special, and that was my goal: to be like Doug. I was positive this was the network I was eventually going to make a deal with.

We met the two Triage Entertainment producers, Stu and Steve, and their agent, Alex, in the waiting room. A few minutes after we arrived, Jeff came out of his office and politely asked us to come in. He shook everyone's hand as we entered, told me it was good to see me again, and asked how my family was doing.

We all sat down, but Jeff did not sit behind his desk. Instead, he joined us on the couches. Brian asked if I could take a few minutes to set up my props. Jeff responded that he had seen me perform four times in the past and did not need to see a performance now. He already knew how people reacted to my act and said he just wanted to hear our TV show concept.

At that point we were lost and everyone started looking at each other for guidance. Jeff totally screwed up our well-rehearsed pitch! Stu jumped in and started to explain the concept. Half of the show would be taped in front of an intimate audience. For the last couple of years I had been performing at private parties, and we wanted to recreate that atmosphere on television. The other half of the show was to be performed on the streets of New York City. I would use my magic skills and the intuitive skills I learned from my father, the New York City detective, to get inside people's minds. People who just happened to be strolling by would be stopped and asked to participate.

Stu gave Jeff examples of the routines I wrote and how the show would look artistically. Jeff just sat there and listened until Stu was finished, and then he had one question for us.

"Every time I see Gerry perform, the audience thinks the same thing—they think it is a setup. How will people at home know this is real, and Gerry is not using stooges who are pretending to be amazed?"

Brian quickly responded, "You cannot fake an authentic reaction."

After a long pause, Jeff said, "I like it. I want the show. NBC will be the network for *The Mentalist.* Which of you two agents will be the point person for the negotiations?"

Brian and Alex looked at each other, and a second later Brian volunteered to be the agent handling the deal for us.

At that point Stu continued his pitch, only to be quickly interrupted by his partner, Steve. "We sold the show. We can stop pitching now."

Everyone in the room chuckled and any tension evaporated. I sat there smiling, looking at everyone like the cat that ate the canary. I knew from the start Jeff was going to come through for me. Everyone chatted for a minute or two and the meeting quickly came to an end. Jeff said goodbye and congratulated us as we filed out of the office. I was the last one out. Jeff shook my hand and said, "Welcome to the NBC family, Gerry. I knew you could do it."

Even though Jeff is three years younger than me, at that moment when he shook my hand, it felt like an uncle or a father expressing how proud he was of my accomplishments. It was almost as if Doug Henning was speaking to me from the grave through Jeff Zucker, and it was a very surreal moment for me. I had dreamt of it for years, and at that very moment, my dream finally became a reality.

As soon as the elevator doors closed and they knew Jeff could no longer hear them, everyone started to congratulate each other and shake hands, acting as if they did not expect to sell the show in the meeting. Brian looked at me and said, "Aren't you excited?" He told me we just made Hollywood history. We started off the day by telling one of the most powerful men in the town to go f*** himself, and we ended the day by selling a TV show during the pitch meeting. "No one ever sells a show during the pitch meeting!"

"This is why I'm here in Los Angeles," I replied. "And this is what I came out to do. But I'm not going to get excited until I actually see myself on TV." In the past, I allowed myself to get overly excited over deals that eventually fell through and left me heartbroken as a result. They laughed at my reserved feelings as we all left the building.

As soon as we got back to Brian's car, he called Richard Pine in New York to tell him we sold the show. Richard asked Brian if I was excited. Brian told him he couldn't believe how calm I was, and again I repeated that I was not going to get excited until I actually saw myself on TV. Brian and I went out for a steak dinner and then he returned me to my hotel room. I had an early flight back to New York the next morning and I needed to pack.

A few days later, Brian called to share a story with me. He said he was in his weekly CAA agents' staff meeting and his boss asked him to tell all the other agents what happened in the Mike Darnell meeting at the FOX Network. All of the other agents applauded and cheered after hearing he told Mike Darnell to go f*** himself. It seemed they'd all had dealings with the short, rude executive in the past, and were quite pleased when someone finally had the balls to tell him off and put him in his place.

On April 9, 2003, Brian received our first official offer from NBC. They offered me $800,000 for the first special and wanted six more specials from me. They also wanted to own the rights to *The Mentalist*. Even though I was excited when I heard the dollar amount, I told Brian I was not giving up rights to my intellectual property. He said it would change after he started negotiating on my behalf. On April 24, Brian called me back and said NBC was sticking to their offer of $800,000 but agreed to give up ownership of the show.

Now that I had an agreement with NBC. I felt it was time to remove something from my life that I hated doing. For years, I hated performing walk-around gigs at Bar Mitzvahs. It was great money, but very boring work. I was paid to walk around from table to table, performing the same three or four tricks over and over again, trying to talk over the band or DJ. I decided the Bar Mitzvah I booked for April 26, 2003 would be my final one. It was one part of performing that I never looked back on.

On Friday, May 2, 2003, my oldest daughter, Kristina had a baby. I was forty years old and I had my first grandchild. I was performing for a private group in Napa Valley, California, so I couldn't be at the hospital with her. But the very next morning I was on the first flight back to New York to visit Kristina, and also to attend a birthday party for my niece Paige.

On May 6, Brian called and said NBC came up with an additional $50,000 and agreed to only two more specials instead of six. I knew we were close to closing the deal. I also knew I needed to get into shape before taping the show. I wanted to drop from 200 pounds down to 190 pounds, so I started to diet and work out religiously. I ran an average of four miles a day on the treadmill, but no matter how hard I worked out, I was never able to get my weight below 192 pounds.

On May 19, I picked up Stu, the executive producer from Triage, at the airport and we went out for a steak dinner.

"The network wants to title the show *Mind Games*," he said.

"No good," I replied. "That's what my friend Marc Salem called his Off Broadway show. I'm not comfortable using it without his permission. Besides, I want to keep the show's title as *The Mentalist* because that's the brand I'm trying to build."

"All right," Stu said. "I'll see what I can do."

NBC SKEDS 'MENTALIST'

By MICHAEL SCHNEIDER

Mental whiz Gerry McCambridge has pulled off his biggest feat yet: landing a one-hour special at NBC.

"The Mentalist" will follow McCambridge as he walks the streets of New York and performs in front of a Los Angeles audience, demonstrating his uncanny ability to read people's actions and determine their innermost thoughts.

McCambridge was discovered at a shindig in the Hamptons five years ago by Peacock entertainment prexy Jeff Zucker.

"He was the executive producer of 'The Today Show' at the time, and I didn't know who he was," McCambridge said. "I went into my demonstration and said, 'This is how I make my living.' He left the show and must have kept my card."

McCambridge

Zucker has since flown McCambridge out to Hollywood several times to perform at private parties, where his audiences have included celebs such as Lisa Kudrow, Courteney Cox Arquette, Larry David, Muhammad Ali and Matt Lauer.

Turn to page 32

NBC SKEDS 'MENTALIST'

Continued from page 7

McCambridge makes it clear to audiences that he's not a psychic. "Psychics talk to the dead," he said. "I don't associate with them; that's not what I do."

Triage Entertainment is behind "The Mentalist." Segments in the special include McCambridge walking into a New York firehouse and toying with the company's firefighters and a stage demonstration with "American Dreams" star Brittany Snow.

"Gerry McCambridge is one of entertainment's best kept secrets, and the special highlights his seemingly inexplicable talents," said Jeff Gaspin, NBC's exec VP of alternative series, specials, longform and program strategy. "Gerry's project should prove equally fascinating to those who believe — and those who don't."

McCambridge and CAA are repped by CAA; McCambridge also is managed by Richard Pine.

Variety Magazine, December 8, 2003

Chapter 39

Taping in New York City

Immediately after NBC signed the deal agreeing to all of the negotiation points, the production company went into high gear. They started to draft budgets and apply for taping permits at locations around New York City. They also started to scout out locations in Los Angeles for taping the part of the show where we would use an audience. I was presented with a shooting schedule on June 20, 2003.

My CAA agent Brian said that NBC would give us one third of the money when we signed the contract, another one third when we started shooting the show, and the final one third when we delivered the completed show. I was a bit concerned that the production company was starting to spend money doing pre-production work when NBC had not yet sent us the first deposit. They assured me it was a done deal and the money would eventually arrive.

Triage Entertainment told me they needed to see and approve a list of the routines I planned to perform in the show. I wanted to hire magical consultants to work on the show with me, and they gave me a budget to do that. Almost a year and a half had passed since Steve "Banachek" Shaw and I ended our partnership. During that time we did not speak, and it bothered me that he was upset with me because his name was not on the bank account. I also had a feeling that his manipulative wife fueled his fire to hate me.

I had no malicious intentions when I opened the account but I wanted to make up for any hard feelings, so he was the first one I called to bring on board as a consultant. It was my way of extending the metaphorical olive branch to a guy I really liked in the past. While chatting a bit and catching up, he told me he decided not to get divorced and was working on his marriage. I asked him to be the lead magical consultant on my TV show, and Banachek said he would be interested in working on the project but needed to talk to his wife first. I always felt his wife had him on a short leash and he was never able to make any type of decision unless asking her permission first. I told him to get back to me with an answer as soon as he could.

The second call I made was to Ted, a fellow member of The Legendary Thirteen and one of the most creative mentalists I had ever met. I told him I was going to hire Steve as the lead magic consultant, and I wanted him to work under him. Ted said he would take the job if he were Steve's equal, because he didn't want to give his ideas to Steve; he wanted to pitch them directly to me.

Within days, both Ted and Banachek agreed and we started having weekly conference calls to come up with more routines for the show. I had two routines that meant a lot to me. I wanted to say thank you to the men and women of the police department and fire department for their service during the September 11th tragedy. The police department passed on our invitation to be on the show, but the fire department loved the idea of participating.

I also wanted to end the show with my blindfolded scooter drive that I pitched to the Amityville mayor years ago. He laughed at me then, but NBC approved the blindfolded drive stunt immediately. I drove to New York City three times a week and practiced driving my gas-powered scooter up and down Broadway, in traffic, so I would get used to all the noise as well as the taxi cab and commuter bus driving patterns. I would use the blindfold skills I learned as a child walking home from school to approximate how far I traveled on the scooter while my eyes were closed, and I would use all the sounds around me to help position myself. I also practiced driving the scooter around my neighborhood for two hours a day. I wanted to learn how to ride it on one foot, with one hand, and alternating feet while it was moving. I jumped from the sidewalk into the street and practiced bouncing off cars without falling off the moving scooter.

On July 17, 2003, the first check from NBC finally arrived, so we started planning a few trips for me to Los Angeles for production meetings at Triage's office. John Bravakis, the Triage Entertainment producer in charge of handling the money, sent me a copy of the check and asked if I was finally getting excited. I told him not yet. I was reserving my excitement until I saw the show on TV.

A corkboard with all our proposed routines and commercial breaks hung in the production office. We were slowly refining how the routines would look and how the show would unfold for the viewer. We reviewed our taping schedule and decided the taping would begin towards the end of July. After we had the show outlined and locked in, I flew back to New York. Every day I headed to Starbucks to sit and write new routines for the show. I loved sitting by the fireplace with my computer, without having Kim around to annoy me during my writing.

On the morning of July 23, 2003, I drove into New York City and checked into the Dylan Hotel on 41st Street. The entire production crew trickled in as the day went on. Later that afternoon, we had our first production meeting with nine of us sitting around a small table. I was there with Ted and Steve, my magical consultants. I met my director Bill Price and Jerrod, the gay African-American man in charge of purchasing my wardrobe. The meeting also included Stu and Stephen, the executive producers, and Mary Donaldson, the coordinating producer from Triage Entertainment. The lady representing the equipment rental company was also present.

We went through each of my routines one at a time. I described to the director what I wanted them to look like on television, and the camera shots I thought we should have. He then told the equipment rental representative all the equipment we needed to tape the segment. It was a long, tedious meeting that took a few hours to complete.

Afterward, we went scouting for various locations that would work best for taping. After a long day, we all went to bed because we had an early call time the next morning.

On July 24, 2003, we officially started taping my television special. When I arrived at Grand Central Terminal, the production crew was already setting up the cameras and lights. After I went through hair and makeup, the taping began.

The routine was simple. I would approach total strangers and show them a train ticket in my hand, but I would not let them see the destination of the ticket. Then I would ask where they were traveling to and what their destination was. After they told me where they were going, I would give them the tickets in my hand, and they would be amazed when they realized I bought a ticket to the very place they were headed before even meeting them. But approaching total strangers with cameras and lights seemed to take people by surprise, and many were scared and hurried away. It was a learning curve we quickly mastered. After lunch that day, we headed down to Times Square and we recorded the newsstand routine.

The newsstand routine is a variation of a routine I have been performing for years. In my live show, I gave a spectator a choice of three or four books and allowed them to select a word or two from any one of the books. Using my mentalism skills, I'd figure out what word they were thinking of. When I performed it in Times Square, I stood in front of a newsstand and randomly asked people walking by to select any book or magazine from the newsstand and pick a random word from inside it. And then I would figure out the word.

After a long day of taping, Banachek and I stayed in the hotel along with the production crew, but Ted took the train back home to New Jersey. The next day, we got an early start taping in Washington Square Park. After lunch, we taped a routine at the Chelsea Pier's Bowling Alley. In this routine, I walked up to random bowlers and predicted how many pins they would knock down before they tossed their ball. The bowling alley routine was a total bust. I could not make the routine look good for television, and we wasted half a day taping and got nothing useable in return.

The next day, July 26th, we taped the Costco routine in Astoria, Queens. This was one of my favorite routines in the show. I randomly approached three different shoppers and told them to walk around the entire store and pick out one item each of them wanted. As they were making their secret selections, I went to the cash register and gave the cashier a random amount of money to hold. When the shoppers returned, I asked the cashier to ring up the three randomly selected items. The total, including tax, was the exact amount I gave the cashier minutes earlier.

My makeup trailer was parked outside the mega store, and while I was getting made up, the crew was setting up the shots at the cash register. Unexpectedly, someone knocked on the door of my trailer. One of the production assistants answered the door and found a little old white lady outside asking to see her son, Gerard. She claimed she was his mother.

The production crew thought she was asking for Jerrod, and they were a little shocked since Jerrod, my wardrobe assistant, was African-American.

The assistant called into the trailer, "Gerard, your mother is here." It was funny to hear Jerrod say "What? My momma is here?"

I heard the entire thing happening and was laughing my head off. Little did the crew realize that my birth name was Gerard, and it was actually my mother at the door looking for me! When Jerrod went to the door, he seemed just as puzzled to see my mother as my mother seemed to be when she saw him. Eventually, they figured out Gerard was actually me and they let her into the trailer.

The Costco shoot went flawlessly. That made me feel good, since I was totally bummed out from the previous day's bowling alley disaster. After the Costco shoot I was done for the day. The crew had to go out and tape B-roll footage for the show. I drove back home to Long Island, Ted returned to his home in New Jersey, and Banachek stayed in the hotel. The producers did not want to pay the crew overtime to work on Sunday, so we had the next day off.

When I returned to the hotel on Sunday night, Banachek was all excited. He told me he'd spent the day walking around in

New York City and he fed the squirrels while sitting in Central Park. He said that gave him the idea for a great routine. What if I had a few different nuts in different colors, and I was able to predict which colored nut the squirrel would choose before they took it? I remember looking at him and thinking this was some kind of a joke, but he was dead serious. When I told him I did not like the routine, he immediately got annoyed with me and walked away. He did not talk to me for the rest of the evening.

On Monday we taped one of my favorite routines in the show at a firehouse. In this routine, six firefighters on the second floor of the firehouse gathered around a fire pole. I was on the first floor of the firehouse with the chief. Without being able to see the firefighters, I was successfully able to predict the order they would slide down the fire pole. We taped the routine in Bloomfield, New Jersey because it was the only firehouse we were able to find with a useable fire pole. We filmed it in one take and the day was over. I was now getting very comfortable in front of the camera and it was becoming a lot easier for me to concentrate on my performance.

The next day, July 29th, we taped the blindfolded scooter routine in Times Square, and it was the day that had me most worried. I had to ride the scooter blindfolded through traffic on Broadway. I told the director we had to get it right on the first take because it was very dangerous. Driving in a car down Times Square with unobstructed vision was dangerous because of the crazy taxi cab drivers, but driving blindfolded on a small scooter bordered on insanity. After I successfully made the drive, the production staff huddled around the replay monitor to see if we got the shots we needed. I was the most relieved when I saw we caught everything on camera.

Later that day we had a matchmaking routine planned, but the casting agency that was hired to send good-looking single people to the nightclub did not do their job very well. When the director showed up, he wasn't happy with the people that were sent to the location and wanted to scrap the entire shoot. When I arrived, I asked how much it cost us to have the crew there. I was told we needed to pay them no matter what because the union required us to pay them for the entire day, whether or not we shot footage. I noticed an outdoor restaurant near the nightclub where we were going to tape and had an idea. Banachek and I put our thinking caps on and immediately started brainstorming. It felt good to have our creative chemistry back.

When Banachek and I finally came up wth an idea we knew I could pull off, I suggested to the producers that I pose as a waiter and asking the patrons to merely think of the food they wanted. I would read their minds and have the cook prepare the meals I thought they had in mind. Then I'd serve the food to the patrons and watch their reactions to see if I was correctly able to mentally figure out their order.

We recorded it in one take and it was successful. Since we recorded extra routines for the show, the "Mentalist Waiter" would never make the television show, but it would be great bonus footage on the DVD. The restaurant routine was the final day of shooting in New York City. After we wrapped at the restaurant, everyone on the crew met back at the hotel bar for cocktails before heading home. Since I did not drink, I had a celebratory soda.

Chapter 40

Taping in Los Angeles

During the month of August, we edited all the New York City routines one at a time. A rough cut was put together and overnighted to me in New York. I reviewed the routine and sent the editor my notes. He re-edited the routine with my input and overnighted me the new version. That process continued until the routines looked entertaining enough to broadcast on television.

I was on the phone constantly with the production company giving them my editing notes. I was also on the phone weekly with my two magic consultants. We were still writing different routines for the September taping of the show, but coming to a consensus was challenging. One of my consultants would pitch a routine and I'd hate it. A routine we both liked would be shot down by the other producers from Triage Entertainment. Or the network would reject a routine we all liked. It was a nerve-racking process of coming up with routines that everyone agreed upon.

On September 20, 2003, I flew out to Los Angeles to tape the second half of the television show. I picked up Banachek and Ted at the airport in my rental car and we drove to the hotel. After checking in, I told the boys we needed to have a meeting in my room in thirty minutes to discuss the routines I was scheduled to tape.

As I started to unpack my production notes in preparation for the meeting, the phone rang. Ted was calling from Banachek's room and said there must have been a mix-up, because Banachek's room was double the size of his. He wanted to know if Banachek might have received my room by mistake and also bet me the view in Banachek's room was much better than mine. I told him both of our rooms overlooked the pool, so our views were similar. He then told me to walk over to the window and look out at the hot tub, where two beautiful girls were soaking topless. We all laughed and hung up.

Two minutes later, Banachek and Ted were walking to my room expecting to have the meeting I just requested. Instead, they found me walking down the hall in my bathing suit with a towel around my neck.

Ted said, "I thought we were going to have a meeting."

I replied, "This is *Hollywood*, baby, the meeting can wait!"

I headed out to the pool and jumped into the hot tub with the topless girls. I figured there was no better way to welcome me to Hollywood than to soak with topless models.

After a nice long soak in the hot tub, the boys and I headed back to my room and we had our production meeting. I gave them some things to work on, got dressed, and headed to a restaurant to meet the Coors Light Twins for dinner. Since they were going to be on the show, I wanted to meet them first. What better way to celebrate my success in Hollywood than having dinner with beautiful blond twins. Everyone in the restaurant was looking at me, wondering who I was, because I was dining with a pair of buxom blond beauties.

After a couple days of production meetings, the big day arrived. On September 23, 2003, I taped all the routines that required an audience. We rented the Park Plaza Hotel in Los Angeles and were scheduled to tape the show two different times in one day. Taping it twice would allow us to pick and choose which version was better suited for television.

The next morning, Ted flew back to New York and Banachek stayed with me for the final day of taping. At this point in time, Banachek and I were not on very good terms. He felt that I rejected every idea he thought was great and pitched to me. During the creative process, he increasingly became irritated with me, so he started giving his ideas to Ted to pitch to me, thinking I'd approve them if I thought they came from Ted. But it didn't matter who pitched it—if it was a bad idea, or I wasn't comfortable performing it, I would reject it.

Around this time, I was starting to get annoyed with how my booking agent, Craig was handling my business. On November 1, 2003, I sent him an email expressing my disappointment with his office system and how they were paying me for all the private shows I was doing. He responded by saying he thought I had too much time on my hands. I sent a follow up note: Was he was kidding? He then said he thought it was time we all moved on. I emailed him on November 3rd and gave him official notice that he was no longer representing me. On November 18, I completed negotiations with Tom Kaufman Productions, and he was now going to represent me for all of my private performances. He told me he wanted to put an intern on just to handle my affairs.

On the final day of taping in Los Angeles, I was scheduled to meet Brittany Snow, the young star of the hit NBC television show *American Dreams,* on her set, where I'd perform a routine with her using a copy of her script. Her show was not doing very well in the ratings, but it was a favorite of Jeff Zucker's. He asked me if I would help cross-promote the failing show, which I agreed to do, and we taped the routine with Brittany. I needed to stay in Los Angeles and supervise the editing and I also had voiceovers to record for the show.

After the show was completely edited, a copy was sent to my CAA agent, Brian, and to my manager, Richard. Brian was not at all happy with what he saw. He said the show did not reflect my true personality. I was coming across very dark and the show didn't reflect my sense of humor. He asked the producers if we could re-edit the show to make me seem more likable. Since my goal was not to be a TV celebrity, I didn't want to start re-taping segments. I just wanted the show to air so I could return to Las Vegas and find a steady job.

NBC originally scheduled the show to air in November of 2003. A few weeks before the show was to air, they changed the air date to February 2004. Soon after, they changed the date again to May 2004, claiming they wanted to save it for the May sweeps period. They also asked me to perform for the media when they introduced me to the press. So immediately following the holidays, I put on my thinking cap and designed a routine that had me making a prediction weeks in advance and publishing it in the *Los Angeles Times* classified ads.

On January 14, 2004, NBC flew me first class to Los Angeles to appear at their press tour, which was held at the Renaissance Hollywood Hotel. My publicist, Heidi Krupp, also arrived, and we went to the Ivy Restaurant for lunch. Heidi introduced me to Paris Hilton. We only spoke for a few minutes, but I thought she was either wasted on drugs or a total airhead. Later that night, we attended a party where the various networks unveiled their new lineup of shows to all of the members of the media. It was the very first time I walked the red carpet. I wasn't sure what was expected of me, so I grabbed Britney Snow and asked her to walk the red carpet with me.

It was an endless sea of photographers and reporters. Everyone wanted photographs and interviews. But what would have seemed overwhelming to the average person seemed perfectly natural to me. I was in my element. This is what I was meant to do with my life—entertain!

After Jeff Zucker welcomed the press to the party, he announced the NBC summer lineup. Then he invited me onto the stage to perform for everyone to officially introduce the media to "The Mentalist." After my short presentation, I revealed my prediction printed in that day's Los Angeles Times, which amazed everyone. I successfully predicted the random words selected by audience members from a stack of books. Then Jeff announced I would be performing my full show in a separate room for all those who wished to attend.

Jean-Paul Aussenard/
WIREIMAGE.COM

JANUARY 28, 2004

Jesse James, left, with producer Neal Moritz

"Behind the Camera: The Unauthorized Story of 'Charlie's Angels'" stars Lauren Stamile, left, Tricia Helfer and Christina Chambers.

Gerry McCambridge, star of NBC's "The Mentalist," wowed the crowd Wednesday at the network's All-Star party with his nearly-impossible-to-believe acts of mental persuasion. "Las Vegas'" **Molly Sims** and "American Dreams'" **Brittany Snow** were among the talent participating in the show at the Highlands nightclub in Hollywood.

The film's Monet Mazur with UTA's Billy Lazarus

Donald Trump of "The Apprentice" and Larissa Meek of "Average Joe: Hawaii"

Left: John Spencer of "The West Wing" and Alison Sweeny of "Days of Our Lives"

"Las Vegas'" Molly Sims, left, and Cheryl Ladd flank NBC's Jeff Zucker.

Motorcycle stunt on Hollywood Boulevard

After my performance was over, I was excited to meet Mark Burnett and his family. Mark was the original creator and executive producer of *Survivor*, which was one of my favorite shows. I told him if he ever did a celebrity version of the show, I wanted to be considered because I was a huge fan. (A request I am sure he gets fifty times a day by every person he meets.)

Soon after returning from Los Angeles, my wife told me we were expecting our third child; she was due the end of August. She was actually very worried about telling me and didn't want to break the news to me alone, so she did it with my 15-year-old daughter Jennifer present. Kim knew I was so excited about moving out to Las Vegas, so she was concerned I would be mad because it was not a planned pregnancy. I told her I would stay with her during the entire pregnancy and delay my Vegas trip until after the baby was born. When we found out the sex of the baby, we named him Luke Vegas in honor of my lifelong dream of headlining Las Vegas.

On March 16, 2004, my agent, Brian, called me and told me the air date of my television special was going to be May 12, 2004 at 8:00 p.m. NBC wanted to wait until network sweeps to air the show, and our competition was going to be the hit television show *American Idol*. Soon after I spoke to Brian, Stu called and told me even better news: *American Idol* was only going to be on during the second half of my show.

On May 10, 2004, my daughter Jennifer and I arrived at Heidi's office in New York City for a radio tour she'd set up for me to promote the show. I sat in a private room wearing a set of headphones. Every ten minutes, a different radio station was scheduled to call in and interview me. I basically answered the same questions over and over again for three hours. After the interviews were over, Heidi introduced me to her neighbor who had an office across the hall from her. Doctor Oz was working on a book and trying to get a television show of his own. He wished me luck with mine.

At this point my media campaign was in high gear. Working hand-in-hand with the publicist from NBC assigned to my show, Heidi set up a lot of media interviews for me. I was doing television appearances, I was on radio shows, and I was in magazines and newspapers. It was pretty cool seeing myself in both the May 17, 2004 issues of *People* and *Star* magazines.

Star Magazine

On May 12, 2004, I woke up really early and headed back into New York City to appear on the *Today Show*. I took one of my best friends, Mark Spiegel, with me to the show. Mark was a very successful on-premise caterer on Long Island who owned a company called Mark of Excellence. We'd met when he was catering a private party where I was performing. I came home from the *Today Show* and took a nap while the entirety of our home was in preparation for the viewing party we were going to have with our family and friends. Mark was catering the party and helped Kim rearrange the house and set up all the food stations. As our guests began to show up around six that evening, they asked if I was excited about the big day. They were surprised to find out I was not. I knew there could still be a chance it would not air. Any number of interruptions could occur, like breaking news or severe weather alerts. A hurricane, earthquake, or tornado could quite possibly destroy my premiere!

At 8:00 p.m., the show officially began. It was the first time I was watching the show on my own television, and I did not have to push the play button on the VCR. It finally became a reality. I actually had my own NBC television special just like my idol, Doug Henning! I had just made one of my lifelong goals come true with a lot of persistence. I had to hold back the emotions in front of my family and friends. My father taught me never to cry in front of people; he said men never cried.

After the broadcast ended, my guests said goodnight and left. The caterers packed up and departed, Kim went to bed, and I was left sitting alone in my office. I looked up at my replica Las Vegas sign and knew I was one step closer to fulfilling my goal. It took me nine years to realize my goal of appearing in my own one-hour NBC special and becoming a name in the entertainment business. But I never gave up the dream, and just like magic, everything lined up the way it was supposed to and the way I visualized it on my mind's movie screen.

The television special received average ratings for the network and I had a great demo reel and credential to use to shop my show in Las Vegas. But the ratings were not good enough for

NBC to pick up their option to do a second special. Brian contacted me and said NBC passed on the option. He had no idea what to do next.

I asked him if the agency wanted to represent me in Las Vegas or in the corporate market. He said the agency was too big and my bookings would not interest them. Just as quickly as CAA jumped on board when I had an idea for a TV special, they vanished when NBC passed on my second special option.

'THE MENTALIST'

Hosting a TV special is all in the head

BY NOEL HOLSTON
STAFF WRITER

"I don't like to tell people what I do," Gerry McCambridge said, sitting in the study of his Dix Hills home surrounded by Batman memorabilia, movies from "Alien" to "Zorro" on DVD and enough self-improvement tapes to stock a Tony Robbins outlet store.

"If you go to school with your kid, and they say, 'What do you do?' and you say, 'I'm an accountant,' they don't say, 'Do my taxes,'" McCambridge said. "But with me — 'Uh, I'm a mentalist, I kind of figure out what you're thinking — it's 'Read my mind! What am I thinking?' I'm always put in situations like that. I just don't tell people."

McCambridge had better savor his relative anonymity while he can. Tonight at 8, NBC will introduce him to the nation in "The Mentalist," a one-hour special that could secure him recurring prime-time gigs like magicians David Blaine and David Copperfield.

In McCambridge's first foray, he impresses a half-dozen New York City firefighters by correctly predicting the order in which they will choose to slide down a fire pole, flabbergasts "American Dreams" star Brittany Snow by predicting the exact word she'll pick from a script and leaves jaded Manhattanites gawking as he rides a motorized scooter blindfolded through midday traffic.

How the 42-year-old McCambridge got to this point would make a better TV movie than most of what networks such as NBC green-light these days. Born Oct. 31 (yes, Halloween), 1962, he grew up in Bayside, the son of a New York City police detective to whom he attributes some of his powers of intuition and observation. By age 10, he was entertaining friends and classmates with feats of memory and "mind reading."

Thinking about thinking

Over time, he learned stage magic and misdirection, studied psychology at Queens College, worked at a psychiatric hospital and voraciously read or listened to the masters of sales, public speaking and personal empowerment, from Robbins to Wayne Dyer to Norman Vincent Peale.

"I studied anything and everything I could," McCambridge said. "I just wondered, 'Why do people's brains work the way they do? Why do they think the way they do? Why do

Predictably (for him), Gerry McCambridge of Dix Hills hosts "The Mentalist" tonight at 8 on NBC.

they act the way they do?'"

He was making a good living, performing 160 or so times a year at casinos, corporate functions and private parties, when, six years ago, he played a fateful date at a Hamptons manse.

"To me, it was just another show, another avenue to feed my family," McCambridge said. Among the guests, however, was "Today" show executive producer Jeff Zucker, who took his card. Four years later, McCambridge got a call from a woman whom

NOW ON NYNEWSDAY.COM
Will you tune in for "The Mentalist?"
Cast your vote online at www.nynewsday.com/tv

he subsequently discovered was Zucker's wife, Caryn. She wanted to hire him for a celebrity party in Los Angeles. When he turned her down because of a prior booking, she changed the date of her bash so he could do it. McCambridge later learned that her husband, Jeff, now president of NBC Entertainment, had salted the audience with production-savvy people to assess his TV potential.

The toughest task that McCambridge faced in making to-

night's special was transferring an intimate, low-tech act to a medium in which the fantastic has been rendered commonplace by computer animation. Moreover, he can't look the audience members he has to impress the most — the ones on their living room couches — in the eye. He can't touch them.

Believe it or not

His solution was to work his first few hits with people likely to inspire confidence, such as the New York firefighters. "A whole firehouse is not gonna lie on my account," he said. "They're credible, ordinary people, and that's how I figured it. If you buy it, OK, then, you'll watch the rest."

Don't misunderstand, though. McCambridge isn't out to persuade you that he can read minds. He doesn't even claim to.

"Jeff [Zucker] asked me what my goal was for the show," McCambridge said. "My goal is watercooler talk. That's it. I don't care that anybody believes what I do is real. I don't care if they think it's a trick. I don't care if they don't understand the line between the two. If they're talking about my show the next day in the office at the watercooler, I've accomplished my goal. I like people to talk."

315

Chapter 41

Douglas Fairbanks Theater

On June 12, 2004, I took a quick trip to Chicago to attend the Psychic Entertainers Association's annual convention, where they honored me with the "Dan Blackwood Award for Outstanding Contributions to the Art of Mentalism." Immediately after the convention, I returned home because Kim was still pregnant, and I didn't feel comfortable leaving her alone for too long with two little ones.

Right after the television show aired, my plan was to keep myself available for any media appearances NBC wanted me to do. Then I would plan my next trip out to Las Vegas to try to get a job. Since I didn't know what NBC would require me to do after the show aired, I did not book any future engagements. So what would I do for the next three months?

One of the things I always wanted to do was to perform my show Off Broadway. I thought if I opened my show just for the summer it would be a great addition to my resume when I finally made it out to Las Vegas. I felt bad when I did not ask my agent, Craig to co-produce my Off Broadway show the first time around, so this time I reached out to him first. He agreed to come on board as co-producer. We hired Heidi Krupp as the show's publicist and we hit the ground running.

We discovered the Douglas Fairbanks Theater had an immediate opening in their schedule. It was the perfect size, so we signed the contract and on Thursday, July 8, 2004, I finally achieved another goal I set for myself: opening my one-man show Off Broadway. We only committed to be a limited engagement for July and August because the baby was due at the end of August.

A lot of friends showed up for the opening of the show, including my ex-agent, Linda. She brought her friend Catherine Hickland, an actress in the soap opera *One Life to Live*. Catherine and I instantly hit it off and became close friends.

Catherine Hickland and Carol Alt

My publicist Heidi also attended, as did a few of her personal friends. Heidi was mainly a literary publicist for writers like the *South Beach Diet* doctor. She was also from the Tony

Robbins' School of Motivation, so she and I were friends as well. She introduced me to her personal friends who, it turned out, worked for Tony Robbins.

Heidi told me Eddie Micone called her office and asked if he could attend my show. At one time, Eddie was one of the biggest agents at International Creative Management, also known as I.C.M., representing artists like Billy Crystal and Robin Williams. He'd recently left the agency to start his own firm and was looking for an act to manage full time. He heard about my show and was interested in seeing my performance.

After the show, Heidi introduced me to Eddie. He asked me what my ultimate career goal was after the Off Broadway show closed. I said that I wanted to have my own show in Las Vegas and occasionally perform for corporate functions. He told me he had a lot of connections in Las Vegas and asked if he could manage me. While I was interested in working with him, I told him I would not sign any exclusive agreement until I saw what he had to bring to the table. Later that week, Eddie and I had a long talk while dining at a Chinese buffet.

He asked where I saw myself performing in Las Vegas, and I told him I admired the success of Steve Wynn. He single-handedly reinvented Atlantic City, and then Las Vegas, with his high-profile, high-end, over-the-top hotels and casinos. He featured headline acts like Frank Sinatra. I remember seeing TV commercials with Steve Wynn delivering towels to Frank Sinatra when Steve owned the Golden Nugget downtown. He knew how to bring in an audience with his advertising and crazy commercials. If he was good enough for "Ol' Blue Eyes," he was good enough for me.

In Vegas, Steve Wynn owned the Mirage, Treasure Island and Bellagio hotels before the MGM Corporation bought him out. His hotels were known not only for their décor, but for their lavish shows. He was responsible for making Siegfried and Roy major stars in Las Vegas. Now that he was building a brand new casino in Las Vegas, I told Eddie I wanted to work for Steve Wynn. Eddie told me he would make some calls to see if he could make it happen.

'The Mentalist' sees Vegas in his future

N.Y. native rides the line between intuition, magic

GERRY MCCAMBRIDGE is part Sherlock Holmes and part P.T. Barnum, though he's better known by his stage moniker The Mentalist, wowing live audiences with his ability to "intuit" the inner-most thoughts of people.

McCambridge, 41, is not a mind-reader and he doesn't have ESP. What he does have — and what he uses in his 90-minute live off-Broadway show — are tricks like reading body language, hypnosis, setting language patterns and what he calls his pitch-perfect sense of intuition.

Showmanship

"If you're not intuitive, you can't take it to the next step, where I can," he says. "Intuition is sensing things without using your five senses."

"There's a very thin line between intuition and magic and where the line is drawn is only something my head knows," he says about his performances.

His showmanship has made him a favorite on the celebrity party circuit (Courteney Cox-Arquette, Molly Sims and Tim Burton are a

few A-listers who have hired him). He works more than 150 performances a year, but most are private events for small groups of people. However, last May he took the first steps towards becoming a household name with a one-hour special on NBC, which was well-received.

Ultimate goal

This summer he has surfaced for a handful of public events and is now at the tail-end of eight shows at the Douglas Fairbanks Theater — tonight is his second to last show. After the curtains fall next week he plans to stop public shows for the next few months to be with his growing brood of kids. After his self-imposed hiatus is over, he plans on resurfacing for public audiences in a much bigger way. "My ultimate goal is to be in Vegas" he says. "Hopefully Vegas within the year."

The Mentalist is performing tonight and next Thursday at 8 p.m. at the Douglas Fairbanks Theater at 432W 42nd St., 212-239-4321.

CATHERINE NEW
catherine.new@metro.us

GERRY MCCAMBRIDGE is known as 'The Mentalist' and uses his intuition to read his inner-most thoughts. He is performing at the Douglas Fairbanks Theater at 432W 42nd St. tonight and next Thursday.

While promoting the show at the Fairbanks Theater, Heidi booked me on a morning radio talk show on WNYC on August 16, 2004. Karen Hunter was one of the co-hosts. During my interview, I explained that my goal was to be a Vegas headliner, and the Off Broadway show was a dream I always wanted to fulfill. During one of those performances, I brought Kim up on stage and we announced to the audience that she was expecting our third child. The two of us then asked my friend Mark Spiegel, the caterer, to come up on stage and we asked him to be the baby's godfather. He was in total shock and gladly accepted the responsibility.

After the radio show was over, Karen and I continued to talk about my career. I explained to her how this all began because an agent approached me to write a book, but I didn't like what he was pitching to the publishers. She asked what I wanted the book to be about, and I told her I wanted it to be about my life and how I overcame obstacles to pursue my goals and dreams.

After years of living with tremendous guilt and shame, I had come to terms with what happened to me and decided, through self-exploration and therapy, that what happened with Mr. Cuales was not my fault. I was an innocent child who was taken advantage of in unthinkable ways. When I finally realized how wrong it all was, I was ashamed to talk about it to anyone because I allowed it to repeatedly happen. It took almost twenty-five years before I could openly speak about it.

I told Karen that during a business meeting, I was talking with an associate and telling him about my experiences and my idea about writing a book. During my description of the book's contents, his face went completely blank. I thought he was in shock with my candor. Halfway through the conversation, he broke down and told me that the same thing happened to him with a police officer when he was a child, and he started to recount his own personal hell. He told me he'd never talked to anyone about what he was sharing with me. After recalling the horrific details, he had a look on his face as if a weight was lifted off his shoulders—a weight he must have been carrying for a lifetime. A weight I knew all too well.

He asked what I did to straighten out my head. He wanted to take similar actions in his life because he was also on a self-destruct course in his marriage because of his childhood abuse. I knew then that I would be able to help him toward his road to mental recovery in a very special way. I knew I had to write this book to try and help others as well.

Karen seemed to really get it. She told me the book should be about me and not about trying to teach others to be like me. The more we talked, the more she understood my vision for the book. She told me her radio job was a part time gig and that her real job was writing. She was the author of a few bestseller books, and she would be interested in ghostwriting this book for me.

I described what had happened with my previous literary agent, and how I wanted to possibly keep him in the equation. She understood and agreed. I told her I would call him and make an appointment for the three of us to meet.

My timing was perfect, because the last performance for my Off Broadway show was on August 26, 2004, and five days later, Luke Vegas was born. When I arrived at the hospital to visit Kim and Luke, I noticed the curtain around her hospital bed was closed. When I opened the curtain, Kim was cradling the baby and Mark Spiegel was sitting at the head of the bed. They were uncomfortably close, and in my mind it looked as if they could have been kissing just before I opened the curtain. I pretended like everything was normal when in fact I was furious with them both. After that night, I never spoke to Mark again. Luke was never baptized, and Mark was not his godfather.

A few weeks after Luke was born, Karen and I met with my literary agent, Richard Pine. For some reason, he was no longer that interested in the project. He listened to the ideas we had for the book, but since they were not even close to his original concept, he didn't seem very enthused. He told us we could draft an outline of the book with a few sample chapters. If he liked what he read, he would take the book to his connections and see if anyone was interested.

Neither Karen nor I had a good feeling about Richard's association with the project, but we decided to see it through. Karen sat with a tape recorder as I told my story to her, and she quickly drafted an outline as Richard requested.

We sent Richard the outline and gave him time to read it. Instead of critiquing the content or subject matter of the outline, he decided to correct Karen's punctuation marks. She was totally annoyed with his attitude and told me she was not interested in working with Richard if he was going to represent our work. I asked Richard if he had any ideas about how he wanted to proceed with the new book idea, but he did not seem interested in the project anymore.

For the second time, my book was dead in the water. His attitude totally turned me off, and I decided to put the book idea on hold and focus on supporting my family by getting a steady job in Las Vegas first.

Chapter 42

Confession is Good for Whom?

A week after we took Luke home from the hospital, my production company notified me that they decided to distribute my television show around the world since it was so well received in Canada and the United States. They brought in a third party distribution company whose sole purpose was to sell the show to overseas markets. They did a good job selling the show to South Africa, Korea, the Middle East, New Zealand, India, Thailand, Australia, Denmark, the Netherlands, Malaysia, and the United Kingdom. Every time they sold the show to another market, I was paid all over again!

When I saw the list of countries my show was scheduled to air in, my heart dropped when I saw New Zealand. It reminded me of when I strayed from my marriage with that girl from New Zealand after performing at a summer camp. What if she wanted to cash in on my fame when she saw my TV show and tried to contact me? My marriage would come to an end! Everything I worked so hard to build would come crashing down. I felt like I was building a house on a faulty foundation. We just had our third child, and I was feeling very guilty about the possibility of putting the family through hell if the New Zealand blond came forward.

The thought of my family going through this kind of pain was too much guilt for me to take. I sat Kim down in the kitchen, and I opened up and told her everything. I told her all the details, saying she would be better off without me as a husband and I was a monster for doing that to her. I did not yet realize why I had strayed, but I knew it was wrong. It was like I was a dog looking at a bag of garbage—it knows it will get in trouble for tearing it apart, yet it still does it.

It felt like a huge weight was lifted off my shoulders when I confessed my sin to my sweet, innocent wife, who never deserved to be hurt. I rested my head on her lap and started to cry. I was worried my house of cards would come crumbling down with my confession. Surprisingly, she was not upset with me. In fact, she did not seem angry at all. She told me it was okay because I was not the only one who strayed from the marriage. I sat up in genuine surprise and asked her what she was talking about.

Kim said she was once attracted to a patient at her job while we were married. They flirted and eventually wound up in a hotel room together, but they never did anything because she was crying so much and felt guilty while they were in the hotel. She said they got dressed and left the hotel before having sex.

Without saying it, she implied that we were even, and that we would get past this. She suggested going to therapy to work all this out. Soon after, she started searching for therapists and found one who worked out of his house. He based his therapy on the book *Men Are From Mars, Women Are From Venus*. After we spent a ton of money on therapy, he basically told us we were both wrong with what we did and we were even. He said we now needed to start over and work on rebuilding our trust with each other.

Kim did not trust me because I was constantly traveling around the country performing, and she was uncomfortable with me being in hotel rooms which offered temptation all around. I tried to convince her that when I was not performing, I was usually alone in my hotel room watching the television, not hanging out in the hotel bars drinking.

I told Kim and the therapist that I traveled with my laptop computer, which allowed her to Skype me anytime she wanted to see what I was doing. She replied that if I had a girl in the room, I would not answer the Internet call. She still didn't trust me, so I offered to keep my camera on twenty-four hours a day, allowing her to watch me anytime she wanted. She accepted that as a compromise she could live with.

After that, as soon as I checked into any hotel room, I set up the laptop in the corner of the room and turned on my web camera. I granted her Skype account unlimited access to view my Internet camera whenever she wanted.

The therapist encouraged us to have a date night and to have more intimacy. Kim complained that I spent all my free time working on my career, and I complained that I felt desired by everyone but my wife. So we made it a point to go out on a date night at least once a week without the children, and to have sex more often.

Eventually, she confessed that she had lied to me about the time she was in the hotel room with her patient and admitted that she had sex with him.

Deep down, I always knew she lied to me about that instance, so it did not come as a total shock to me, but it was nice to hear her finally admit it. She said he was a total stranger, she never saw him again, and it was a big mistake. She called it a onetime occurrence, like my "New Zealand affair."

When we brought it up in therapy, Kim again admitted she lied to me. She didn't have sex with a total stranger in the hotel room—it was actually her boss, the doctor she was working for.

At this point I was getting really frustrated. How many more lies would Kim admit to? How many more details would she confess to? I thought about it and realized what my marriage had come to. I was checking into hotel rooms and setting up web cameras so my wife could spy on me to make sure I wasn't fooling around with anyone, while she was out fooling around herself. Even though Kim said she only strayed one time, after all the lies, I never truly believed her. At that point I decided my marriage to Kim was over. I needed time alone to think about my future, and what better place to be alone, then in the desert. I decided to focus on my Las Vegas goal instead of dealing with my failed marriage.

Chapter 43

Success and More Challenges

In this chapter of my life, I learned how to pitch a television show to the networks, and how people in power could be extremely rude.

While witnessing how everyone but me got excited when we sold my show to NBC, I realized how big the wall had become around my emotions. I had been burned so many times in the past with deals that were promised, it was easier to maintain the wall instead of getting emotionally connected to a person or project that would eventually disappoint me.

I learned how insincere people quickly befriend you, when in reality it is nothing more than a false friendship based around money. When the promise of possibly making a buck disappears, so does their friendship.

The one person I thought was wholesome, innocent, and family-oriented was just as bad as I was. Temptation would always be around us, and thinking we were strong enough to always resist it was a foolish notion.

Again, my brain was reinforced to learn not to let anyone close to me. No matter how much I trusted someone, they would eventually betray me or hurt me—even someone as close as my wife.

The final brick in the metaphoric wall around my heart had been cemented in place. I finally became cold and turned off to everyone in my life except my mother, my friend Steve (who is like a brother to me), and my children. My mind manipulating skills and my acting ability allowed me to easily convince people that I liked them and enabled me to form a false bond with them.

Heading to the Desert

Chapter 44

Auditioning for Steve Wynn

Now that I had the television special under my belt, it was time to head out to Las Vegas and bang on some doors. As always, I started at the top when reaching for my goals and worked my way down. Who was the biggest person in Las Vegas? It was a high-profile skeptic named Steve Wynn. If you were an entertainer and you wanted to perform at a casino, you wanted to be at a Steve Wynn casino. This was the man I needed to start with.

Steve Wynn sold his Vegas hotels to the MGM Grand Corporation in 2000 for more than $4 billion, and announced his plans to build the most luxurious, ritzy, out-of-this-world hotel and casino ever. It was to be completed in the spring of 2005 and would feature a Lamborghini and Maserati dealership in the lobby of the hotel. He was going to build a mountainside with a cascading waterfall in front of the casino that would serve as the entryway for people approaching the casino. Wynn also vowed to top the shows he had at the Mirage.

My new manager, Eddie, sent a copy of my NBC television special to his friend Steve Wynn with a note saying that he should consider me as an act for his new hotel and casino. One day while Eddie was in a crowded elevator in a New York office building, Steve Wynn called and literally screamed so loudly at Eddie that he had to quickly exit the elevator because everyone around him was able to hear Steve on the phone.

"How dare you make me watch this!" he shouted. "You want to make me a laughing stock? I know all about magic acts like these. This is all staged and the audience is full of plants." After Wynn had finally calmed down, Eddie told him that my act had no audience "plants" and that it was 100 percent legitimate.

Eddie asked me if I still wanted him to book a meeting with Wynn, knowing his attitude and the fact that he was such a skeptic. I told him I was not intimidated in the least and to go ahead and plan a meeting. On October 18, 2004, Eddie and I were on a plane to Las Vegas to prove to Mr. Wynn that I did not use stooges at any time during my performance.

The night that we arrived in Las Vegas, Eddie made arrangements for us to see *The Danny Gans Show* at the Mirage. Danny was an impressionist and singer, and after the performance, Eddie asked me what I thought of the show. I said Danny was very talented, but he appeared to be bored while he was performing. He seemed like he was just going through the motions and would have put on the same exact show whether the audience was there or not. Eddie agreed with my review and said it could be the result of performing the same show night after night for so many years.

Danny Gans and Gerry

334

Since his new casino was still under construction, Mr. Wynn's temporary office was in a small, unmarked building along an industrial/commercial strip in Vegas. Needless to say, it was nothing like his office at the Mirage. His assistant, Joyce, met us in the lobby. Eddie told her that I would need a conference room and about fifteen people as an audience. She showed us into a long, rectangular room with a big wooden conference table in the middle.

I needed to get a vibe for the room. I wanted to get acclimated to the surroundings, to the seating and the lighting. I wanted to see the room from every angle. I needed to set up my act and have it arranged the way I liked it, so that I did not have to think about anything while performing.

I have a pre-show ritual in which I stand alone where I am about to perform and visualize the show and my performance. It usually takes about ten minutes to go through the whole ritual. This time, however, I had done most of my prep the night before. I spent only two minutes alone in the conference room before Joyce escorted Eddie and me to see Mr. Wynn in his private office.

Eddie walked in first. Mr. Wynn shook his hand and said, "Hi, Eddie! How are you doing?"

He then shook my hand and quickly said, "Glad to meet you." He did not look at me and I didn't know what to make of it at first, because I knew that he had vision problems. He walked behind his desk and sat down, and invited us to sit in the chairs in front of his desk.

Mr. Wynn then started to tell us a story about *Avenue Q*, the hit Tony Award-winning Broadway play that was going to be a show in one of the three theaters in his new casino. Sitting on a chair in the corner of his office was a big puppet replica of Steve Wynn that the folks at *Avenue Q* made especially for him. He told Eddie how he bought the show for his new casino and had recently flown the entire cast somewhere on his private jet for a performance off-Strip.

Wynn was very animated telling his story. He admired the puppet of his likeness as he spoke, and also looked at Eddie during the entire story. He looked at his assistant Joyce when she entered with a tray of coffee and placed it in front of him, and also at the cream and sugar he put in his coffee. He seemed to be looking at everything, but he never looked at me. Eddie had warned me that Steve loved to talk about himself. He instructed me to sit quietly and just let Steve go on, and eventually he would get around to our main purpose.

At this point I remembered this was the look, or the lack of the look, that I get all the time by people intimidated by what I do for a living. People often think that if they do not look at me, I cannot read into their thoughts. I have even had people say to me that they are scared to *think* in my presence.

After Wynn went through his *Avenue Q* story, he finally looked directly at me for the first time. "I saw your TV show," he said, staring me square in the face. "It was quite impressive. You have the look and charisma of a star, but I can't put you in my casinos because I only have top-class entertainment and there's a bust-ability with you. Your act can be busted, and if word gets out that the audience is full of stooges, I'll be a laughing stock in Las Vegas."

"Eddie tried to convince me that your act is not a setup," he continued, "but I know how reality television shows work and I know how those things are all staged. I was the first to discover Siegfried and Roy, so I know how all that magic stuff works." He then listed a bunch of magicians that he knew and threw out a few magic buzz words to imply his knowledge of magic. He told me how he helped design the *Siegfried & Roy* show and knew the entire inside workings of the illusions.

"I know everything there is to know about the craft," he insisted. I sat there and listened to him. I did not say a word.

"Now look me in the eye and tell me that nobody on your television show was a plant," Steve Wynn said.

"Is that your only concern?" I asked.

He repeated how his hotel would be the most prestigious ever built and would have the hottest shows in Vegas. For those reasons, he said, he couldn't afford to be made a fool of by having a show that could be busted as a fraud.

"If that's your only concern," I said, "then step inside, and I will prove your theory wrong and put your mind at ease."

Joyce led us into the conference room where she had already assembled all of his employees. It was a lot more than the fifteen we requested. In fact, people lined the walls. Even Wynn's wife, Elaine, was there. Steve Wynn took a seat and thanked everyone for coming. Before I started my act, he grilled the room.

"We have Mr. McCambridge here," he said. "I saw a DVD of his performance and he does some very impressive stuff. He had a special on primetime NBC. Six and a half million people watched it. Did any of you see it?" A couple of hands went up.

"Have any of you, besides Joyce, spoken to this gentleman today? He's been in the office here for about a half an hour. Did he talk to or approach any of you? Did his manager approach any of you? Have you received emails or any correspondence from either of them?" Everyone answered "no" to each question.

"So, he knows nothing about you or anyone here? He never had any correspondence of any kind at any time about this?" Again, everyone replied in the negative.

"Okay, Mr. McCambridge," he said, emphasizing the second syllable of my name. "Go ahead and do your thing. You now have my complete attention."

He sat back in his chair and folded his arms, and I began my pitch. I started with my book routine, the same warm-up routine

I used in the TV special. That's where I asked people walking the streets of New York to pick any word from any page of a book or magazine they selected at the street newsstand, without telling me what the word was. I then told them the word that they randomly selected.

Wynn sat with his arms folded and a nay-saying scowl on his face, ready to say, "I see the string or hidden mirror! This is all bullshit!"

By the time I got to my final routine more than sixty minutes later, and asked for my final volunteer, Wynn practically jumped out of his seat to participate. He was like a kid in a classroom who knew the correct answer.

"Pick me, pick me!" he said with a childlike enthusiasm in his voice.

Since the beginning of the pitch, I had one person holding a sealed envelope. For my final routine, I asked three different people to name something at random. I asked one to name a random city in the world, another to name a random celebrity, and the third to name a random amount of money. Wynn was one of the three volunteers. I asked the person who had been holding the envelope since the beginning of the performance to open the envelope. Written on the paper inside were the exact three things my volunteers just named, all woven into a little story.

"I was going to say something else!" Steve Wynn said. "I don't know why I changed my mind at the last minute…son of a bitch! You got me!"

He sat there with a big grin on his face. He turned to his group and said, "By a show of hands, how many of you enjoyed watching Gerry perform?"

Every single hand in the room went up.

"How many of you would pay to see Gerry perform?" he asked.

And every hand was raised again.

"How many of you would tell your friends to see this show?"

All hands went into the air a third time.

He thanked them all and they went back to work. Eddie and I stayed behind and Wynn started making phone calls while I packed up my props. He did not expect to be wowed, so now he had a dilemma. The new casino had three theaters and Steve Wynn had already booked three shows with long-term contracts for those theaters. There was no place to put my act.

He talked to the builders and planners and made many phone calls in front of me, but everyone told him that it was too late in the game to build another theater. The casino was scheduled to be finished on time and on budget in the spring of 2005.

"Let me see what I can do to fit you into my plans and get back to you," he told us. "I have to try to fit this square peg into a round hole. Gerry is the most unique entertainer I have ever seen."

It was a bittersweet moment. My dream of being in Las Vegas was so close. Steve Wynn actually said I was the most unique entertainer he had ever seen—this after vowing to "expose" me as a fraud—yet he had no place to put me. Eddie and I returned to New York after Steve promised to make more calls to his connections in Las Vegas.

Our trip to Las Vegas made me realize something very important about my dream. Over the years, most of my performances were usually one-night corporate events, or two-night comedy club bookings on Friday and Saturday nights. I wondered how I would adapt to performing every night in the same venue. Would I quickly get bored of performing my show like Danny Gans seemed to be? I decided I needed to give it a try.

I called Craig who was now the owner of all of the Catch A Rising Star comedy clubs. I told him I wanted to work in a casino environment every night to see if I could adapt. He booked me to perform in his Atlantic City club from March 29 to April 3, 2005. I was not sure if I would like it, and I didn't.

I *loved* it!

Every time I performed at a corporate function, I had to rehearse my show and teach my cues to the sound and light man. Having the same sound and light man who knew all my cues during the entire run in the casino, and not having to pack and unpack my props every night, was *awesome*! I felt I would have no problem adapting to the daily routine of a Las Vegas casino gig.

I have always been able to achieve my goals. I turned doubting billionaire Steve Wynn into a believer and convinced NBC to give me a television show. All my accomplishments first started as a mere thought, maybe a dream, but I always had the belief that I could eventually do it. If Steve Wynn didn't have a showroom for me to perform in, I didn't take it personally. Someone else in Las Vegas would. I refused to give up.

Chapter 45

The Student Becomes the Master

Before I decided to throw in the towel on our marriage, Kim and I decided to go to marriage counseling once more. During a session, the therapist told me he noticed that every time any part of my childhood concerning Mr. Cuales came up in conversation, I'd clench my fists and get angry. He likened it to an anger button that was very easy to trigger. He suggested I start to see a therapist for the sexual abuse in addition to marriage counseling, which I did.

After many therapy sessions, I came to realize I did nothing wrong. I was just a child when Mr. Cuales sexually molested me. I was trying to rationalize my decisions now as an adult when, at the time the abuse occurred, I was just a child. People like Mr. Cuales prey on little kids like me. They have a pattern of what kind of children to look for. And unfortunately, boys find it way too embarrassing to report sexual molestations and rapes, so they usually go undetected.

I gave a lot of thought to what my counselor said, and decided it was time for the student to become the master. I tried to track down Mr. Cuales using the Internet. Unfortunately, all I was able to locate was his age and the town he lived in. Any other information would cost me money to acquire. I suddenly remembered Mr. Cuales's children's names—names I had not recalled in years. I did a search on his son, Michael, and the search returned a couple hundred matches. I looked over the list, focused on it, and randomly selected just one name in California. On March 27, 2005, I sent the following email to that randomly selected name:

Dear Mike,

I am looking for my old Bayside High School teacher, Hector Cuales from New York. Any chance that is your father?

ESPecially,
Gerry McCambridge

Evidently, I selected the correct name because his son emailed me back. Michael was excited to hear from me. He remembered me most of all as the boy who "cut off" his finger and magically restored it. In less than twenty-four hours, I received the following response from him:

Are you kidding me? Gerry McCambridge? The magician who's tricks and illusions entertained me through most of my childhood? I still swear you cut off your finger once, then stitched it back on right before my eyes. You found the right guy. My father would love to hear from you.

- mike cuales

He had no clue that his father made my innocence disappear. Michael quickly contacted Mr. Cuales and told him that I had reached out to him. Mike must have passed on my email address to Mr. Cuales because he emailed me the next day. This is exactly what he sent me:

Gerry McCambridge, as I live and breathe, a voice from the future! Yes, this is Hector, Mike's father. Michael couldn't believe it was you; he remembered you so well with all of your illusions. Melissa just walked in the door, I'm sure she will remember you as well. I think of you on occasion as I do many other students. I am in touch with quite a few from Bayside High, from Florida to Connecticut.

I'm happy to hear that you hit the big screen; Michael was very excited. I will talk to you soon.

Your friend,

Hector

He wanted me to know that he was still in contact with other students, and that everything was still okay. *Everybody's doing it.* The words echoed in my mind.

For the time being, I decided I was not going to return his email. I would keep him wondering—wondering why I reached out to his son out of the clear blue, wondering what I was up to, wondering what I was thinking… This time, I was in control. The student has become the master. This time, *he* was thinking twice about *my* actions.

After the casino gig ended at the Catch a Rising Star comedy club, I returned home knowing I would have no problem performing my show night after night in Las Vegas when I finally booked my show.

The work in Atlantic City had displaced my pain. A few weeks later during a flight from New York to Las Vegas, I decided to draft a response email to Mr. Cuales on my cell phone. Midpoint in my travels, I had a short layover in Dallas and was able to go online. While sitting in the Dallas terminal, I sent Mr. Cuales the following email:

To: Hector Cuales
Sent: Mar 28, 2005 4:47 PM
Subject: Your Turn

Dear Mr. Cuales,

I searched you on the internet and was able to get your age and home address, but was not able to get your email address.

I remembered your children's names and did a search on Michael. Many Michael Cuales' came up. I used my intuition, selected only one and sent out an email... And low and behold, your son responded! It was nice to read that he remembered me and my magic from so many years ago.

After the world wide success of my *NBC* special titled "The Mentalist," I was offered a book deal. The publisher loved the story of how a boy went from an orphanage to international stardom, even after overcoming obstacles such as coming from a broken family and repeated sexual abuse by a person of authority.

I hope the book will motivate others to go for their dreams, no matter what obstacles they have. Since I have kids in high school, I hope the book also teaches kids how not to allow themselves to be physically and sexually abused.

The reason I did an internet search on you is so that I could send you a copy of my book, since you have a big part in it.

ESPecially,

Gerry McCambridge
NBC's The Mentalist

Surprise, surprise! He never responded to my email. I also felt good about letting Mr. Cuales know my intentions to include him in my book. I am sure my email must have ruined his day.

Chapter 46

My First Vegas Show

My manager Eddie contacted me and told me the Rampart Casino in Summerlin, Nevada was interested in booking my show. They had a small showroom with a comedy club that was hosted by Sandy Hackett, the son of legendary comic Buddy Hackett. The casino comedy club was only open on Friday and Saturday nights, but they wanted another show Monday through Thursday. Eddie said it wasn't located on the Strip, but it was a good place for us to start. If I performed there, he would be able to send other casino entertainment directors to see my show.

Tom Willer, the entertainment director at the Rampart Casino, wanted to meet me before offering me the gig. I told Eddie I was going to be in Las Vegas from June 10th to the 15th, 2005, to attend the three-day Psychic Entertainer's Association convention. After the convention, I planned to spend two additional days in Las Vegas with my Uncle Joe and my friend Daniel Dunninger. Daniel was a relative of the legendary mentalist Joseph Dunninger. Eddie told me he would set up a meeting with Tom while I was in town.

On Friday, June 10, 2005, Daniel and I flew out to Las Vegas and checked into the Golden Nugget Hotel and Casino. Later that night, we watched David Brenner perform at the Las Vegas Hilton in the Shimmer Cabaret. After the show, Daniel's wife, Donna, made arrangements for us to meet David Brenner.

I told David about the offer I had at the Rampart Casino. I told him I heard it was far off the Strip and I really was not interested in performing my show only for the locals; I wanted a casino on the Strip. He told me to reconsider and take the job, explaining that if I eventually worked on the Strip, the locals could be up to 15 percent of my audience every night. To get the locals on my side before I booked a steady gig in a Strip casino would eventually work to my advantage.

The next day, Daniel and I took a long taxi ride from the Golden Nugget Casino to the Rampart Casino. I met with entertainment director Tom Willer and the casino general manager, Sal Semola. They showed me the Addison Lounge Showroom, said they were interested in seeing my show before booking me, and asked when I'd be performing on the West Coast.

I didn't have any gigs planned in the next few months on the West Coast, so I offered to fly back to Las Vegas to audition for them. I said if they gave me an audience, I would knock their socks off. I also said that I would pay for my own flight if they would give me a room and cover my meals while I was there. They were excited over my offer and agreed to let me perform an audition.

Daniel and I returned to the Golden Nugget Casino and shared the good news with a few of my closest friends in the Psychic Entertainer's Association.

The next day, on June 11, 2005, the Psychic Entertainer's Association presented me with their most prestigious award, the Dunninger Memorial Award for "distinguished professionalism in the performance of mentalism." It was not a surprise because the awards committee let me know in advance I was getting the award, hoping I would show up in person to accept it.

The previous winner of the award usually presented it to the current winner. I wanted to make the presentation very special, so I asked if I could have a member of the Dunninger family present it to me instead. Having a member of the Dunninger family at the convention was very exciting for the P.E.A. membership, so they enthusiastically agreed to have a non-member of the organization present at the awards ceremony.

I contacted Eddie when I returned to New York and told him to set up a date for me to audition with the Rampart Casino. A little over a week later on June 20, 2005, I flew back out to Las Vegas and performed for a packed showroom. Tom and Sal sat in the back of the showroom and watched the audience reaction. Everyone loved my performance and they wanted to offer me a contract to perform at their casino starting on July 10, 2005. I would perform four nights a week with the comedy club performing on Friday and Saturday evenings. We shook on the deal and I returned to New York.

On July 8, 2005, two days before my show opened at the Rampart Casino, the entertainment director asked if I wanted to book the entire month of August because every July performance was already sold out. He wanted to extend my contract, and I agreed to stay on through August.

On the night of July 11, 2005, I stepped onto a Las Vegas stage for the first time as a performer with my own show. It took many years to realize my goal of performing in Las Vegas, but I never gave up the dream. And just like magic, everything lined up the way it was supposed to, the way I visualized it on my mind's movie screen.

The press about my show opening at the Rampart Casino included an interesting article by Mike Weatherford in the July 14, 2005 edition of the *Las Vegas Review Journal* newspaper. He interviewed Rampart Casino entertainment director Tom Willer, who said, "I think I may have found the new Danny Gans, but Gerry is not an impressionist." Tom mentions he was the entertainment director at the Stratosphere Casino when Danny Gans crossed over from the corporate and trade-show circuit and introduced the impressionist to ticket-buying audiences on the Strip. Now Willer handles marketing at the Rampart and Cannery casinos. "I really see the potential for (McCambridge) to have a nice career in Las Vegas," Willer says, and the show is "very good for our customers."

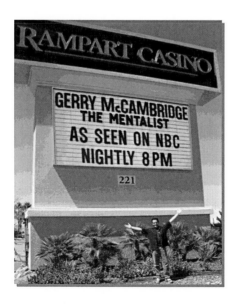

Because of positive press coverage like that, the tickets for all of my scheduled August shows at the Rampart Casino disappeared as quickly as the July tickets. Tom extended my contract another month, through the end of September, and decided to get rid of the comedy club. He wanted me performing in the showroom full time. When the comedy club shared the showroom with me, I performed during the week and took the red-eye flight back to New York to spend time with the kids on the weekend. Now that I would be performing six nights a week during the month of September, I was not able to visit my kids in New York as much.

The support I received from the Las Vegas magic community was awesome. Lance Burton came out one night to the Rampart Casino to see my show, and a few days later Siegfried and German magician Jan Rouven attended my show. The night Lance Burton attended, we went out to dinner together after my show. Afterward he drove me back to my hotel in his Corvette, and I told him my goal and my dream was to eventually be a headliner on the Las Vegas Strip just like he was. He told me to be careful what I wished for, because it just may come true. I found Lance to be one of the nicest people in Las Vegas. He never said a bad word about anyone, and he was a true gentleman.

I had read that *The Magic Show* with Doug Henning went on to play 1,920 performances at the Cort Theater on Broadway, so I set my new goal: I wanted to perform in my show, *The Mentalist,* at least that many times in Las Vegas.

I quickly grew tired of living in the casino, so I contacted a real estate agent and spent most of September looking for a house. I knew I would be traveling often, so I looked for something close to the airport.

Three weeks later I purchased a house in the Legacy development. Since I was not taking any furniture from New York with me, I needed to furnish the entire house. The man selling the house was moving onto a houseboat and had no use for all the furniture, so I purchased everything in the house from him. On October 13, 2005, I signed the papers and moved in to a fully furnished house. It was a turnkey transaction and was so much more comfortable than living at the Rampart Casino.

I needed a way to get back and forth to work every night, so that night after my show, I took a red-eye flight back to New York. I landed at seven in the morning and went home to sleep. Later that night, ever-faithful Steve and I loaded my car and began our three-day cross-country drive back to Las Vegas. I felt like I was in the 1988 movie *Rain Man* with Dustin Hoffman and Tom Cruise. There is a scene in the movie when Charlie Babbitt and his brother, Raymond, are driving cross-country to Las Vegas. Raymond, also known as "Rain Man," was a savant who was great with numbers, just like Steve. During the three-day cross-country drive, Steve kept a log of everything: how many miles between each gas stop, how many gallons we pumped to fill up the car's gas tank, how much the gas cost, how many hours we drove, and how many times Steve used the restroom. We finally arrived in Las Vegas on Sunday night, October 16, just before I lost my sanity, and just in time for me to be back on stage performing the next night.

While we were driving cross-country, Rain Man Steve informed me that the anniversary of our meeting was rapidly approaching. We had been best friends for thirty years! I told him I was going to do something special for him for our anniversary, and also because he took the long cross-country drive to keep me company. I asked him to think about what he wanted and to let me know.

As we were approaching Las Vegas, Steve saw a billboard on the side of the highway advertising George Carlin, who was performing at the Stardust Casino. Steve pointed to the billboard and told me he wanted to see that show for our anniversary. When we arrived at my new house, I purchased two tickets to see George's show. When we were seated in the showroom, a strange chill came over me, because I realized Steve and I were sitting in the very same booth where I sat when I saw Wayne Newton perform eight years earlier in 1997.

When I returned to the Rampart Casino, the boss informed me ticket sales were strong, so my contract was extended through the end of November. Every night, audience members came up to me after the show and told me it would only be a matter of time before a casino on the Strip wanted my show. They asked me to notify them when I eventually moved my show to the Strip, so I started to collect email addresses from anyone who wanted me to let them know when I made the move.

Since I had not returned to New York for a month, I asked Kim to bring the kids to Las Vegas for Thanksgiving.

Soon after Kim and the kids visited, her father and grandfather decided they were selling their New York houses and moving to a retirement community in Florida.

Kim decided there was nothing left for her to stay in New York for, and she said she wanted to give our marriage another try. She fixed up the New York house and put it up for sale after the holidays.

Immediately after my show on January 24, 2006, I flew back to New York. I helped Kim pack the last of our belongings into a portable moving pod, which was then hauled by truck to Las Vegas. The morning of January 27, 2006, I drove Kim and the kids to the airport and put them on a plane. They landed in Las Vegas in time for lunch that day.

After I dropped my family off at the airport, Steve and I loaded the family dog and Kim's huge pot-bellied pig into the van and started driving cross-country for the second time. The van was also packed with all the delicate items we did not want to pack in the moving pod.

Kim knew I was not a big fan of her pet pig. She thought I wouldn't feed the pig on the road trip, so she decided to overfeed her before we set out. Less than twenty minutes into our cross-country drive, the pig puked all over Kim's van. The smell was wretched! We pulled over and purchased a case of paper towels to try to clean up the puke. No matter how hard we tried, the smell would not dissipate. Pulling over to a carwash to have the carpet shampooed was not an option since the van was packed solid with household belongings and stuffed boxes.

Two hours into the drive the pig vomited again, and again a few hours later. Basically, the pig puked in each of the first three states we drove through: New York, New Jersey and Pennsylvania. Before we drove the first five hours of the three-day trip, we used an entire case of paper towels cleaning up after the pig. When Kim and the kids landed in Las Vegas and made it to the house safely, she called to check in with us. She could not stop laughing when I told her the story.

We arrived in Las Vegas on Sunday in time for dinner, and Kim and the kids came out to meet us when we pulled up. Immediately, she slid open the van door to greet her pig. When the foul stench of vomit hit her nose, she backed away from the van and covered her mouth like she, too, wanted to vomit from the horrible smell.

I stepped out of the van, looked at her, and said, "Good to see you too Kim." I told her since I had to drive for two days with that horrific odor, she was going to be the one to clean it all up. After saying hello to the kids, I took a long, well-deserved shower.

Soon after making the cross-country drive, I did an interview for a local magazine that was going to publish a feature story about my show at the Rampart Casino. They also scheduled a photo shoot for me at a local photographer's studio. Immediately afterward, the photographer was scheduled to do a photo shoot for the brand new Hooters Hotel and Casino, which was opening soon where the old San Remo Hotel once stood.

The photographer was going to take some promo shots of Michelle Nunes, the newly crowned "Miss Hooters International." She and her entourage arrived just before my photo shoot ended, so Michelle and I took a few shots of me goofing around with her crown. Kim was furious when she saw the photos.

I always have loved eating at the Hooters Restaurant when I lived in New York, and the opening of the new Las Vegas casino seemed to be creating a lot of buzz. I asked the Hooters Hotel and Casino promotions director, who happened to be at the photo shoot, what the new casino planned to do for entertainment. I thought she could help put me in contact with the entertainment director if they didn't yet have a show planned. But she informed me that the Hooters girls were the entertainment for the property—they would be the poker dealers, restaurant servers, and casino bartenders—and management did not feel any other entertainment was needed.

I realized what a big mistake the Hooters management was making. I told my photographer that a Hooters restaurant in a small town outside of Las Vegas was fun to eat at because of the sexy girls in tight orange shorts and low cut tops. But in Las Vegas, every casino had sexy girls working as dealers and cocktail servers. What the Hooters management thought would be their main draw was available in almost every other property in town. I winked and told the photographer I would eventually be working at the Hooters Hotel and Casino.

Needless to say, after the initial fanfare of the Hooters Casino grand opening died down, they quickly realized they needed something other than sexy girls to attract customers to the property. While I was keeping track of the Hooters Hotel and Casino's fading success, I continued to work at the Rampart Casino. My three-week contract kept getting extended due to popular demand. I performed there for forty-six sold-out weeks.

Chapter 47

The Stardust Time Bomb

I jumped at the opportunity to move my show from the Rampart Casino to the Las Vegas Strip when an offer from the Stardust Hotel and Casino was presented to me. The entertainment director at the Rampart Casino was very happy for me when I told him I was moving my show to the Strip. He thought I would have received an offer to perform at a Strip property much sooner than I did.

I performed 162 shows at the Rampart Casino, with my last performance on May 31, 2006. My success at the Rampart indicated to me that my show was a perfect fit for Las Vegas audiences, and I should have a long, successful career in this town. I sent an email to all the people on my list and announced my big move. I received hundreds of emails in return from the locals who were very loving and supportive of my move.

In 1991, I set a goal for myself to become a Vegas headliner performing on the world famous Las Vegas Strip, and on June 1, 2006, that goal was accomplished. I was now a Las Vegas Strip headliner performing in the Stardust Hotel and Casino, proving that with persistence and hard work, dreams and goals can come true.

When I was given the opportunity to headline at the Stardust, the entertainment director, Terry Jenkins, informed me the casino was eventually going to close down. He said Boyd Gaming, the company that owned the Stardust, was going to implode the casino and build a huge complex named the Echelon that would contain a casino, hotel, shopping mall, and condos. Terry couldn't tell me when the doors of the casino would eventually close for good. He just wanted me to be aware that my employment at the Stardust could be as short as a week or as long as a year. Terry is one of the nicest guys in Las Vegas, and I admired his honesty and candor.

When I took the job at the Stardust, I was scheduled to perform nightly at 5:00 p.m. in the Hypnotic Lounge. It was a small, intimate showroom with two hundred seats. The problem was that time slot was really bad and would have been almost certain death for most shows. But I thought taking the gig would get my foot in the door at the casino, and I'd figure out a way to make things happen after I was situated.

When I opened my show on June 1, 2006, my assumptions were correct: the Hypnotic Lounge showroom was like a ghost town. The audiences were small, mainly because of the show time. Everyone in Las Vegas was having dinner at that hour. A hypnosis show that always seemed to have great crowds followed my show. The first thing I needed to do was to get the media to see my show and write about it. Since I was a kid, I always wanted to own a Corvette like the one Bill Bixby drove on the television show *The Magician*. I purchased a 1973 Corvette Stingray and wrote it into the show's introduction.

When the audience entered the showroom, the projection screen explained that I was not in the building, and I did not know who was in the audience until I stepped out onto the stage. When the show began, the projection screen cut to a live shot of the Stardust parking lot, and the audience could see me drive up in the car and enter the showroom. Unfortunately, the Corvette was old and broke down often, so I sold it soon after my media night. But I promised myself that I would eventually purchase another one.

That summer, my daughter, Jennifer, and my son, Scott, came out to Las Vegas to spend some of the summer with us. Scott fell in love with the city and asked if he could live in Las Vegas with us. His mother, Kathy, was very upset with his decision, but eventually supported his wishes. Jennifer returned to New York when the summer was over and Scott stayed. I enrolled him in school and also gave Scott a job as my stage manager. Every night we drove to work together and enjoyed some quality father and son bonding time.

A few weeks after I opened my show, the general manager's wife came to see my show. She loved it and asked her husband Tony, if she could use one of the hotel suites to have a girls' party for her friends. She then asked if I could stop by the suite and put on a private show for her and her girlfriends, and I agreed.

No matter how small the Stardust audience was, I never canceled my show. A few weeks after the show opened, I caught the lucky break I was hoping for. There was a show in the main showroom called *Headlights and Tailpipes*, which was a topless dance show in which the girls danced on and around fancy automobiles. I heard that the show suddenly decided to close down, and that meant their 9:00 p.m. time slot was immediately available.

I contacted Tony and asked if Kim and I could take him and his wife out to dinner. A few nights later, we met at Hank's Steakhouse in the Green Valley Ranch Casino. If there was any time I was going to use all of my persuasive mental skills to work to my advantage, this would be it. I told Tony that I loved the Stardust Casino and I would love to continue performing my show on his property, but the showroom rent and advertising expenses were killing me. I asked if he had another show coming into the main showroom to replace the topless review. He said he was receiving a lot of inquiries, but he did not promise the time slot to anyone yet.

During dinner we continued to chat, and I used my mental persuasion skills on Tony. By the time the dinner was over, he offered me the time slot in the main showroom. He also told me I did not have to pay any rent for the time slot, and he would give me four billboards around the town to advertise my show.

Soon after Tony promised the main showroom time slot to me, Richard Keeley, the producer of the hypnosis show that shared the small showroom with me, contacted him and asked to move his show to the main showroom. Richard was pissed at me when he found out I beat him to the punch.

I only performed forty-seven shows in the Hypnotic Lounge before moving to the Stardust's main showroom on July 20, 2006. Every night I stood on the very stage that magicians Siegfried and Roy stood on at the start of their Las Vegas careers. I was performing in the very same showroom where I saw Wayne Newton perform his show nine years earlier. It was the showroom I swore to my agent, Craig, that I would be headlining in some day.

One night after my show, I was doing a meet and greet outside the showroom. A Las Vegas showgirl named Marie Claire, who was a big fan of my show, came up to talk to me. When we were done talking, she planted a huge kiss directly on my lips. When the showgirl walked away, I noticed that Kim had unexpectedly shown up at the casino and had witnessed the inappropriate kiss. By the look on her face, I knew Kim was thinking her moving to Las Vegas to start over was a mistake.

I performed seventy-six shows in the main showroom before the Stardust closed its doors for good. My final performance there was on October 24, 2006.

360

Chapter 48

Show Tickets 4 Locals

On October 24, 2006, I walked out onto the Stardust's main showroom stage for the very last time. They were locking their doors for good and preparing the building to be imploded. I decided I wanted to take some time off from performing my show in Las Vegas since I was performing there seven days a week, and never did have any type of vacation.

Part of my success in Las Vegas was due to the locals. They helped make my dreams and goals come true. During my self-imposed hiatus, I wanted to find a way to give back to the community.

A few days after I closed my Stardust show, I was visiting my friend Anthony Cools, a hypnotist who was also a Las Vegas headliner. While we were relaxing in his backyard, as I watched him puff on his stinky cigar, he received an unexpected call from Mike Weatherford, the entertainment reporter from the *Las Vegas Review Journal*. Mike said he was bringing a photographer to Anthony's show later that night and was going to review the show for the local newspaper.

Anthony was very happy about the news until he called his box office and learned his ticket sales were a little slow that night. He frantically started texting everyone in his address book and offered them comp tickets to that night's show. He knew a packed house would ensure he gave a better performance, and he really wanted to put on a great show while Mike was in attendance.

I volunteered to send an email to all the names on my email list of locals, offering free comps to his show to help him pad the room. The locals on my mailing list responded enthusiastically, despite the fact that it was a last minute ticket offer. Later that night, Anthony's show was packed and Mike Weatherford gave him a good review.

Gerry and Hypnotist Anthony Cools

The next day, I received emails from people on my email list who attended Anthony's show. They thanked me for the opportunity to see my friend perform, and some asked me to let them know if I ever had any other friends offering comp tickets at the last minute. I was looking for a way to give back to the locals, and at that moment the concept for my comp ticket website was born.

I thought it would be beneficial to all parties involved if I could start a website offering the locals last minute comp show tickets. First I would collect a list of local email addresses for people who had the ability to see a show on short notice. Second, I would offer access to the list to any performer who needed a packed audience. The locals would get to see free shows, and the performer would be guaranteed a full showroom if they needed one. It was a win-win for everyone.

At first I thought the concept would only be used by shows needing to fill empty seats on slow nights. Then I started learning other reasons that even the most successful shows could use such a website.

For example, shows like the *Danny Gans Show* were required to put aside a certain number of tickets every night for the casino to purchase. The pit bosses gave them to the high rollers and the casino hosts gave them to the VIPs. If the casino used them, they would compensate the show's producer for the tickets. If the casino did not purchase them by a certain time of day, small blocks of tickets were released back to the show's producer so the casino would not have to pay for them. If the producer couldn't sell the tickets to the public on such short notice, they would be offered as comps to friends, family, or casino employees. I figured my website could assist show producers with filling the empty comps on short notice.

I was a full-time dad and a Las Vegas performer who did not have much time to operate an Internet website, so my son, Scott, and I had the challenge of designing a website that was at least 80 percent automated. I started to research website developers who could build my new vision from the ground up and have the website operate exactly how I wanted it.

After interviewing many website development companies, I selected a company called WebSlingers out of Texas. The company was owned by Rick, the older brother of my ex-magic partner Floyd, from Fort Totten, New York. Rick informed me the website concept I designed would take months, and thousands of dollars to write the code. I decided to break the new website down into phases and roll it out a little at a time. I added Google ads to the web pages to generate the revenue needed to cover design and operating costs.

Word began to spread like wildfire, and the email list of locals grew rapidly. A year after I started the website, my membership list for *ShowTickets4Locals* grew to over ten thousand! I started by offering one show a week. It quickly became so popular with show producers that it grew to at least one show a day.

The best part of operating this website are the members who post nice comments on Facebook or bring me little gifts to my showroom. They are excited because they have lived in Las Vegas for years, many on a fixed income, and could never afford to attend a show. But now with my website, they can now start to have date nights and see shows again.

From the day I created the website to present time, over 100,000 locals have joined the site and have enjoyed the tens of thousands of complimentary show tickets I have distributed to them. I have given the locals over $1 million worth of free show tickets! I do not draw a salary from the website; the contribution of my personal time is merely a labor of love. It certainly has been an interesting journey for me. It feels very rewarding giving back to the community that I now call my home.

Chapter 49

Barry Manilow

While I was performing at the Stardust Casino, I had the pleasure of meeting Ian, who was the bass guitar player in the *Barry Manilow Show* playing at the Las Vegas Hilton. He told me quite a few of Barry's cast and crew members had attended my show, and they were amazed with my performance. He was curious and had to check out my show. Afterward, we chatted a bit and he invited me to see come see his show.

I was working seven days a week at the Stardust and didn't have any time to take Ian up on his offer. But when the Stardust closed, and I spent my days working on my website, I had plenty of time available at night to attend shows.

On Friday, February 23, 2007, I attended the *Barry Manilow Show*. I found myself singing most of the songs along with Barry because I was a big Barry Manilow fan when I was a kid. Finally getting to see him live was an awesome experience. After the show, Ian took me back stage to Barry's green room.

Barry always had a meet and greet after his Hilton show for the high rollers and anyone who shelled out the cash to purchase a VIP meet and greet ticket. Afterward, Ian introduced me to Barry. He seemed very happy to meet me and knew exactly who I was.

Barry told me he did not get a chance to see me perform at the *Stardust*, but heard a lot of good things about my show from many of his staff members. A member of his staff gave him a copy of my DVD to watch on his flight home one night. Barry lives in California and took a short flight home every night to be home with his dogs. The only nights he'd stay at the Hilton were Fridays.

Since he didn't have a chance to see me, I said I'd gladly bring my show to him. He was thrilled at my offer, and asked me if I could perform for him and his cast and crew in a few weeks at his second anniversary celebration at the Hilton. Barry wanted to do something special for his group for their loyalty, and I gladly accepted his invitation to perform for this special occasion. Ian would give me the details when the party night was finalized.

Barry excused himself so he could change out of his show clothes, and invited me to attend his "Frank Friday" party. Seems every Friday, since Barry slept at the Hilton, Barry and his musicians and backup singers met in the Hilton bar outside his showroom. The bar manager bar roped off the back area to give Barry and his group privacy. Barry would have one cigarette and one cocktail a week, only on Fridays. He explained it was a routine Frank Sinatra also use to do.

Ian took me upstairs to the roped off area of the bar, and soon after we got comfortable, Barry arrived. We all sat around and chatted like old friends. They were asking me questions about my show and begged me to perform something for them. If Barry Manilow was asking me to perform, you bet I was going to grant his request! I performed two or three mentalism effects for the group and they were all amazed at what I did. We stayed around for a few hours and enjoyed the evening.

A few weeks later, I attended Barry's performance for a second time. After the show, the musicians and crew gathered in a large backstage room for a bite to eat. Barry always made sure there was plenty of food available for his crew after the show. While everyone was eating, I set up my props in the corner of the room. After Barry finished his formal meet and greet, he joined us and I began my performance. The intimate group of twenty-five people sat on couches and on the floor in a semi-circle around me.

There I was, entertaining the man who entertained me for years. I enjoyed his performances on television, and now the living legend was enjoying one of my performances. The entire evening was very surreal for me.

Barry was so impressed with my performance, in December of 2009 he asked me to be his opening act on his holiday theater tour. We had multiple performances in California and Chicago. Some theaters held 1,700 people and others held up to 3,000. The tour was completely sold out. I took my son, Scott, and my assistant, Danica, on the tour with me as my onstage assistants.

After my performance each night, I'd walk off stage and Barry would be standing in the wings with a big smile on his face. He watched my performance on a television monitor and listened to the audience reaction to my routines. He liked to tell me how great I did after each performance.

Back on April 5, 2009, realizing my marriage had been over for a while, I decided to move out of my marital residence and into the small two-bedroom condo I had purchased for Steve. When the kids came to visit me, they had to sleep in sleeping bags on the floor. Christmas 2009 was my first Christmas without my family, and it was difficult for me. But listening to Barry sing his holiday songs every night, and watching him make it snow in the theater, was just the boost of Christmas spirit I needed to help me make it through the holidays. I took the money I made from the tour and purchased a 3,100 square foot, five-bedroom house so the kids and Steve would have their own bedrooms.

In January 2011, Barry asked me again to be his opening act, but this time it was on his Florida arena tour. We performed in many different arenas including the St. Petersburg Times Forum in Tampa, the Jacksonville Veterans Memorial Arena in Jacksonville, the Amway Center in Orlando, and the Sunrise Florida at Bank Atlantic Center.

Each night I walked out on stage to the applause of over ten thousand Barry Manilow fans, or "Fan-alows" as they called themselves. They were the largest audiences I had ever performed for, yet I was not a bit nervous when I walked out on to the stage. Every single time I set foot on the stage, the energy from the large crowds caused the biggest unexplainable surge of electricity to explode in my spinal cord. Again, I took Scott and Danica on the tour with me as my onstage assistants.

Watching how the roadies unpacked all the eighteen-wheeler tractor-trailer trucks and assembled the concert stage, sound equipment, and lights every night was amazing to me. It was an experience most people do not get a chance to be a part of, and it will remain a happy experience burned in my memory forever.

Chapter 50

Hooters Casino

While I was still building the *ShowTickets4Locals* website, I received a call from Kim, the Hooters Hotel and Casino food and beverage manager. He told me he'd heard about my ticket website and asked for details about using it to help with their failing comedy show. Comedian Bobby Slayton had been hired to perform two shows a night, five nights a week, and he was not selling any tickets at all. The casino desperately needed help putting butts in seats immediately.

I told him how my service worked and without hesitation, he asked me to start promoting Bobby's shows for all five nights a week. Then I asked what they had planned in the showroom on the two nights Bobby's show was dark. He said they invested too much money in Bobby's show and could not afford to bring on another show.

I told Kim, or K.T. as he liked to be called, that I recently had a successful show at the Stardust Casino before they closed down. I said I was looking for a new casino to perform at, and I would love to perform in the Hooters showroom when Bobby's show was dark. He repeated that they didn't have any money left in the entertainment budget to hire another performer. They were actually losing money every week with Bobby's show, but they were under contract and had to keep him there for a certain amount of time.

I asked if they were more concerned with generating money from show ticket sales or getting bodies into the casino, so they would gamble, eat, and drink while on the Hooters property. For years, the Hooters restaurants brand targeted men. Very few women were coming into the casino, and women made up seventy percent of Las Vegas slot machine players. K.T. said the casino wanted more women on the property, and hoped the Bobby Slayton comedy show would have accomplished that.

I made him an offer he could not refuse. "I have an idea how I could perform for you for free," I said, "and get bodies into your property." He was intrigued enough to grant me a meeting.

I did a little research and discovered the Hooters Hotel and Casino was a joint venture between the original owners of the Hooters restaurant chain and the owners of the old San Remo Hotel. A few days later I met with K.T., who was put there by the Hooters side of the partnership. Any time Hooters opened a new location, K.T. was on site supervising the construction of the new restaurant from start to finish. Gary, the COO for the Hooters Hotel and Casino, was also in the meeting. He'd been put there by the San Remo side of the partnership. Together, the two men ran the Hooters Hotel and Casino, but did not appear to always see eye-to-eye.

I started by telling them I would immediately offer Bobby Slayton comp tickets to the locals as they requested. When I asked what each body I sent to the show would be worth to them, they said they'd be willing to pay me five dollars for each person. Since I didn't charge for them to use my website, I said it wouldn't cost them a dime.

I explained that I wanted to perform in their showroom on Sunday and Monday when the Bobby Slayton show was dark, and I'd do it for free. If all they wanted was bodies in the casino, they could pay me five dollars for each person who attended my show. If no one showed up to see my show, it wouldn't cost them anything. They loved the idea, but admitted they never saw my show when it was at the Stardust Casino.

I offered to audition for them for free. "Give me your showroom, and I will fill it with audience members so you can see my show and how an audience reacts to my performance." They jumped at the chance and scheduled me for that Saturday afternoon, which was May 18, 2007.

Since my website membership of Las Vegas locals was growing by leaps and bounds, filling the showroom for the audition was very easy. When I arrived at the showroom, Bobby Slayton greeted me and immediately started to bitch at me. "So you are the mental case who is looking to take my showroom away from me," he said.

"Not at all!" I explained I was only looking to perform on his dark nights. My website took a great deal of my time, and I just wanted to keep my act fresh in my mind since I hadn't performed it in a few months. He barked at me a little more as he walked away to go sit in the audience with Gary and K.T.

Right after my audition performance ended for the packed showroom, Gary and K.T. made me an offer: I could perform my show on Monday and Tuesday at 8:00 p.m. when Bobby's show was dark, but they also wanted me to perform on Saturday and Sunday at 6:00 before Bobby's show. I graciously accepted.

Hooters Hotel and Casino needed time to promote my show. They asked if I could start performing on Sunday, June 10, 2007. I told them I could start on that day, but I'd need time off in two months for a family cruise I had already planned. They had no problem with my time off vacation request. While I was waiting those few weeks before my show opened, I gladly filled the empty Bobby Slayton seats for the casino.

When I told Kim that I had accepted a job at Hooters Hotel and Casino, she was furious. She hated when I occasionally ate at the Hooters Restaurant in New York. Kim has a major self-esteem problem, and she viewed any female with a bigger chest than hers as a threat. Now I was going to be working on a regular basis with the sexy Hooters girls, who were known for having big chests. At this point, I was so over being married to her that I didn't care what she thought about my new job.

On June 10, 2007, I showed up to perform my very first show at Hooters Hotel and Casino. My audio engineer, Jim, greeted me and we did a full sound and lighting rehearsal before the show.

My first performance was on a Sunday night. The showroom audience was filled to 70 percent capacity, as was my next show on Monday night. My third performance on Friday at 5:00 p.m. was a little light, around half full, but I knew it was because of the time slot. I'd learned from performing at the Stardust, that a 5:00 show time is a tough sell.

Immediately after my show ended on Friday, the audience for the Bobby Slayton show started to enter the showroom. While I was reviewing my show notes with my soundman, Jim, Bobby interrupted our conversation to point out that he had a bigger audience than me. He said he was at 80 percent capacity, and this is how it was every single night at his show. He gloated that I should learn from the master how to fill a showroom.

"Did you know the casino is using a seat filling company to fill your show with audience members who did not pay?" I politely asked. "My entire audience paid to see my show."

"You're lying," he shot back. "I've never heard of such a company. Everyone here is a fully paid customer."

"Actually, I'm pretty sure most of the audience members were complimentary ticket holders, because I'm the one who owns the company that distributed all of the comp tickets."

When I asked Bobby where he was staying, he said he stayed at the casino when he was performing and flew back to his home in California when his show was dark.

"Once or twice a week, I pay a visit to the ticket brokers and concierges to promote my show and boost ticket sales," I said. "I bring them donuts and DVDs of my NBC TV special. If you want to join me sometime, I'll gladly pick you up. We can go together, representing the Hooters Hotel and Casino showroom as a team."

He looked at me, laughed, and again insisted his audience was all paid customers. "I refuse to go to the brokers and shake hands and kiss little babies like some cheap politician," he said.

I quickly realized he was totally clueless how shows in Las Vegas operated, and I didn't want to be the one to school him. I wished him a good show that night and left the showroom.

For the next few weeks, Bobby kept showing up after my Friday show to point out that his crowds were always bigger than mine. I quickly figured out he was a lonely, miserable old man. My soundman Jim said Bobby was usually high on cocaine, though I never witnessed him doing it. Jim told me to ignore his childish ranting.

Just before I took time off to go on my family cruise, I decided I had enough of Bobby's attempt at playing childish head games with me. I felt I was more than kind to the aging comedian, and it was time he felt the wrath of my mental games. It was time I showed him who the mastermind manipulator really was at Hooters Hotel and Casino.

Right before I left town, I changed the Hooters Casino password that the box office manager used to log into the *ShowTickets4Locals* website. That meant they were not able to log in and offer comp tickets to the locals. For the entire length of my cruise, Bobby Slayton's show had no audience. His show died a fast death while I was relaxing at sea.

Bobby was waiting for me at the showroom the night of my first performance after my vacation.

"What the hell did you do to my audience?" he snapped.

"I don't know what you're talking about," I replied.

He proceeded to tell me that he had fewer than twenty people a night in his audience, and it was because the box office manager could not log into my ticketing website.

I had to use all my acting skills to put on a confused look and pretend like I didn't know a thing about the situation. "I thought you knew nothing about the casino using a seat filling service for your show. Now you're an expert?"

He told me to fix the problem immediately, and as he walked away he told me to "go f***" myself.

I changed the password back, apologized to the box office manager, and told him I had no clue what went wrong with the website. I thought knocking Bobby down a peg or two would stop his childish shenanigans, but unfortunately it did not.

After each and every show, I loved to greet my audience and take photos with them. As they left the showroom, I shook their hands and thanked them for coming to my show. Bobby didn't like that. He felt they should leave the showroom quicker so his audience could be seated faster and have the opportunity to drink more. Apparently the more they drank before his show, the funnier he seemed.

On Fridays, Bobby started to approach my audience as they waited to take a photo with me and rudely rush them out of the showroom. He'd walk over to the soundboard and kill the music that played while the audience walked out of the showroom. If my show ran two or three minutes late, he complained to the showroom manager and to the big boss Gary. No matter what I did, he was a miserable old grouch who was threatened by my presence. I really tried to be his friend, and to bond with him over work-related issues. But no matter how hard I tried, he retaliated by trying to intimidate me to quit, and trying in every way possible to get the boss to fire me.

Chapter 51

Phenomenon

The Successor, also known as *The Next Uri Geller,* was a live TV show starring Uri Geller, in which contestants performed acts of mentalism, illusion, escapism, and other feats in an attempt to win over the panel of judges, Uri Geller himself, the studio audience, and telephone voters at home. It was like an *American Idol* for mentalists and magicians.

The show, which Uri created, premiered in Israel in early 2007. In the summer of 2007, while I was still headlining at Hooters Hotel and Casino, the show's Los Angeles casting director called to tell me the producers were bringing the show to the United States.

The show was a smash hit in Uri's home country of Israel, so Uri and the production company were going to try to recreate that success in the United States. Unfortunately, his popularity in the United States had faded, especially after Uri's appearance on *The Tonight Show* with Johnny Carson. Since Johnny was an amateur magician, he knew Uri's tricks and was able to foil all of Uri's attempts to demonstrate he had real psychic abilities. James Randi also wrote a few exposure books about Uri's tricks. Uri's career could not take the exposure, and his popularity in the states faded fast.

NBC purchased the rights to the show in the United States but realized Uri did not have enough star power to carry the show. They needed another magician, along with Uri, to act as a judge for the competition. I had heard David Copperfield turned down the offer, so the network offered it to Criss Angel. They also decided to change the name of the show to *Phenomenon*. British TV presenter Tim Vincent was brought on as the host.

The casting director asked if I wanted to appear as a contestant on the show, but I said I didn't want to perform on any show that had Criss Angel as a judge. Criss had quickly risen to fame with his successful cable television series *Mindfreak*, but I didn't feel he was enough of an authority on mentalism to give advice or critique other mentalists.

I also wasn't interested in appearing on any show that had magicians competing against mentalists. I explained to the casting director that putting mentalists up against magicians was a bad idea. They were two completely different forms of magic, and it was like comparing apples to oranges.

Since I turned down the offer to appear on the show, the casting director asked if I could suggest any other mentalist or magicians who would be interested. They specifically were looking for female performers. I told them I would get back to them if anyone came to mind. When I eventually called them back, they had already found a female magician for the show.

A few weeks later, the casting director called again. The producers decided they were not going to cast magicians. The show would be exclusively based on mentalism, and the winner would receive a $250,000 cash prize and a TV show of their own. Now I was interested and could look past the fact that Criss Angel would be a judge on the show.

I wanted to know if there would be a neutral mentalist to oversee the competition. I explained that some mentalists do something known as pre-show work to secretly gather information from the audience before the performance. Unless they had guidelines in place, and a mentalist who was not competing on the show to supervise the pre-show information collection, the competition wouldn't be fair. When she asked if I knew anyone who would be good for that job, I suggested Ross Johnson, Eugene Burger, or Banachek.

Several weeks after that, the casting director said they hired Banachek as a liaison between the producers and the performers. He would oversee the mentalists' routines and keep the pre-show work in check. But when she asked if I would now commit to the project, I said I was no longer interested in performing on the show because they hired Banachek.

She was completely baffled by my response. "First you tell us to hire the guy, then when we do, you still refuse to be on the show. What's the problem now?"

"Since I already had my own NBC prime time television special, it would look like a fix if NBC hosted a reality talent show for mentalists, and the mentalist who had a special on the same network won the competition," I explained. Also since Banachek and I were partners in the past, and now he is on the staff as a creative consultant, that would also look like a fix if I won the competition.

She agreed with my line of thinking and ended the conversation.

A week or so later, the casting director called again. A production crew was coming to Las Vegas to hold auditions at the Luxor Casino. Because my television special aired more than three years ago, the producers decided it would not be a conflict if I competed on the show and she asked me to audition. I told her that the producers could come to my Las Vegas show, or they could watch my NBC television special. My days of auditioning were far behind me.

The day before the Luxor auditions were scheduled to begin, I received yet another call from the casting director requesting two comp tickets to my show. After my performance, I sat with the producers.

"How's casting going?" I asked.

"I swear, if we see another magician bend a spoon, we're going to shoot ourselves!" one replied. "We've just been inundated with audition videotapes, but every one is the same."

The other producer congratulated me on the performance I just gave. "You're exactly what the show needs. You're funny, likable, entertaining first, and amazing second."

That made my day, because little did they know, that was the ultimate compliment anyone could ever give to me. After my friend Roy from The Legendary Thirteen told me I needed to be more likable many years ago, it was always something I tried to work on.

The producers said they had some good talent booked for the show, and each person was being cast in a specific role: A Middle American blue collar worker. A contestant who lost the Israel version of the show. A female magician. A person who could talk to the dead. A bad-ass karate performer. A young, cocky magician who still had a lot to learn. And since Uri Geller was the judge, they had a few Israeli mentalists to make him happy. They wanted me to be the "seasoned performer" on the show—a guy who had his own Las Vegas show, and who could possibly assist the younger generation of upcoming mentalists.

Now I was intrigued. "The only way I will consider the offer is if I can mention that I perform in Las Vegas nightly every time I appeared on the show," I said.

"We can do that. But we'd still like you to come to the Luxor Casino to perform a few routines on video and tape a short interview."

"I'll stop by for the interview, but I'm not performing," I replied. "That's too much like an audition, and I don't do auditions anymore."

The next day I met them in a private room at the Luxor and recorded a short interview. Then they asked me to perform a few routines on camera. I reiterated that I would entertain them if they shut off the camera, but I refused to audition. They laughed, thanked me for stopping by, and mentioned they also had auditions in other cities around the country.

A few weeks after my interview, I received a call informing me that I was one of the few selected by the production company and the network for the final round of auditions. All of the finalists would be flown to Los Angeles and spend a few days in a hotel while the final interviews were taking place.

I reminded the caller that I performed my Las Vegas show every night, and closing the show to spend a few days waiting for an interview was not going to happen. I said I would fly into Los Angeles and they could have two hours of my time before I returned to Las Vegas. I wanted to be interviewed as soon as I arrived at the hotel, and then I wanted to immediately leave. They eventually agreed to my terms.

When I arrived at the hotel in Los Angeles, it looked like a mentalist convention with performers all over the place. The person in charge told me I would get to talk to the producers as soon as the mentalist currently being interviewed was finished. While I waited, a few of the other guys in the waiting room asked for my autograph and wanted me to pose for photos with them.

In the interview room, the three executive producers were seated behind a long table. The casting director was also there, as was Banachek. They questioned me for a while and then asked if I would perform something for them, so I performed my phone book prediction routine. They thanked me for making time in my busy schedule to come to Los Angeles and indicated the interview was over.

But we weren't done just yet. Now it was *my* turn to interview *them*.

"I've heard a rumor that the network is going to have an online discussion group so viewers can voice their opinions and discuss how they think we're performing the tricks," I said. "I don't want any part of a show that encourages the exposure of my craft." They assured me that no such online forum was going to happen.

I also asked them what part they thought Banachek was going to play in the show. Would he be present when the performers would pre-show the celebrity guests? Would we have a set of rules in place that each performer needed to follow? They assured me the suggestions I made previously were being taken very seriously, and every effort would be taken to keep the pre-show down to a minimum, with guidelines each performer would have to follow.

The producers wanted all performers to spend two months in Los Angeles rehearsing and performing while the show was airing. I told them I would not be able to spend the entire time in L.A. during the taping, but I could give them three days a week. Then I wanted to drive back to Las Vegas to be with my family and perform in my show, which I did not want to close completely for two months. I also needed to know immediately if they wanted me for the television show, because I had to make arrangements to close my Vegas show on those dates.

They again thanked me for making the trip and told me I would hear from them very soon. A few days later, the casting director called to tell me I would be on the show, but I needed to keep it a secret since they hadn't yet selected the other contestants. They just wanted to give me the advance notice I requested to arrange for time off from the casino. At that point, I committed to the project. I was excited to help bring mentalism to television, and I was also excited to possibly patch things up with Banachek.

The first episode was scheduled to air live on Wednesday, October 24, 2007, but the casting director wasn't able to tell me how many weeks the show would last. If the ratings were good, NBC would add additional weeks onto the series. The entire cast had to be in Los Angeles on October 1st to start rehearsals. Since it was going to be a live show, they wanted everything tight and perfect. There is no room for screw-ups when you go live.

A week before I had to report to the set, a camera crew showed up at my house to interview me and get some of my backstory. They also interviewed my wife and children. That night they attended my Hooters Hotel and Casino show to tape the performance. Afterward, they taped B-roll footage of me walking up and down on the Las Vegas Strip.

The First Phenomenon Cast

When I checked into the hotel in Los Angeles, I met some of the other performers in the hotel lobby. We introduced ourselves to each other and chatted a bit before going to our rooms. The producers hosted a cast dinner that night so everyone had the chance to meet one another. The cast of the show was Jan Bardi, Jason Scott, Ehud Segev, Angela Funovits, Jim Karol, Guy

Bavli, Wayne Hoffman, Jim Callahan, Eran Raven, and Gerry McCambridge.

From the very first day, almost all of the cast members bonded and became close friends. We were not allowed to rehearse on the set together since it was a competition show, but when we were in our hotel rooms at night, we'd help each other with the routines we were going to perform.

Angela, Jim Karol, and I had a special bond. Jim and I were like Angela's two surrogate fathers who watched over her the entire time we were in L.A. We were together most of the time; where you would find one of us, you would most likely find the other two close by. Every night, the three of us would go out to eat dinner together at the Saddle Ranch. Many nights other cast members would join us.

The only performer who did not interact with the group was Jason Scott, a young man who also lived in Las Vegas. He performed walk-around magic and mentalism in The Foundation Room, an exclusive members only club located at the top of the Mandalay Bay Hotel. He also performed at many private celebrity parties. Jason and I shared a dressing room and we were both from Las Vegas, so we bonded a little, but he remained distant. He always had his headphones on listening to music, tuning the rest of us out.

About two weeks before our first episode was scheduled to air, Jan Bardi had a death in his family and he had to return to Belgium for the wake. When he tried to return to the United States, he discovered his paperwork had expired. The show producers did not know if Jan would be able to get his visa straightened out in time to return for the first episode. The producers contacted magician Mike Super and asked him to report to the set and be on standby just in case Jan couldn't make it back in time.

The cast welcomed Mike and we quickly made him feel like part of the group. Four days before the first show was set to air, we were notified that Jan had his papers in order and he was on the plane heading back to the United States. We were all glad Jan was able to get things straightened out in time, but at the same time, we were sad to say goodbye to Mike. Before the cast went out for our Sunday night dinner, we said our goodbyes to Mike in the hotel. As we exited the elevator in the hotel lobby, the three executive producers were getting on. We assumed they were going to say goodbye to Mike as well.

The next morning, we all met in the hotel lobby as we did every Monday morning, and waited for the studio to send over our transportation. Mike was there waiting with us, so we asked him what happened but he said he couldn't tell us. At the studio, the executive producers told us that Mike was back in the show because they released Jason Scott. They didn't feel he was producing what his agent promised and said he was not growing as a performer.

Jason never said goodbye to the rest of the cast; he just quietly checked out of the hotel and returned home to Las Vegas. I think he was embarrassed to be fired from the show; quite a few of his family members were flying into Los Angeles to watch him perform on the broadcast. Even though we both lived in Las Vegas, I never heard from Jason again. A year later, on July 15, 2008, sadly Jason was found dead in his home. The Clark County coroner's office ruled it "alcohol and OxyContin intoxication." He had about ten beers and two prescribed pain pills.

I met Eran Raven's girlfriend in the elevator without realizing who she was associated with. She introduced herself to me and we chatted a bit. She was living with Eran in the hotel room because he had a back injury just before we were required to report to Los Angeles. Eran couldn't walk without a cane, and he was very unstable on his feet and in pain most of the time.

Eran and I also instantly bonded. When we were on the set for rehearsal or during the actual television show, I was usually walking next to him, supporting him and holding him up. When the show went live, I walked Eran out onto the set and physically held him up because we did not want the home viewers to see his cane. A second or two before we went live, I stepped away from Eran and he balanced himself. When the director yelled cut, I immediately grabbed him and walked him off the set. There was a cot for him to lie on backstage. Lying down took the pressure off his back and made it a little more bearable for him.

After the series ended, Eran's mother came to me and thanked me for taking such good care of her son. She said I treated him like he was my brother, and she appreciated the love and support I showed to him.

While rehearsing for the show, the producers hired actor and magician Bob Fitch to give the cast some acting and breathing lessons. Bob was the actor who played Rooster Hannigan in the Broadway show, *Annie*. (He was the one who made the switchblade knife disappear in the show.) I introduced myself to Bob and told him how I was a big *Annie* fan when he was in the show. We reminisced about the Broadway show, and he told me a lot of stories about the production, the cast, and how they eventually made it to Broadway.

Each week, *Phenomenon* had different celebrities in the audience for us to use in our routines, including Carmen Electra, supermodel Rachel Hunter, Actress Tia Carrere, Dayna Devon, Kim Kardashian, Ross Mathews from *The Tonight Show*, actress Raven-Symoné, Holly Madison, and Miss USA, Shandi Finnessey.

The first episode aired on October 24, 2007 with four of the ten cast members scheduled to perform while Criss Angel and

Uri Geller reviewed our performances. Uri was also scheduled to perform one of his psychic stunts each week on the show.

I performed my phone book routine on the first episode. It was the same routine I used to open my Las Vegas show for years, and I had performed it hundreds of times in the past. My performance was well rehearsed and thought out. The first television show was viewed by almost 8.5 million people, and NBC was very happy with our ratings.

However, Uri Geller's psychic stunt routine was extremely boring and not at all clever. After the first episode, the network and the producers decided Uri would not perform on any future episodes.

All week long, while we were rehearsing our routines, Uri Geller quietly watched us from the back of the room. He was very supportive and complimentary of my rehearsals. But when we went live with the broadcast on October 24th, he threw me under the bus and told me the routine was boring and predictable. This review came from the man who just performed so badly that he was excluded from performing on his own series!

I was pissed at his criticism, but I was even more surprised by his remarks. When I went backstage, all the cast and crew told me my performance was great and they didn't know what got into him. I was sure his remarks would cause the home viewing audience not to vote for me, but his rudeness backfired because the home viewers didn't agree with him. I was voted through to the next round of the competition.

The next day, I was on the set saying goodbye to some of the crew because I was about to drive back to Las Vegas to perform for the next three nights at Hooters Hotel and Casino. We were talking about how big a jerk Uri was for talking to me like that on television.

Suddenly, Uri came bolting into the building through the large loading dock doors. He walked right up to me and stood in my face; he was actually uncomfortably close to me. The crew all looked worried because they didn't know what was about to happen. Uri reached out and grabbed my shoulders with both hands, looked directly into my eyes, and said he was sorry for being so hard on me last night. He apologized for his rude remarks, then waited in silence for me to offer him forgiveness.

It was my turn to speak, and no one had any idea what I was about to say. The tension was so thick you could have cut it with a knife.

I met his stare and said, "You can go f*** yourself! You trashed me in front of millions of people, and think an apology in front of three people will make up for it?" I pushed his hands off of my shoulders and walked away from the stunned, fallen superstar. I turned to the crew and said, "Maybe I will see you in a few days. Then again, since this is Uri's bullshit show, maybe you won't."

I strode out of the loading dock doors, got into my car, and headed back to Las Vegas. Immediately the producers started calling my cell phone, worried if I was going to return in three days for the show rehearsal. I refused to return their messages for the next two days.

Unfortunately, the series went downhill fast from there. The second week, only 5.9 million people watched. The third, fourth, and fifth weeks averaged 6 million viewers. Because of the low ratings, NBC did not extend the show, and the series was limited to only four weeks, including a double show on Halloween.

In the fourth episode, Guy Bavli and I were both eliminated but each of us had one last chance to impress the judges by performing a routine. In the end, the judges had to decide who to save and who to eliminate. After telling Uri to go f*** himself, I knew I was going to be the one eliminated.

Mike Super, the magician who was a last-minute stand-in for Jan Bardi, and later the replacement for Jason Scott, was eventually crowned the winner of the competition. The producers promised all of the mentalists that agreed to compete in the show that it would not be a magic show, yet an appearing motorcycle trick, disguised to look like a mentalist trick, won the competition.

As much as I fought it at the beginning, when the experience finally ended, I totally enjoyed myself. The people I met, the close friends I made, and the experience of making a live television show made it all worthwhile.

When I made my own TV special, it was taped and we had plenty of time to edit it so it was perfect. Making *Phenomenon*, a live television show, was a new experience for me, and I always love learning new things about my craft. I never would have thought of clearing everyone out of the studio an hour before we went live so that bomb-sniffing dogs could sweep the studio, or having each and every audience member pass through a metal detector looking for explosives. The producers explained a bomb going off during a live television broadcast was something the network always worried about.

The Second Phenomenon Cast

389

Chapter 52

The Presidential Rolex

"With great power comes great responsibility" is a line from one of my favorite movies, *Spiderman*. But unfortunately, every once in a while, I am tempted to use my mental ability for bad instead of good. When I returned from doing the television show *Phenomenon*, Bobby Slayton became even more annoying to me, and I realized he was not going to stop until one of us was fired. I knew it was either going to be him or me—and I was staying put. I had achieved my goals of having an Off Broadway show, my own NBC television special, and becoming a Las Vegas headliner. It was time I set a new master goal for myself: to get rid of Bobby Slayton.

I set a total of five mini-goals, each one aimed at taking one of Bobby's 7:00 p.m. time slots away from him. First the casino took away one of his 7:00 shows on his slowest night and offered it to me. Then a second night fell to me, and then a third, and within a few months of setting my goal, I had all five of his 7:00 p.m. time slots. He was now working one show a night, five nights a week.

I wanted to rub it in his face, so I came up with a media stunt to annoy him and mentally mess with him. My five-hundredth Las Vegas performance happened to be right around the same time Hooters Hotel and Casino offered me Bobby's last 7:00 time slot.

I had always wanted a Rolex watch, so I approached Gary, the COO, and told him I was going to buy myself a diamond studded Presidential Rolex watch. I wanted to invite all the media to an anniversary performance of my show on June 25, 2008. At the end of my performance, Gary would come on stage to announce that Hooters extended my show schedule to six nights a week, and then he would present the watch to me as if it was a gift from Hooters in honor of my five-hundredth performance and my contract extension. Gary agreed to the idea and it went according to plan.

COO Gary presenting Gerry with a Rolex watch

Besides giving me a sixth night a week, Hooters also decided to change my pay. Instead of being compensated for each body I brought into the showroom, they decided to put me on a weekly salary. The very next day, Bobby Slayton stormed his way into Gary's office and demanded a diamond Rolex watch. Gary told

Bobby it was a publicity stunt, and Hooters Hotel and Casino didn't pay for the watch.

Bobby then approached me and chuckled about knowing the story behind the publicity stunt. I pretended it was all legitimate, and that Gary was lying to him about who paid for the watch. Not knowing the truth about the watch sent Bobby into a tailspin, and he became even more miserable than ever.

I thought for sure that taking all of Bobby's 7:00 time slots would let him see I was just as valuable as he was on the property, but he still kept complaining to Gary about every little thing he could. His cocaine usage increased, and his performances became worse and worse. Every night, people got up and walked out in the middle of his show because he was so rude to the audience.

In August of 2008, I received a note from *CBS* employee Rick Hack from the *Entertainment and Business Development* department. On September 23, 2008, the network was airing a new television series called *The Mentalist* starring Simon Baker as Patrick Jane. The Jane character was a consultant with the California Bureau of Investigation assisting in a double murder investigation of a pro golfer's wife and her doctor who were killed in Palm Springs.

Rick explained that Simon Baker was an actor and knew nothing about performing mentalism or explaining it to other people. The network executives remembered me from my NBC television special, and they wanted to know if I could assist with promoting the pilot episode. They wanted a real mentalist to do the interviews and explain to the general public what a mentalist was. I asked him to send me a copy of the show so I could preview it and decide if I wanted to assist with the project. After watching the pilot episode, I thought it was very good and Simon was going to be a very likable mentalist. I agreed to help promote the show, knowing that if the show was a success, it would help the general public understand what my Las Vegas show was about. And since CBS decided to name their show after my television show, it would help with my brand recognition. On September 22, 2008, I flew to Los Angeles and checked into the Sofitel Luxury Hotel. The media campaign began the next day.

Between all the media attention I received from the Rolex stunt and the new CBS television series, I thought I'd finally proved my worth to Gary. But every time I approached him with marketing ideas to further promote my show, or suggestions to boost my ticket sales, he gave me the same response: "I'm sorry, but the answer is no, we will not consider it. If you feel you must find another venue, we understand and wish you luck." Soon after any of my suggestions were rejected, my idea would be executed to promote the Bobby Slayton show instead.

I expressed my frustration to my soundman, Jim Thayer, about having all my ideas shot down and given to Bobby Slayton. He decided to let me in on the truth. About a year earlier when Hooters was considering adding a show to the property, K.T. and Gary flew to Florida to watch Bobby Slayton perform in a local comedy club. Gary and Brook Dunn, Bobby's manager, were good friends, and they struck a deal to have Bobby headline at the Hooters Hotel and Casino. It was agreed that Bobby would pay Brook his agent's commission each week, and Bobby would also kick back cash under the table to Gary Greg.

K.T. eventually decided to leave his position as food and beverage manager at Hooters Hotel and Casino and open his own Hooters Restaurant on Rainbow Boulevard, located quite a ways off the Strip. After he quit, I asked K.T. if Jim's allegations were true, and he said that Bobby did, indeed, have Gary in his back pocket.

K.T. also explained to me that the Hooters Hotel and Casino board of directors had monthly meetings. The owners of the Hooters franchise flew up from Florida in their private jets for the mandatory meeting, and they listened as Gary described how the property was doing financially—the Hooters Restaurant, the casino, the hotel, and the showroom.

My show was always very profitable for the property, and Bobby's show was always in the red. But if Gary told the board that Bobby's show was losing money, they would close the show and Gary would lose his under-the-table kickbacks. So Gary mixed my profits with Bobby's losses to give the board the impression the showroom as a whole was profitable for the corporation.

K.T. told me that no matter what promotion idea I suggested to Gary, he would reject it and use it to help promote Bobby's failing show. The only reason he went along with the Rolex watch publicity stunt was because it would have never worked to promote Bobby's show.

Since K.T. was responsible for bringing me to Hooters Hotel and Casino, and Gary was responsible for bringing Bobby Slayton to the casino, there was always a silent competition between Gary and K.T. regarding the two shows. From the day I was hired, Gary always did more to promote Bobby's show before he did the same for mine.

The time came when Gary could no longer hide the financial losses from Bobby Slayton's show, so he did not renew the contract. Bobby left Hooters Hotel and Casino and moved his show next door to the Tropicana Hotel.

I continued to work for Hooters Hotel and Casino in the 7:00 p.m. time slot. Eventually Gary brought in a male strip show to fill the empty 9:00 p.m. time slot, hoping to lure young women to the property. They would arrive early and want to drink before the show, so Gary told me he wanted my seventy-five minute show to end at 8:05. That would give the staff time to clean up the showroom and allow the young women in to start drinking. He said if my show kept ending at 8:15, his staff wouldn't be able to turn the room over in time for the 9:00 male strip show.

Gary also informed me that he was considering changing my show start time to 6:30. I told him that I would be looking for another venue for my show if he made that schedule change. My threat fell on deaf ears, and on March 14, 2009, he switched my time slot to 6:30 p.m.

Around this time, David Saxe, one of the biggest show producers in Las Vegas, contacted me and asked me to headline in his new V Theater showroom located in the Miracle Mile Shops at the Planet Hollywood Hotel and Casino. I scheduled a meeting with David and on April 27, 2009, we struck a 2 year, million dollar deal. David said the contract would be typed up and ready for us to sign the very next day.

I went home and decided it was now time to play a mind game with Gary. On April 27, 2009 at 4:14 p.m., I sent Gary an email asked if he could change me back to a 7:00 p.m. time slot. I told him I was not comfortable in the 6:30 time slot, knowing full well his response would be the same as it always was. As predicted, five minutes later at 4:19, he responded by saying:

> I'm sorry, but the answer is no, we will not consider it. If you feel you must find another venue we understand and wish you luck.

Six minutes later at 4:25, I sent him an email that said:

> I understand your position. I would like to officially give you my two-week notice and close my show at your casino.

He took some time to think about my decision, and at 6:04 p.m. he responded:

Gerry, we appreciate having your show here and hope you will reconsider. I suggest that we take 24 hours to think about it and if you still want to pull out it would be a shame because we do like having you here.

The next day, David Saxe and I signed our contract. The emails between Gary and I went back and forth for two days. I told him that I was aware of his special financial arrangement with Bobby's manager, and how I disagreed with the way he operated his property. I also informed him I was not going to change my mind. I was leaving his casino. One of his final emails to me read:

If I did not appreciate the work you are doing, I would not beg you to stay.

Interesting how two days earlier he wished me luck in finding another venue, and now he was begging me to stay. I performed 487 shows at Hooters Hotel and Casino, with my final performance there on May 14, 2009. My first performance at Planet Hollywood Casino was the very next day, on May 15, 2009.

My master goal was to break Doug Henning's 1,920 performance record in *The Magic Show* on Broadway. When I closed my show at Hooters Hotel and Casino, I had performed my show 772 times in Las Vegas. On May 10, 2013, I officially broke Doug's record when I performed my 1,921st show in Las Vegas. But since my first show in Las Vegas was at the Rampart Casino, which was not on the Las Vegas Strip, I decided to set up another mini-goal for myself. I wanted to perform on the Las

Vegas Strip at least 1,921 times to break Doug Henning's Broadway record.

That happened on November 19, 2013, when I performed my 1,921st show on the Las Vegas Strip, headlining in my own show. And as of August 4, 2013, I performed my show 2,300 times in Las Vegas, making it the longest-running mentalist show in the history of Las Vegas.

Chapter 53

The Second Divorce

Many years ago, when I was working at Fotomat, I was introduced to the rock group Pink Floyd and *The Wall* album. The hit album was made into a full-length movie about a boy who lost his father at a young age and who was also abused by his schoolteacher. The boy went into the entertainment business and found out his wife was cheating on him while he was on the road. Each event that was happening in his life was like another brick in the wall being built around him, to protect him from the outside world. I felt I was able to relate to the album and the movie on many levels.

My friend at the time, Doug, told me *The Wall* concert was one of the best concerts he had ever attended. But since the band broke up, I never had a chance to see their theatrical event. Eventually Roger Waters would leave Pink Floyd, and after a long court battle, he was legally able to perform the concert without the rest of the band. On June 11, 2012, I attended Roger Waters' *The Wall* concert in Grand Rapids, Michigan, and I watched my life story unfold on the stage in front of me. It was such an emotional experience for me that I started to cry while watching the concert. It helped put my life into proper perspective.

Kim felt that "retaining information" was not considered a lie. The more I thought about Kim's lies and slow confessions about her affair, and the humiliation she put me through by having an affair with her boss, the more I realized I would never love her or trust her the way a man should love and trust his wife. I know I put her through a lot of humiliation as well, and I also knew our marriage was truly over and beyond repair.

After I returned home from the concert, Kim and I never slept in the same bed again. I decided I would never be able to get over what she did, and a divorce was inevitable. I knew how emotionally taxing the divorce process was, and before I sat down to write this book, I needed to get my personal life in order. We both knew it was truly over, but neither of us wanted to say the words out loud.

Soon after I met Kathy's lawyer during my first divorce, I knew I would be able to manipulate the entire divorce process. As it turned out, I controlled Kathy's lawyer's mind during the entire divorce negotiations and eventually manipulated him into accepting the settlement I predicted he would accept.

Kim hired a female lawyer to defend her in court. I needed to see Kim's lawyer because it would help me get a better read on the type of person I thought she was. I could then decide if I would have the ability to mentally manipulate her, and to what extent.

Soon after I filed the divorce papers as the plaintiff, my lawyer and I were in court with Kim and her lawyer. In my opinion, her lawyer looked as if she was the short, ugly duckling girl in high school, who overcompensated for her looks by becoming an academic over-achiever. I knew she would be a little bit of a challenge, but I knew I could beat her at the game.

From the very start, Kim told her lawyer I was a master at playing mind games and what my capabilities were. In their initial documents submitted to the court, her lawyer stated that I was a well-trained stage entertainer who makes a living tricking and deceiving people. She said I carefully observed and manipulated people, and I was trained to trick, fool, and lie to people as part of my craft. She concluded with a statement saying that these manipulation skills must be at the forefront of all communications coming from me during the divorce process.

Her lawyer was basically acknowledging my superior mental skills, and decided to take the case against me anyway. Part of the beauty of mental manipulation is letting the other person think they have the upper hand, and letting them believe they are winning the battle. If I did my job correctly, Kim and her lawyer would walk away from the divorce thinking they won the battle. It would take many months for me to win the war, but luckily I am a very patient man who can stay focused on my master goals, even during difficult parts of the fight.

After meeting Kim's lawyer in court I realized the only way to get the case to settle the way I wanted was not to use mind manipulation on her, but mind misdirection on her instead. I had to keep her focused on the small issues in our case, so she would completely forget about the big issues. Eventually my game plan worked like a charm. I kept distracting her with issues like car purchases and house purchases, so she would forget about the big issues Kim forgot to tell her about during the discovery process. I wanted the divorce from Kim to be quick and inexpensive. She and her attorney drew the battle line in the sand and did not play fair from the start, so I just followed their lead and eventually knew I outplayed them.

Eventually our divorce negotiations ended and we went to trial on January 15, 2014. The judge officially pronounced us divorced after the lawyers hammered out the details of our divorce decree wording. Soon after the divorce was final, I fulfilled the plateau reward I made to myself and bought myself a new Corvette. But no matter how long the divorce process took or how much money was wasted on legal fees, if I had the chance to turn back time, I would get married to Kim all over again. We did have many good times together. Plus my second marriage produced three beautiful children: Ronny, JoAnn, and Luke.

Being a single father has taught me how to be a better father and a better person. Unfortunately, fatherhood was something I was not very good at with my first three children. I hope they find it in their hearts to forgive me for not always being there for them.

On August 3, 2010, while I was going through the divorce, I received a certified letter from Tracy Woelfel, a litigation assistant from Simon and Schuster. She said her editorial staff never received the completed manuscript for my book and they wanted their retainer back.

Since all of our money went to hiring lawyers for our divorce, I didn't have the cash advance to return to them. I sent a letter back to Tracy informing her that I still wanted to write the book and tell my story to the world, but her ghost writer, Karen Hunter, was the one who did not follow through with our deal. To date, Karen refused to return any of my calls or emails. I told them if they wanted a refund they needed to talk to Karen first. I still intended to write my book, and that was the last I heard from Simon and Schuster.

Chapter 54

Tony Robbins

When I had my one-man show Off Broadway in New York City, my publicist, Heidi Krupp, invited some of her personal friends to my show. These friends of hers happened to work for Tony Robbins. They loved my show and word got back to Tony, who decided he had to see me perform for himself.

He had his people reach out to me to see if I could perform at one of his "Platinum Member" events at the Sun Valley Resort in Sun Valley, Idaho, on February 19, 2011. Tony has an exclusive group of people who, after attending one or more of his seminars, decided to enroll in his exclusive "Platinum Partner Program." Joining as a "Plat" for one year allows them unlimited access to attend any of Tony's seminars around the world, and it also allows them to attend all four of Tony's "Platinum Only" events during the year. Tony wanted me to perform at the "Platinum Only" event focusing on finances.

I considered Tony to be one of my mentors and a very big influence on my life and career. To be asked to perform for him was a huge honor for me, and I immediately agreed to perform at the event.

Tony was on stage speaking when I arrived. When he finished and told the audience to take a break, he came over to me and expressed how excited he was to be able to see me perform. He also thanked me for closing my Las Vegas show to make the trip. I told him I was a huge fan of his work and explained how much he helped me achieve the successes in my life.

I told Tony that when I saw his commercials many years ago, I purchased his "Personal Power" thirty-day course. I confessed I didn't have the money to afford the program at the time, so I copied the cassette tapes and the workbooks that came with the course and then sent the course back for a refund. Tony looked at me, wondering why I was confessing this to him right before he was scheduled to introduce me. I explained that many years later, when I became successful, I purchased his thirty-day course again because I felt I owed it to him. I also purchased all of his other available tapes and books. Tony chuckled at my story and thanked me for my honesty.

A few minutes later, he went back on stage to introduce me. Instead of using the written introduction his staff provided for him, he decided to share my confession. He told the audience how I had the nerve to copy his tapes and return them for a refund, and then admit it to Tony. Everyone laughed at the story. I walked out on stage and we shook hands. He exited the stage and sat in a private area in the back of the room reserved for him and his staff. His seat was elevated above the rest of the audience, so I was able to see him clearly during my entire performance.

I was so happy when I told the audience a joke and, glancing over at Tony, saw that he was laughing and applauding for me. He was enjoying my show just as much, if not more, than his audience. After the show was over, he returned to the stage and hugged me as I received a standing ovation from his "Platinum Members" and event staff. It was another surreal moment that will be burned into my memory for the rest of my life.

After the performance, Tony invited me back to his house for dinner. Tony and his wife, Sage, are beautiful, warm people, and the most gracious hosts I ever met. I asked Sage to take a photo of Tony and me together while we were in his basement playing video bowling.

Gerry and Tony Robbins

Being asked to perform for Tony was an honor, because he had heard how good I was through others and not by seeing the show himself. But when Tony called and asked me to return a year later, that was the ultimate compliment. I knew he would only hire me back a second time if he really liked my show.

On March 21, 2012, I flew to Whistler, British Columbia, to perform at the Four Seasons Hotel for the same financial seminar. This time Tony greeted me with a huge bear hug. We were now friends, and he asked how I was and how my Vegas show was going.

The following year, I performed for Tony and his group a third time at the Four Seasons in Whistler, British Columbia, Canada, on March 14, 2013. A few days after the performance, Tony left me a five-minute voice message that was the best compliment I ever received. He told me he was my biggest fan, and apologized for one of his audience members who tried to bust my chops while she was on stage with me. He said I was the consummate professional, because no matter what was thrown at me on stage, I was able to take the situation and turn it into gold for the audience.

He said I had him and his staff laughing their asses off during my show, and told me he has never booked the same speaker three years in a row. He also mentioned that he was very sorry to hear I was going through a divorce, and assured me I would be so much better off when it was all over. He personally invited me to his relationship seminar, which he only gives once every other year. Ironically, I was scheduled to be in divorce court the same week as the seminar, so I was unable to take Tony up on his generous offer.

I listened to Tony's voice message a few times, and shared it with my mom and children, who were very proud of me. I never expected Tony to call me again, but I was wrong. Tony wanted me to perform a fourth time for the same group back at the Sun Valley Resort, in Sun Valley, Idaho on February 12, 2014. This time, Tony asked that I put on a totally different show for the group since a lot of the attendees had already seen my previous performances.

A day before I was to fly out to Sun Valley, I went into my mentalism studio and looked over all the routines I could perform for the group. I spent some time picking out the effects I thought Tony and the group would enjoy. I packed my props in my travel case and planned on rehearsing the routines when I arrived at the hotel. I was scheduled to fly in on the 11th so I would have all the rest of that day to rehearse as well as the next day, since I wasn't scheduled to perform until later in the evening on the 12th.

When I arrived, Tony came over, gave me another bear hug, and told me I looked ten years younger. He said the weight of the divorce was off my shoulders, and it really showed in my appearance. I asked him what I should do now that I was a single man with two divorces under his belt. He advised me to start making a list of everything I wanted in a partner, and to be very specific and detailed. The list would slowly grow, and I could continually add to it as I thought of more things. If I preferred blonds, add it to the list. If I liked thin ladies, add it to the list. If I liked tall ladies, add it to the list. When I finished creating my list, he instructed me to read the list to myself a few times a day. After a month or so, I was to read it to myself once or twice a week.

He said if I remained positive, my dream girl would appear in my life. He pointed across the room to his beautiful wife Sage, and claimed he made his extensive list after his divorce, and that beautiful woman entered his life. She was everything he put on his list, and more. I knew the power of positive thinking and goal setting, so I knew exactly what he was talking about. Tony went back on stage to continue his talk, and I checked into my hotel room and started creating my dream girl list.

A few minutes later the phone rang. Tony's assistant was calling to say that Tony had changed the schedule. Could I perform my show immediately? I did not want to let her know I'd planned on rehearsing my routines for the next two days, so I agreed to get dressed and return to the conference room. Being around Tony is such a confidence booster that I put on my show without rehearsing, and received a standing ovation when I was done performing. They loved it, and the best part was I now had three days to relax and enjoy the conference. As always, I made friends with a bunch of his "Plat" members.

Since I started performing for Tony's group, many of his students have attended my Las Vegas show. They returned home from a Tony Robbins event and told their spouses about my performance. Then, when they visited Las Vegas, they brought their spouse to my mentalism show so that they could be amazed as well!

In 2013, when Tony was putting on a seminar in Las Vegas, Sage contacted me to ask if she could bring her parents to my show. My mother happened to be visiting from New York at the same time, and Sage and my mother met after my show. Sage could not say enough nice things about me to my mother.

Later that night when my mother told me about their conversation, she was glowing with pride over her son's accomplishments. My father never told me how proud of me he was before he passed away on April 22, 2012, but my mother more than made up for it. A child, no matter how old, loves to hear that his parents are proud of him.

Sage, Gerry and Tony Robbins

Chapter 55

The Power of Self-Confidence

In this chapter of my life, I learned not to be intimidated by people in power. If you are confident in your abilities, you have nothing to fear from them. Performing for Steve Wynn, Tony Robbins, and Barry Manilow never made me nervous one bit. I was excited to be entertaining them, but never intimidated.

I decided it was time that Mr. Cuales learned his student had become the master. I carried many years of guilt over what he did to me, and now it was his turn. I was going to hold him accountable for his actions, and make sure everyone knew what a monster he was.

I know some goals are easily attainable, and others take quite a while and a lot of persistence. My mini-goal of headlining on the Las Vegas Strip took fifteen years to accomplish.

I was also reminded that special abilities could be used for evil as well as good. I am not a confrontational person, but when someone gets in my way, or decides to take what is rightfully mine, I will do everything in my power to stop them—and possibly destroy them.

Persistence Achieves Goals

Chapter 56

Time to Tell His Son

After some time had passed since my ghostwriter, Karen, and I tried to sell my book idea to my literary agent, she reached out and contacted me again. She told me she now had a unique agreement with the book publisher Simon and Schuster. Since she wrote so many best sellers for them, she now had the ability to negotiate her own book deals on behalf of the publisher. She said my life story had to be told, and she wanted to be the one to tell it to the world. If I was still interested in writing my book with her, she said I would receive a contract from her publisher. If I agreed to the terms in the contract, they would send me a cash advance to write the book and she would start writing.

I signed the contract with Simon and Schuster and they sent me a large cash advance against book sales. David Kokakis, who worked for Karen, sent an email saying that Karen would contact me as soon as she finished a few projects she was currently working on. He thought she should be contacting me around May of 2008. May passed with no word from Karen. I waited until July of 2008 and decided to reach out to her to see how soon we could start the project. She never returned any of my emails or Facebook messages. For the third time, the book was dead in the water.

Around this time, Mr. Cuales's son, Michael, sent me an email. He was going to be in Vegas for a bachelor party and would love to see my show, get together with me for a drink, and catch up on old times. His email made it painfully obvious that Mr. Cuales never told his son what he had done to me, or why I reached out to him. It looked as if my book was never going to be published, and the truth about Mr. Cuales was never going to surface. I felt it was time to at least let his family know the truth about their father. I took the time to compose an email to Michael in which I fully explained my intentions when I contacted him. I briefly told him what his father had done to me without getting into too much detail. I was surprised when he emailed me back, especially after I told him those things about his father.

In his email, Michael told me multiple times how truly sorry he was. He said that reading about what his father did to me didn't come as a total shock to him, and it seemed to answer some questions he and his sister had regarding events that happened in the past. He explained that when his father was a kid, he lived in an orphanage where he was sexually abused by other boys. Michael's statement was sincere, but also implied that it was partial justification for his father's despicable actions.

The next morning, a nightmare awakened me, likely triggered by the email from Michael. It was the same topic that had surfaced its ugly head for years, and that had affected my life in a very negative way. As a fifteen-year-old boy, I was molested by my high school woodshop teacher. The ordeal often haunted me in my dreams as my brain recalled the mental manipulation and physical molestation Mr. Cuales had put me through. The thought of him seemed to haunt me at least once a day, every day of my life since it happened.

I felt the molestation had been a factor that contributed greatly to my relationship and marital problems. I knew what happened to me negatively affected my relationship with my children and other family members, and I decided enough was enough. It was time I took action to regain my sanity. I needed to put an end to the nightmare and finally hold him accountable for what he did to me. Since my ghostwriter, Karen Hunter, disappeared again, I needed to figure out another way to expose Mr. Cuales for his actions. At the same time, I thought perhaps it was time to channel my negative feelings in a positive way to help others.

As long as I carried the guilt, and as long as I carried the rage, I felt any of my future intimate relationships would be continually affected by the aftermath of the crime committed against me. Could I still press charges against him? I assumed the statute of limitations was up a long time ago, and there was nothing I could legally do against him. However, a quick Internet search indicated that in 2006 the statute of limitations was lifted from five years to infinity.

My knee jerk reaction was that I should press charges against him, but I had no proof other than my word against his. It had been years since the crime occurred, and there was no physical evidence. I felt I could not win the battle in court. It would cost me thousands of dollars in legal fees to bring it to trial, and unless he confessed, there would not be enough evidence to convict him.

It was something I needed to look at from all angles before I made a decision, so I called my friend and mentor, Ross Johnson, in Chicago. Ross was a schoolteacher who later turned professional mentalist; I trusted him completely. I explained the situation, and he told me every time this happened, there was always more than one victim. If I was brave enough to come forward, others would most likely surface as well, especially if this was well publicized in the media. He assured me that bringing my former schoolteacher to court would bring his actions out into the open, and maybe other students in the school who were also molested or raped by the woodshop teacher would come forward as well.

I immediately went silent. I could not speak and had to hang up the phone. My brain went deep into overdrive—too many thoughts were swirling around in my head, and I didn't know how to sort them or process them. The only thing that I was certain of was that I did not want this life-changing horror to happen to another innocent child. I did not want parents to trust people in authority without being vigilant. I wanted men to know it was okay to put the shame aside and come forward and report the incident to the proper authorities. And I wanted men to know it was okay to bring it to light, even many years after it happened.

While all this was going on, Steve received notification that his Social Security benefits were stopped. It seems his employer, Wal-Mart, gave him a one dollar per hour raise just in the summer months since he was working out in the heat, and it put him $42 over the amount he was entitled to earn before forfeiting his benefits. That meant he no longer received any financial assistance and he lost all of his medical benefits. They also sent him a bill to pay back the government $19,000 because they said he fraudulently collected the funds and was not really entitled to assistance. This was a situation Steve did not have the ability to correct on his own.

As far as I am concerned, my past did not create the man I am today; it only helped me define the man I chose to become. I feel when tragic events happen to a person, they define, destroy, or strengthen that person. I decided I was a man who was willing do everything in his power to prevent other innocent children from being molested, including holding a man accountable for his actions forty years after the fact.

I spoke to a lawyer and asked what could happen if I used Mr. Cuales's real name in the book. He said it would be up to him to prove I was lying if he took me to court. The burden of proof is on him, and if he decided to take a person like me to court, the media attention I attracted would likely draw other victims of his molestation out of the woodwork.

After getting that legal advice, I decided I was going to write the book myself instead of taking him to court, even if it meant being sued for libel. If Simon and Schuster did not want to publish my story because Karen no longer wanted to write it, I would self-publish the book.

When the first edition of the book was published, I hired a private investigator to find out where Mr. Cuales was now living. After discovering he moved his family to North Carolina, I mailed a copy of my book to his wife and another to his son and daughter. I also sent a copy to all of his neighbors. If they have small children, I think they should know who their neighbor is and what he likes to do to small children. I also sent a copy to the Holly Springs Police Department, which is his local police station and a copy to the Child Protective Services in his area.

After his family received a copy of the book, I heard all hell broke loose in his household. I was sure I was going to receive a cease and desist letter from his lawyer. Instead, I was told his family called the Wake County Human Services Department to investigate if he molested his grandchildren. After an investigation, the department concluded any concern from the family was unsubstantiated and the case was closed on November 14, 2014.

Everyone in his immediate family as well as his neighbors and the local authorities were now on alert. In my opinion, if writing this book and making them aware of who Hector Cuales is, and what he likes to do to children, helps prevent just one child from going through what I went through, then it would all be worth it.

I hope readers of this book become more vigilant with their children, and learn not to put their full trust in people of authority. Young boys are just as susceptible to sexual molestation as young girls are.

Gerry's family

Chapter 57

Starting All Over

I took Steve to the Social Security office and helped him reapply for all of his benefits. The representative said it would be easier and faster to reapply while Steve's case, and Steve's outstanding bill for $19,000, was under reconsideration. The process took over a year of applications and doctor exams and tests. Eventually, we received word that he was denied for any Social Security benefits because he was no longer considered disabled. I found their response to be very strange since he was born this way, and nothing had mentally or physically changed with him since they granted him benefits.

I set a goal to get his full benefits reinstated, have his $19,000 bill wiped out, and have all of his past benefits paid to him retroactively. I decided it was time to get the media on our side in this battle. I started a Facebook page for Steve and fully explained his plight to everyone. I encouraged other Facebook members to share the story and get the word out. The page quickly grew and collected over five thousand "likes." I contacted the local news stations along with our local Congressman. The news reporters came to our house and asked me to give an interview explaining what happened. I insisted they interview Steve instead of me. Seeing and hearing him talk would be all the proof that was needed to show everyone he clearly needed financial assistance from the government. I think it was the first time in my life I ever declined to give an on camera media interview.

Soon after the story hit the media, I received a call from a Social Security representative in Washington with instructions on how I could make this situation better. A short time later, we went before a judge so Steve could tell his story. He was in the courtroom for about a half hour before I was asked to testify. The judge told me he reviewed a list of Steve's monthly expenses and noticed his Wal-Mart paycheck was not enough to cover his living expenses. The judge asked me where he was getting the extra money from, and I said I was giving it to him. When the judge asked if Steve had to pay back all the money I gave him if his benefits were reinstated, I said "no." Then he asked why I was helping Steve if we weren't related. He didn't seem to understand the concept of one human being helping out another with no strings attached. It was like the word *friendship* was not in his vocabulary. A few weeks later, we were notified that all of Steve's benefits were reinstated and he would be reimbursed for the lost benefits over the past eighteen months. Since Steve is not allowed to maintain a large amount of money in his bank account, I took the reimbursement check and helped Steve pick out a new car for himself. It was the first time in his life he ever had such a nice vehicle, and he was so proud to own it and drive it.

After a year and a half of fighting for Steve's social security benefits, and fighting with my ex-wife's lawyer in and out of divorce court, I wanted to celebrate. I also wanted to announce to the world that I was a single man again, so I agreed to appear on the television show *The Millionaire Matchmaker* with Patti Stanger. My goal was not necessarily to find the next love of my life, but mainly to promote my Las Vegas show. Secretly, I knew it would irritate Kim and her lawyer when they found out I appeared on the show as a millionaire bachelor. Her lawyer was never smart enough to find my money during the divorce discovery process, even though it was right there under her nose the entire time. The mental manipulation and distraction techniques I used worked like a charm, and this was a way of rubbing her lawyer's face in it. Did I really have the money and used the television show as a way to stick it to her lawyer? Or did I appear on the show and write the above paragraph as a continued form of mental manipulation, knowing Kim would eventually read this book, and show her lawyer in hopes of reopening the divorce case? Only I will know the answer to that question.

It took three days to tape the television show, and it was a complete blast to do. It reminded me how much fun I had making television shows. The very first time the show aired in March of 2014, my social media profiles exploded. I received hundreds of Facebook friend requests after the show aired and gained many more Twitter followers. The very next day, my email box was packed with letters and photos from ladies around the country who wanted to fly into Las Vegas to meet me, others who wanted to date me, and some who knew they wanted to marry me.

One thing that I noticed from watching myself on the television show was my weight gain. I had packed on thirty pounds over the previous two years while going through all the legal proceedings. Since Kim always wanted me to be a muscular weightlifter gym rat, my brain apparently decided to rebel and go in the opposite direction. Seeing myself on the television show made me realize I needed to focus on my mental and physical health before focusing on dating again.

On June 1, 2014, I publicly announced on Facebook that I was going to go on a diet. My master goal was to get my weight down from 229 pounds to 199 pounds before Labor Day. In the first month of dieting, I lost twenty-two pounds! I officially reached my goal on July 17, 2014—only 47 days. I set up little mini-goals and remained focused and did not let anything, or any food, get in my way. The last time I dieted was in 2003 while I was training for my television special. I was never able to get below 192 pounds that time, so after I reached my goal and hit 199 pounds this year, I reset my goal and decided to drop to 190 pounds, just to prove to myself that I could. My second goal of losing 40 pounds was also achieved before Labor Day.

I also felt I needed to take a break from being in a serious relationship. Between my two marriages, I was married for the last twenty-five years of my life. I needed to find myself first and determine what I really wanted in a partner before I tried to commit to anyone again. I wanted to finish the list Tony Robbins instructed me to make, and make it the next goal after getting my weight back in control. I decided I only wanted to have female friends who enjoyed going out after my show for dinner or catching an occasional movie or show, with no relationship strings attached.

After the divorce was over my lifelong friend, Brian Thorsen, asked me if I had read the new Paul Stanley book (Paul was the lead singer from the rock group KISS). I confessed to Brian that I had an attention problem that prevented me from reading anything of great length. He told me the book was also released in audio book form, and his excitement about the book motivated me to download it on iTunes. It took me about three days to listen to the entire book.

Listening to Paul Stanley read the book fascinated me. It felt as if he was sitting next to me, having coffee, telling me his life story in little chunks. I thought if I could sit and tell my life story into a microphone, I could possibly write my story on my own. Even better, if I could find a computer program that transcribed my words into text, I would not have to type out the entire book.

My close friend Eran Raven, who appeared on the television show *Phenomenon* with me, told me about a program called Dragon Dictate that would do exactly what I wanted. He also said he'd recently sent one of the Dragon Dictate company executives to see my Vegas show, and he loved it. Eran contacted him on my behalf, and a few days later a copy of the Dragon Dictate Program and a headset were delivered to my house.

I felt the stars had finally aligned for me: Brian telling me about the Paul Stanley book around the same time that a man who worked for the Dragon Dictate software company attended my show. I decided it was now time to write the book myself. I did not want to wait for anyone else to ghostwrite my story. I have never read an entire book in my life, so writing one would be twice as difficult for me, but I felt it would be well worth the journey.

Since 1988, when I used a Porsche in the routine at my VFW Hall performance, I've wanted to own one. I set up a plateau reward for myself and decided to buy a Porsche after I completed the first draft of my book.

Chapter 58

Taking Back My Power

In this chapter of my life, I finally took back my personal power. I was no longer carrying all the guilt from the sexual molestation because I passed it back to my molester. I felt bad for telling his son Michael, because he is an innocent victim in this, but then again, so was I. Because of what his father did to me and others, I am sure his relationship with his children and grandchildren will never be the same. Even if his son did not tell him that I revealed the details of his father's past, Mike would always have it in the back of his mind and never leave his children alone with their grandfather for any extended period of time.

I realized bringing his actions to light through the legal system could cost a lot of money and take a lot of time, and still might not ever become public knowledge. But writing this book will instantly force his actions to be out into the public realm. If he decides to take me to court for writing about him, it will just add to the book's publicity and increase his exposure. I decided if going to jail means I can help prevent this injustice from happening to other children, I am willing to take that chance.

I was also able to take back my independence by divorcing the person who I felt humiliated and embarrassed me while she tried to play the innocent victim. When she betrayed me, my hate for her ran much deeper than any little love I may have had for her. It took some time before I realized what she did was unforgivable, and I tried to civilly end the marriage.

I took on two different divorce lawyers in my life and had no problem beating them both at their own game. It will be interesting to see what Kim and her lawyer do when they read this book, because I am positive one of the two will want to take some sort of action. She was never able to fully let go of me after the divorce. I knew she was constantly checking my social media sites and Facebook pages to keep track of my personal business. I hope Kim is not foolish enough to take this book to her lawyer and tell her this is the smoking gun that they need to prove to the judge that I manipulated them during the divorce process. If she does, she will be wasting more of her money that she could be spending on our children. When an author writes a book like this, he has the artistic freedom to embellish a story and make it seem more interesting to the reader. Were the details I described in this book fact, or did I make them up to seem like I am a mental manipulation master? Only I know the answer to that question.

Making the Mentalist

Chapter 59

Life Lessons

Writing this book made me realize that my young life was full of disappointments that contributed to my abandonment issues. Immediately after I was born, I was placed in an orphanage. I am sure a newborn baby requires constant contact and bonding with its mother, which I did not get for the first three and a half months of my life. When I was twelve years old, my best friend Tommy left me to join his father in heaven. Less than a year later, my older brother Mal left me after he got married. A month after that, my adoptive father left our family to be part of another family. All of these departures left a huge void in my life.

My heart realized the best way to prevent itself from constantly getting hurt was to build a wall around it and not to let anyone in. I did not know it at the time, but all of the things happening in my life were the first few bricks of the emotional wall I would build around my heart. If I did not let people in, when they eventually left my life—which history showed me would always happen—it would not hurt as much.

When my adoptive father moved out to be with another family, my mother spent a lot of time in her bedroom. Unfortunately, our house was very small and more often than I care to remember, I heard my mother sobbing. The only time she seemed happy was when she went out disco dancing with her boyfriend on the weekends; dancing became her escape. After they returned home from the disco, I heard them laughing in her bedroom. My brain did not like it when I was alone with my own thoughts, so hearing my mother's laughter in place of sobs subconsciously taught me that quality time with someone of the opposite sex was one of the ways I could avoid loneliness. It was very easy for me to mentally manipulate the girls into thinking there was an emotional connection just to get them into bed so I would not have to be alone.

I think I initially became friends with Steve because my heart was looking to fill the void left by Little Tommy's death. To this day, I still feel I was responsible for his death; partly out of guilt, I decided to take care of and protect Steve, and become his guardian angel here on earth. I think part of my life's calling was to protect this innocent soul from the cruelties of the world. Eventually, Steve and I formed a lifelong friendship that was stronger than any blood connection. Steve does not judge my actions, and he is my biggest cheerleader in life. I understand his personal issues and do not judge him for anything he does. I may never get married again, but I truly think Steve and I will be together until death.

I feel I got lost in my parents' divorce shuffle. My father was preoccupied with starting his life all over again with another family, and my mother was forced to work full-time to make ends meet. When she wasn't working, she was looking to put the pieces of her life back together by going out dancing with her friends. The only way I could get any attention from my family was to perform my magic.

When I was a very young boy, I had an accident and banged my head into a brick wall while playing with my friends in the schoolyard. I didn't realize it, but it split my skull open and blood was pouring down my face. The school nurse realized it was too big a wound for her to bandage, so she called my parents to come and take me to the hospital emergency room. I remember lying there on the hospital emergency room table. The doctor was about to cover my face with a piece of blue paper, which had a hole cut out to expose the wound so he could stitch me up. The last thing I saw was my mother's face looking at me through the window in the emergency room door, and she was crying her eyes out. The entire time I was laying there, I was really scared and felt alone. I focused my mind and imagined I was lying at home in the comfort of my own bed. It was almost as if I taught myself to teleport my mind out of my body to the comfort of my own bedroom to distract myself from the pain of the doctor stitching me up.

My brain learned how to focus on things I really wanted, and keep that laser-like focus on the thought or goal until I made it my reality. I was able to manifest some of my thoughts into reality pretty quickly, and others took a great deal of work and persistence. I knew no matter how big my realistic goal was, persistence would always pay off.

My father neglected his fatherly duties, causing my brain to search for a male father figure to look up to during my preadolescence. A pedophile schoolteacher took me into his life and made me a part of his loving family. After he gained my trust and my mother's trust, he took advantage of my mental instability and mentally manipulated me to think his repeated molestation was normal. Soon after, two other adult men would try the same thing on me. I learned to trust no one. The wall I constructed around my heart kept me well-protected from pain, but it also kept me from getting too close to anyone.

I discovered mentalism as a defense mechanism to deal with people like them. Mentalism gave people the illusion that I had access to their innermost thoughts and allowed me to mentally control them. People loved watching me perform using my mental skills, but they also wanted to stay at arm's length away from me. And if anyone happened to get to close to me, the wall was there as my second line of defense.

I became uncomfortable letting people get close to me, but I always wanted to maintain control. Performing on stage allowed me to have total control over my surroundings and the people watching me perform. I became more comfortable on stage than I did dealing with people one on one. I realized that when someone drank alcohol, they lost control. As a result, I promised myself I would never drink so I would never lose control in public.

Being an altar boy at a young age taught me how to be comfortable in front of an audience. Watching my father fight to the death when it came to winning an argument taught me how to voice my own opinion and stand strong to defend it. And watching him be the life of the party taught me how to make people laugh. When my father moved out of the house and left my mother financially devastated, I learned not to rely on others for financial support. My mother taught me how to earn money and support my family and me.

I took my performing and verbal skills, added my own version of comedy, and combined them with my mentalism tricks. Every day, I laid in bed with my eyes closed and imagined performing on stage, making people laugh and smile while I was also amazing them. I set my goals and refused to stop until I achieved them. Patience and persistence became the keys to my success.

My friend and lawyer Jason, contacted Simon and Schuster on my behalf and informed them I was writing the book, despite the fact their ghostwriter never returned any of my correspondence over the years. We asked if they were still interested in publishing my book.

I was secretly hoping they would pass on the project, and revert all rights back to me. Since so many years had passed when I signed the contract with them, self-publishing now became the path many authors decided to take. If I self-published the book, I would not have to follow the publisher's legal requirements and change my molester's name out of fear of legal retaliation.

On July 22, 2014, we received an answer from Simon and Schuster. They decided not to acquire the project for publication, and we were ecstatic. They gave me back all of my rights, title, and interest in the book, so I was now free to self-publish it and include my molesters' names.

Using my verbal manipulation skills allowed me to easily talk a lot of ladies into my bed. At first I thought women were disposable pleasures used to keep me company when I was alone. After I came to know and truly understand myself, I learned casual sex was not as interesting to me as creating a real mental and physical bond with a woman; I really wanted to find a meaningful relationship. I made my list outlining exactly what I am looking for in a woman, as Tony Robbins instructed me to, and I will not stop looking until I find her. In December 2014, I attended a six-day Tony Robbins seminar in Florida called *Date with Destiny*. When I finished the seminar, I had a detailed blue print for my new life.

Unfortunately, due to my past, I still have a very tough time trusting people. As much as I understand why I have a problem trusting others, it is still something I struggle with daily. I have really good people in my life who love me and have my best interest at heart, but sometimes I think the scars run too deep for me to fully open up and trust anyone. Steve, my mother, and my children are the only ones who I expose any part of my heart to. No matter what I tell my mother, my daughter Jennifer, or my son Scott, I know they trust me and would never judge me.

When Jennifer, Scott, and I are together we have a secret bond we have named The Core. We are open and honest with each other, and feel we can tell the other two anything in the world without fear of being judged. Relationships are based on trust, and aside from those three people, trusting someone is a major problem for me. I am hoping when that someone special comes into my life, I am not going to push her away because of my emotional scars. I am aware I will never fully understand another person unless I walked a lifetime in their shoes. I hope to find someone who feels the same way. It is easy to tell me it is okay to trust them, but unless they have walked a lifetime in my shoes, they will never truly know how I feel about trusting another person.

I went after the career I really wanted to have, and against all odds, I succeeded. I wanted to perform in my own Off Broadway show, and I did. I wanted my own prime time NBC television special, and I made it happen. I wanted to be a Las Vegas headliner on the Strip, and I am proud to be the longest-running mentalist show in Las Vegas history with thousands of performances to date.

But I have realized that my greatest achievement has to be my children. They are the love of my life, and I would give my life for any of them in a second. They are amazing, each and every one of them, and I am so fortunate to have them in my life. I hope they feel the same about me being in their lives.

Writing this book has been an interesting process for me, both personally and professionally. It has also been very therapeutic for me as it forced me to look at all the pieces of my life from many different perspectives. Looking back at things that happened in my life, years after they occurred, allowed me to learn a lot about why I became the person that I did. Finding the proper words and labels to describe myself to the reader allowed me to better understand what I liked about myself and what I disliked. It indicated to me which of my titles and labels needed to change, and which ones I was proud to have.

After a few failed attempts with my literary agent, Richard, and my ghostwriter, Karen, I never gave up on writing this book. On April 26, 2014, I officially started writing the book on my own. My master goal was to have the first draft completed by September 1st, Labor Day; that was 127 days after I officially began. My goal was to write a book containing at least 300 pages of text, not including any photos. That gave me a realistic goal of writing two pages per day to complete my task. I spent quite a bit of time organizing my journals and scrapbook. On July 21, 2014, the first draft was officially complete at 404 pages. I reached my goal in 87 days—forty days ahead of schedule.

While going through my journals to gather information for this book, I noticed an entry I made on March 8, 1993. It said: "My children are growing up so fast. I enjoy watching them developmentally and physically. I wonder if the fact that I feel they are growing so fast is a sign that I am not spending enough time with them." I heard that a study shows that the average father does not spend more than fifteen minutes a week with his kids. I am making a great effort to spend at least fifteen minutes each day with each child, separately. I want to be a major part and influence in their lives. Since I didn't have that with my father, I know what I missed. I know how little time I did spend with my father, and how important that time was to me. I have very few memories of my father and I doing things together. I want my children to have lots of good memories about me after I am gone.

I was not the best father for my oldest three children when they were young, and have tried to correct it. I hope they find it in their hearts to forgive me for all I did wrong. If I was only allowed to pass one thing on to my six children before I die, I would tell them to be persistent with their dreams and goals, but do not neglect their family while doing so. Do not keep their eyes exclusively focused on the end of the journey; rather, enjoy the entire journey with their family as they are taking it.

I want my children to have lots of good memories about me after I am gone. Currently I only have one goal. I do not want my own reality television show, I do not want to be a movie actor, and I do not need to have a huge Las Vegas showroom. My current goal is to be the best father I can be for my children. They will be grown and out on their own quicker than I care to think about. Spending quality time with them and making memories has become my newest goal. Being a television and movie star can wait. I have more important things to focus on right now.

I am honored that you took the time to read my life story. Announcing publicly on Facebook that I was going on a diet, and posting my weekly results, has influenced a lot of my friends and fans to take control of their own health and seek out better ways of eating and improving their physical appearance. I hope this book has the same effect on my readers by inspiring them to reach for their dreams. I hope you learned that realistic goals are attainable. I hope I reinforced you to understand people are not always what they seem to be, and to be trusting, but cautious.

And if you were ever molested, I hope I gave you the courage to seek assistance, either dealing with the pain or shedding light on your abuser and exposing them for the monster that they truly are.

By writing this book, I have taken the first major step in my life to opening my heart and revealing myself to strangers, and removing some of the bricks from the wall. The cover of the book is an illustration of me hiding behind an 80's Comedy Club stage brick wall, but some of the bricks have been removed. By telling you my story, you now know what made this man "The Mentalist."